Questions & Answers
Public Law

Questions & Answers Series
Series Editors: Rosalind Malcolm and Margaret Wilkie

The ideal revision aid to keep you afloat through your exams

Q&A Company Law
Stephen Judge

Q&A Criminal Law
Mike Molan

Q&A Employment Law
Richard Benny, Michael Jefferson, and Malcolm Sargeant

Q&A Equity and Trusts
Margaret Wilkie, Rosalind Malcolm, and Peter Luxton

Q&A EU Law
Nigel Foster

Q&A Evidence
Maureen Spencer and John Spencer

Q&A Family Law
Ruth Gaffney-Rhys, with Chris Barton, Mary Hibbs, and Penny Booth

Q&A Human Rights and Civil Liberties
Steve Foster

Q&A International Law
Susan Breau

Q&A Land Law
Margaret Wilkie, Peter Luxton, and Rosalind Malcolm

Q&A Law of Contract
Adrian Chandler with Ian Brown

Q&A Law of Torts
David Oughton and Barbara Harvey

Q&A Public Law
Richard Clements and Philip Jones

- advice on exam technique
- summary of each topic
- bullet-pointed answer plans
- model answers
- diagrams and flowcharts
- further reading

Questions & Answers

Public Law

SIXTH EDITION

Richard Clements
Principal Lecturer in Law, Bristol Law School, University of the West of England

Philip Jones
Senior Lecturer in Law, Bristol Law School, University of the West of England

2011 and 2012

OXFORD
UNIVERSITY PRESS

OXFORD
UNIVERSITY PRESS

Great Clarendon Street, Oxford OX2 6DP

Oxford University Press is a department of the University of Oxford.
It furthers the University's objective of excellence in research, scholarship,
and education by publishing worldwide in

Oxford New York

Auckland Cape Town Dar es Salaam Hong Kong Karachi
Kuala Lumpur Madrid Melbourne Mexico City Nairobi
New Delhi Shanghani Taipei Toronto

With offices in

Argentina Austria Brazil Chile Czech Republic France Greece
Guatemala Hungary Italy Japan South Korea Poland Portugal
Singapore Switzerland Thailand Turkey Ukraine Vietnam

Oxford is a registered trade mark of Oxford University Press
in the UK and in certain other countries

Published in the United States
by Oxford University Press Inc., New York

© R. Clements and P. Jones 2011

The moral rights of the authors have been asserted

Crown copyright material is reproduced
with the permission of the Controller, HMSO
(under the terms of the Click Use licence)

Database right Oxford University Press (maker)

Third edition 2004
Fourth edition 2007
Fifth edition 2009

All rights reserved. No part of this publication may be reproduced,
stored in a retrieval system, or transmitted, in any form or by any means,
without the prior permission in writing of Oxford University Press,
or as expressly permitted by law, or under terms agreed with the appropriate
reprographics rights organizations. Enquiries concerning reproduction
outside the scope of the above should be sent to the Rights Department,
Oxford University Press, at the address above

You must not circulate this book in any other binding or cover
and you must impose the same condition on any acquirer

British Library Cataloguing in Publication Data

Data available

Library of Congress Cataloging in Publication Data

Data available

Typeset by Laserwords Private Limited, Chennai, India
Printed in Great Britain
on acid-free paper by
Ashford Colour Press Limited, Gosport, Hampshire

ISBN 978–0–19–959995–0

10 9 8 7 6 5 4 3 2

Contents

Preface vii
Table of Cases ix
Table of Statutes xvii

1. Introduction 1
2. Constitutions; the Nature and Sources of the United Kingdom Constitution 5
3. Prime Minister and Cabinet 21
4. The Royal Prerogative 40
5. Parliament 56
6. Parliamentary Sovereignty 83
7. The Rule of Law; the Separation of Powers 99
8. The Human Rights Act 1998 109
9. Freedom to Protest and Police Powers 132
10. Freedom of Expression 155
11. Administrative Law: Judicial Review 176
12. Public Authority Proceedings 202

Index 221

The Q&A Series

Key features

The Q&A series provides full coverage of key subjects in a clear and logical way. The book contains the following features:

- Questions
- Commentary
- Bullet-pointed answer plans
- Diagrams
- Suggested answers

online resource centre
www.oxfordtextbooks.co.uk/orc/qanda/

Every book in the Q&A series is accompanied by an Online Resource Centre, hosted at the URL above, which is open-access and free to use.

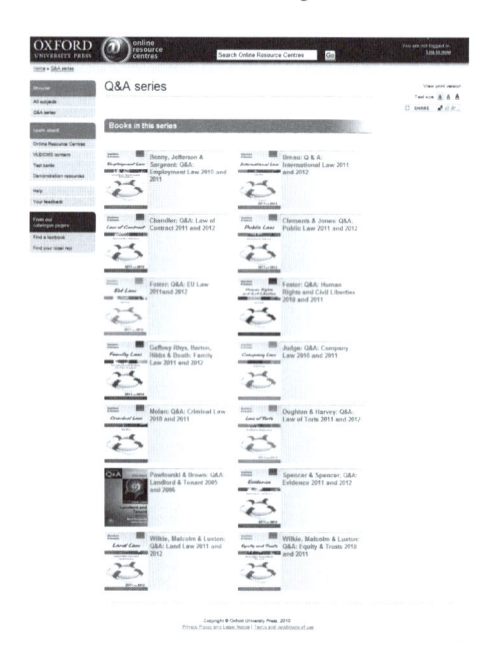

The online resources for this title include revision and exam advice, a subject-specific glossary, and links to websites useful for the study of public law.

Preface

When this book was *first published,* in 1997, a new Labour government replaced the Conservatives who had been in power for 18 years. The incoming administration had a long list of intended constitutional changes. There followed measures such as the Human Rights Act 1998, Freedom of Information Act 2000 and Constitutional Reform Act 2005 to name but a few. Similarly, with this *new edition* much is changed or changing. We have a new government replacing Labour after 13 years in office. This new government too has a long list of proposed constitutional reforms. There is one major difference however, the government itself, the first coalition government in 60 years. This new edition considers the present and future significance of this highly unusual development. So what else is new to this edition?

We consider the new government's constitutional reform agenda. Its Programme for Government 2010 includes, for instance, a controversial plan for fixed-term Parliaments; a wholly or largely elected House of Lords (by proportional representation); a referendum on replacing First Past the Post with the Alternative Vote system for general elections; greater devolution including full implementation of the 2009 Calman Commission; more powers to backbench MPs such as election of Select Committee Chairs; Petitions and other adaptation to the legislative procedure to enhance public participation; and measures on the thorny issue of the EU and sovereignty, a Sovereignty Bill declaring the ultimate sovereignty of the Westminster Parliament and a 'referendum lock' on any further attempted transfer of sovereignty by EU treaty.

The Human Rights Act 1998 continues to generate a lot of legal interest. The newly elected Conservative-Liberal Democrat coalition government has continued the previous government's policy of investigating whether the Human Rights Act 1998 should be replaced by a Bill of Rights specifically tailored for British conditions. A commission has been established to that end. The new UK Supreme Court has also decided that, although the courts of the UK must take into account decisions of the European Court of Human Rights, they are not bound to follow them: *R v Horncastle* [2010] 2 WLR 47.

Anti-terrorist legislation has been subject to repeated legal challenge, in particular control orders, as seen in *Secretary of State for the Home Department v AP (Nos. 1 and 2)* [2010] UKSC 24 and 26 and *Secretary of State for Home Department v AF (No. 3)* [2009] 3 All ER 643, with some success for the claimants. The police had been allowed to stop and search, without the need for reasonable suspicion, but this was condemned by the European Court of Human Rights in *Gillan and Quinton v UK* (2010) 50 EHRR 45. Amending legislation will be forthcoming.

The 'right' to assisted suicide continues to generate much media interest and Debbie Purdy had some success in *R (Purdy) v DPP* [2010] 1 AC 345, with the Director of Public Prosecutions being required to issue new guidelines on the prosecution of such cases.

The Iraq war has also thrown up many human rights issues, notably whether the Human Rights Act 1998 extends beyond UK territory. Soldiers discovered that they only enjoyed its protections when they are on their base: *R (Smith) v Secretary of State for Defence* [2010] 3 WLR 223.

Police discretion to control public order situations continues to be evaluated by the courts, with the additional requirement that human rights should be respected. The controversial police tactic of 'kettling' was held not to be a breach of Article 5, the right to liberty, in *Austin v Metropolitan Police Commissioner* [2009] 4 All ER 227.

The right to freedom of information continues to develop with some amendments to the law in the Constitutional Reform and Governance Act 2010 and rulings that Cabinet minutes and details of MPs' parliamentary expenses should be revealed.

Judicial review is always changing. The right of natural justice has been reinforced by Article 6, the right to a fair trial, in *RG v Governors of X School* [2010] 2 All ER 555. Another possible basis of judicial review, mistake of fact, continues to develop, in *R (March) v Secretary of State for Health* [2010] EWHC 765.

We have tried to give flavour to this book by giving views and getting under the skin of how aspects of the constitution really work. You may disagree with a given 'slant' here and there: in a democracy, that is your entitlement!

Our thanks are due to Jane Kay, one of the original authors of this book, who has now retired. Much of the structure of the book and its contents are still the product of her hard work and insight into the workings of the UK constitution. Any errors in the book remain the responsibility of the current authors alone.

Richard Clements
Philip Jones
August 2010

Table of Cases

A v B plc and Another [2003] QB 195 . . . 173, 174

A v Secretary of State for the Home Department (No. 1) [2005] 2 AC 68 . . . 103, 113, 114, 129, 131

A v Secretary of State for the Home Department (No. 2) [2006] 1 All ER 575 . . . 103, 113

A v UK (2009) 49 EHRR 29 . . . 124

Abdillaahi Muuse v Secretary of State for the Home Department [2010] EWCA Civ 453 . . . 205

Adams v Naylor [1946] AC 543 . . . 209

Agricultural Training Board v Aylesbury Mushrooms Ltd [1972] 1 WLR 190 . . . 183

Agricultural, Horticultural and Forestry Training Board v Aylesbury Mushrooms [1972] 1 WLR 190 . . . 197, 198

Air Canada v Secretary of State for Trade [1983] 2 AC 394 . . . 219

Al Saadoon & Mufdhi v UK (2009) 49 EHRR SE11 . . . 210

Al-Khawaja and Tahery v UK (2009) 49 EHRR 1 . . . 125

Allen v Gulf Oil Refinery Ltd [1981] AC 1001 . . . 203

Anisminic v Foreign Compensation Commission [1969] 2 AC 147 . . . 180

Anns v Merton LBC [1978] AC 728 . . . 214, 216

Argyll v Argyll [1967] Ch 302 . . . 171

Arrowsmith v Jenkins [1963] 2 QB 561 . . . 135, 141, 147

Ashworth Security Hospital v Mirror Group Newspaper Ltd [2004] 4 All ER 1 . . . 163

Associated Provincial Picture Houses v Wednesbury Corporation [1948] 1 KB 223 . . . 183, 192

Atkins v DPP [2000] 2 All ER 425 . . . 159

Attorney-General v Blake [2001] 1 AC 268 . . . 163, 166

Attorney-General v De Keyser's Royal Hotel [1920] AC 508 . . . 40, 42, 51, 52

Attorney-General v English [1983] 1 AC 116 . . . 159

Attorney-General v Guardian Newspapers (No. 2) [1990] 1 AC 109 . . . 166, 172

Attorney-General v Hislop [1991] 2 WLR 219 . . . 160

Attorney-General v Jonathan Cape Ltd [1976] QB 752 . . . 10, 12

Attorney-General v Punch Ltd [2003] 1 All ER 289 . . . 164

Attorney-General v The Observer, The Times (Spycatcher) [1990] 1 AC 109 . . . 156, 164

Attorney-General v The Times [2001] 1 WLR 885 . . . 164

Attorney-General v Wiltshire United Dairies Ltd (1921) 37 TLR 884 . . . 197, 199

Attorney-General's Reference (No. 3 of 1977) [1978] 3 All ER 1166 . . . 158

Attorney-General's Reference (No. 4 of 2002) [2005] 1 AC 264 . . . 115

Attorney-General ex rel Tilley v Wandsworth LBC [1981] 1 WLR 854 . . . 190

Attorney-General of Duchy of Lancaster v Overton Farms Ltd [1982] Ch 277 . . . 43

Attorney-General of New South Wales v Trethowan [1932] AC 526 . . . 87

Attorney-General of New South Wales v Bardolph (1934) 52 CLR 455 . . . 211, 212

Austin v Metropolitan Police Commissioner [2008] 1 All ER 564; [2009] 3 All ER 455; [2009] UKHL 5 . . . 143, 144

Austin v MPC [2009] 4 All ER 227, HL . . . 139

Author of a Blog v Times Newspapers [2009] EMLR 22 . . . 174

Averill v UK (2001) 31 EHRR 839 . . . 115

BBC v Johns [1965] Ch 32 . . . 42

Baggs Case (1615) 11 Co Rep 93b . . . 178

Bailey v Williamson (1873) LR 8 QB 118 . . . 199

Barrett v Enfield LBC [2001] 2 AC 550 . . . 206

Barrs v Bethell [1982] Ch 294 . . . 192

Beatty v Gillbanks (1882) 9 QBD 308 . . . 138, 140, 144, 148

Bennett v Horseferry Road Magistrates [1993] 3 All ER 138 . . . 103

Table of Cases

Bernstein v Skyviews Ltd [1978] 1 QB 479 . . . 171

Bici v Ministry of Defence [2004] EWHC 786, QBD . . . 209, 210

Birmingham City Council [2008] 1 AC 95 . . . 130

Blackburn v Attorney-General [1971] 2 All ER 1380 . . . 40, 51

Boddington v British Transport Police [1998] 2 All ER 203 . . . 201

Bradbury v Enfield London Borough Council [1967] 1 WLR 1311 . . . 183

Brannigan and McBride v UK (1993) 17 EHRR 539 . . . 115

Bribery Commissioner v Ranasinghe [1965] AC 172 . . . 87

British Coal Corporation v R [1935] AC 500 . . . 86

British Oxygen v Board of Trade [1971] AC 610 . . . 190

British Railways Board v Pickin [1974] AC 765 . . . 85

Brogan v United Kingdom (1988) 11 EHRR 117 . . . 113, 128

Bromley LBC v Greater London Council [1982] 1 AC 768 . . . 191, 192

Brooks v Commissioner of Police of the Metropolis [2005] 2 All ER 489 . . . 214

Burmah Oil Co. v Bank of England [1980] AC 1090 . . . 206

Burmah Oil v Lord Advocate [1965] AC 75 . . . 40, 51, 52, 102, 212

Buron v Denman [1848] 2 Ex 167 . . . 51

Bushell v Secretary of State for the Environment [1981] AC 75 . . . 187

Campbell v Mirror Group Newspapers [2004] 2 AC 457 . . . 119, 124, 156, 173

Caparo Industries v Dickman [1990] 2 AC 605 . . . 214

Carltona v Works Commissioners [1943] 2 All ER 560 . . . 31

Case of Proclamations, The (1611) 12 Co Rep 74 . . . 45

Chahal v UK (1997) 23 EHRR 413 . . . 50, 113, 123

Chandler v DPP [1964] AC 763 . . . 42, 50, 53, 54, 161, 162

Chapman v Earl [1968] 1 WLR 1315 . . . 183

Chorherr v Austria (1993) 17 EHRR 358 . . . 146

Christians against Racism and Fascism v United Kingdom (1980) 21 DR 138 . . . 145, 146

Christie v Leachinsky [1947] AC 573 . . . 151

Church of Scientology v Johnson-Smith [1972] 1 QB 522 . . . 75

Churchward v R (1865) LR 1 QB 173 . . . 211

Clark v University of Lincolnshire and Humberside [2000] 1 WLR 1988 . . . 194

Commissioners of Custom and Excise v Cure and Deeley [1962] 1 QB 340 . . . 199

Coney v Choyce [1975] 1 WLR 422 . . . 182, 183

Connor v Surrey County Council [2010] EWCA Civ 286 . . . 206, 216

Conway v Rimmer [1968] AC 910 . . . 180, 205, 212, 217–20

Cook v Alexander [1974] QB 279 . . . 77

Cooper v Wandsworth Board of Works (1863) 14 CB (NS) 180 . . . 178

Cork v McVicar (1984) Times, 31 October . . . 164, 172

Corporate Officer of the House of Commons v Information Commissioner [2009] 3 All ER 403 . . . 168

Costa v ENEL (6/64) [1964] CMLR 425 . . . 89, 90, 94, 96, 97

Council of Civil Service Unions v Minister for the Civil Service [1985] AC 374 . . . 40, 41, 44, 50, 53, 54, 197–9, 211

D v NSPCC [1978] AC 171 . . . 220

Daily Graphic HC 27 (1956–7) . . . 76

Derbyshire v The Times [1993] AC 534 . . . 156

Dimes v Grand Junction Canal Co (1852) 3 HLC 759 . . . 187

Doherty v Birmingham City Council [2008] 3 WLR 636 . . . 125, 131

Douglas v Hello! [2001] QB 967; [2002] 1 FCR 289 . . . 156, 173

DPP v A & BC Chewing Gum [1968] 1 QB 519 . . . 158

DPP v Clarke, Lewis, O'Connell & O'Keefe [1992] Crim LR 60 . . . 136

DPP v Fidler and Moran [1992] 1 WLR 91 . . . 136

DPP v Hawkins [1988] 3 All ER 673 . . . 151

Table of Cases

DPP v Hutchinson [1990] 2 AC 783 . . . 200
DPP v Jones (Margaret) [1999] 2 AC 240; [1999] 2 All ER 257 . . . 133, 136, 139, 141, 142, 147
DPP v Jordan [1977] AC 699 . . . 158
DPP v Orum [1988] 3 All ER 449 . . . 137
DPP v Whyte [1972] AC 849 . . . 158
D'Souza v DPP [1992] 4 All ER 545 . . . 151
Dudgeon v UK (1981) 4 EHRR 523 . . . 170
Duke v GEC Reliance Ltd [1988] AC 618 . . . 91
Duncan v Cammell Laird [1942] AC 624 . . . 179, 217, 218
Duncan v Jones [1963] 1 KB 218 . . . 138, 145
Dunlop v Woollahra Municipal Council [1982] AC 158 . . . 205, 214
Dunn v R [1896] 1 QB 116 . . . 211
Dyson v Attorney-General [1911] 1 KB 410, CA . . . 178

E (a child), Re [2009] 1 All ER 467 . . . 135, 139, 148
E v Secretary of State for the Home Department [2004] QB 1044 . . . 192
Ellen St Estates Ltd v Minister of Health [1934] 1 KB 590 . . . 86, 90, 95, 96
Engel v Netherlands (No. 1) (1976) 1 EHRR 647 . . . 162
Entick v Carrington (1765) 19 St Tr 1030 . . . 101, 116, 149, 152, 153, 171
Eszias v North Glamorgan NHS Trust [2007] 4 All ER 940 . . . 187

Factortame (C-213/89) [1990] 3 CMLR 375 . . . 91, 94
Factortame (C-221/89) [1991] 3 CMLR 589 . . . 91, 94
Factortame (No. 2) [1991] 1 AC 603 . . . 9
Fairmount Investments v Secretary of State for the Environment [1976] 1 WLR 1255 . . . 186
Financial Times v UK (2010) 50 EHRR 46 . . . 163
Foster v British Gas [1991] 1 AC 306 . . . 96
Fox, Campbell and Hartley v UK (1991) 13 EHRR 157 . . . 129
Francome v Mirror Group Newspapers Ltd [1984] 2 All ER 408 . . . 172
Franklin v Minister of Town and Country Planning [1948] AC 87, HL . . . 179

Garland v British Rail Engineering [1983] 2 AC 751 . . . 90
Genner v Sparks (1705) 6 Mod Rep 173 . . . 151
Ghani v Jones [1970] 1 QB 693 . . . 153
Gillan & Quinton v UK [2010] 50 EHRR 45 . . . 114, 147
Golder v United Kingdom (1975) 1 EHRR 524 . . . 129
Goodwin v UK (2002) 35 EHRR 44 . . . 170
Gouriet v UPW [1978] AC 435, HL . . . 42, 54

HK, Re [1967] 2 QB 617 . . . 186
HM Treasury v Ahmed & Others [2010] 2 WLR 378 . . . 114
HM Treasury v Information Commissioner [2010] 2 All ER 55 . . . 168
HRH Prince of Wales v Associated Newspapers Ltd [2008] Ch 57 . . . 174
Halford v UK (1997) 24 EHRR 523 . . . 170
Handysides v UK (1976) 1 EHRR 737 . . . 159
Harris v Minister of the Interior 1952 (2) SA 428 . . . 87
Hashman and Harrup v United Kingdom (2000) 30 EHRR 241 . . . 147
Hatton v UK (2003) 37 EHRR 28 . . . 204
Hellewell v Chief Constable of Derbyshire [1995] 1 WLR 804 . . . 172
Hello! v Douglas [2001] 2 All ER 289 . . . 119
Helow v Secretary of State for the Home Department [2009] 2 All ER 1071 . . . 188
Hetley v Boyer (1614) Cro Jac 336 . . . 178
Hill v Chief Constable of West Yorkshire [1989] AC 53 . . . 206, 214
Hirst v Chief Constable of West Yorkshire (1987) 85 Cr App R 143 . . . 147
Holgate-Mohammed v Duke [1984] AC 437 . . . 151
Home Office v Dorset Yacht Co [1970] AC 1004 . . . 207, 216
Howard v Secretary of State for the Environment [1975] QB 235 . . . 184

Ireland v UK (1978) 2 EHRR 25 . . . 112, 113, 115, 130

Jackson Developments v Hall [1951] 2 KB 488 . . . 184
Jain v Trent Strategic Health Authority [2009] 1 All ER 957 . . . 206, 215

Table of Cases

James v Minister of Housing and Local Government [1966] 1 WLR 135 . . . 184
Jeffrey v Black [1978] QB 490 . . . 152
Johnstone v Pedlar [1921] 2 AC 262 . . . 51
Jordan v UK (2001) 11 BHRC 1 . . . 112

Kaye v Robertson [1991] FSR 62 . . . 171
Khan v Commissioner of Police of the Metropolis [2008] EWCA Civ 723 . . . 152, 153
Khan v UK (2001) 31 EHRR 1016 . . . 170
Klass v Germany (1978) 2 EHRR 214 . . . 162
Kulkarni v Milton Keynes Hospital [2009] EWCA Civ 789 . . . 187
Kynaston v DPP (1987) 84 Cr App R 200 . . . 151

Laker Airways v Department of Trade [1977] QB 643 . . . 42, 51
Lawless v Ireland (No. 2) (1961) 1 EHRR 15 . . . 115
Lawless v Ireland (No. 3) (1961) 1 EHRR 15 . . . 129
Lewis v Chief Constable of South Wales [1991] 1 All ER 206 . . . 151
Lister v Forth Dry Dock [1990] 1 AC 546 . . . 90
Littrell v USA (No. 2) [1994] 3 All ER 203 . . . 51
Liverpool Taxi Fleet Operators' Association, Re [1972] 2 QB 299 . . . 192
Liversidge v Anderson [1942] AC 206 . . . 128, 179
London & Clydeside Estates v Aberdeen District Council [1980] 1 WLR 182 . . . 182
Lord Advocate v Dumbarton Council [1990] 2 AC 580 . . . 209

M v Home Office [1992] QB 270 . . . 107
M v Home Office [1994] 1 AC 377 . . . 33, 103, 212
Macarthys Ltd v Smith [1981] QB 180 . . . 92, 97, 98
Madzimbamuto v Lardner-Burke [1969] AC 645 . . . 12
Magee v UK (2001) 31 EHRR 822 . . . 115
Malone v Metropolitan Police Commissioner [1979] Ch 344 . . . 102, 117, 171
Marbury v Madison (1803) 1 Cranch 137 . . . 10, 105

Marcic v Thames Water Utilities Ltd [2004] 2 AC 42 . . . 204
Marleasing (C-106/89) [1992] 1 CMLR 305 . . . 91, 94
Marleasing SA v La Commercial Internacional de Alimentacion SA [1990] ECR I-4135 . . . 97
Marshall v Southampton and SW Hants AHA [1986] QB 402 . . . 96
Matthews v Ministry of Defence [2003] 1 All ER 689 . . . 118, 210
Mayor of London v Hall [2010] EWCA Civ 817 . . . 148
McCann v UK (2008) 47 EHRR 40 . . . 125
McE, Re [2009] 4 All ER 335 . . . 115
McGann, Farrell and Savage v UK (1995) 21 EHRR 97 . . . 112
McLeod v United Kingdom (1999) 27 EHRR 493 . . . 147
McLorie v Oxford [1982] QB 1290 . . . 152
Mersey Docks and Harbour Board Trustees v Gibbs (1866) LR 1 HL 93 . . . 213
Metropolitan Asylum District v Hill (1881) 6 App Cas 193 . . . 204
Mitchell v R [1896] 1 QB 121 . . . 211
Mortensen v Peters (1906) 8F(J) 93 . . . 85, 95
Mosley v News Group Newspapers [2008] EMLR 20; [2008] EWHC 1777 . . . 124, 174
Moss v McLachlan [1985] IRLR 76 . . . 143
Mulcahy v Ministry of Defence [1996] 2 All ER 758 . . . 210
Muller v Switzerland (1991) 13 EHRR 212 . . . 159
Murray v Express Group Newspapers [2008] HRLR 33, CA . . . 174
Murray v UK (1996) 22 EHRR 29 . . . 115

Nagy v Weston [1965] 1 All ER 78 . . . 141
Netz v Chuter Ede [1946] Ch 224 . . . 50
Nissan v Attorney-General [1970] AC 179 . . . 209
Nissan v Attorney-General [1970] AC 179, HL . . . 51

O'Reilly v Mackman [1983] 2 AC 237 . . . 182, 194
Observer v UK (1991) 14 EHRR 153 . . . 164
Osgood v Nelson (1872) LR HL 636 . . . 187
Osman v United Kingdom (1998) 29 EHRR 245 . . . 130, 207, 215

Table of Cases

Padfield v Minister of Agriculture [1968] AC 997, HL . . . 180

Parlement Belge, The [1879] 4 PD 129 . . . 51

Pearlberg v Varty [1972] 1 WLR 534 . . . 186

Percy v DPP (2002) 166 JP 93 . . . 136, 143

Percy v DPP [1995] 3 All ER 124; [1995] 1 WLR 1382 . . . 138, 143, 146

Phelps v London Borough of Hillingdon [2000] 4 All ER 504 . . . 216

Pickin v BRB [1974] AC 765 . . . 9, 95, 97, 198

Pickstone v Freemans plc [1989] AC 66 . . . 90, 98

Pinochet, ex parte [1999] 1 All ER 577 . . . 187

Platform Arzte fur das Leben (1988) 13 EHRR 204 . . . 136, 138, 148

Poplar Housing v Donoghue [2001] 3 WLR 183 . . . 117

Porter v Magill [2001] UKHL 67; [2002] 1 All ER 465 . . . 188

Pretty v UK [2002] 2 FCR 97 . . . 120

Prince Albert v Strange (1849) 1 Mac & G 25 . . . 171

Prince of Wales v Jim Regan The Times, 7 May, 1981 . . . 172

R v A (Complainant's sexual history) [2002] 1 AC 45 . . . 117

R v Abdroikov [2008] 1 All ER 315 . . . 187

R v Anderson [1972] 1 QB 304 . . . 158

R v Barnsley MBC ex parte Hook [1976] 1 WLR 1052 . . . 190

R v Bottrill ex parte Kuechenmeister [1947] KB 41 . . . 50

R v Budimir [2010] 2 Cr App R 29 . . . 159

R v Chief Constable of Devon and Cornwall ex parte CEGB [1982] QB 458 . . . 135, 146, 148

R v Chief Constable of South Wales ex parte Merrick [1994] 2 All ER 560 . . . 114

R v Chief Constable of the West Midlands Police ex parte Wiley [1994] 3 All ER 420; [1995] 1 AC 274 . . . 205, 218, 220

R v City Panel on Takeovers and Mergers ex parte Datafin Ltd [1987] QB 817 . . . 198

R v Criminal Injuries Compensation Board ex parte A [1999] 2 AC 330 . . . 192

R v Criminal Injuries Compensation Board ex parte Lain [1967] 2 QB 864 . . . 43

R v Crown Court at Northampton ex parte DPP (1991) 93 Cr App R 376 . . . 153

R v Dairy Produce Quota Tribunal ex parte Caswell [1990] 2 AC 738 . . . 195

R v Davis (Iain) [2008] 3 WLR 125 . . . 129

R v Department of Health and Social Security, ex parte Camden LBC (1986) Times, 5 March . . . 199

R v Disciplinary Committee of the Jockey Club ex parte Aga Khan [1993] 1 WLR 909 . . . 193

R v DPP ex parte Kebilene [2000] 2 AC 326 . . . 118

R v Employment Secretary ex parte Equal Opportunities Commission [1995] 1 AC 1 . . . 97

R v Foreign Secretary ex parte Everett [1989] AC 1014 . . . 43, 50, 54

R v Foreign Secretary ex parte Rees-Mogg [1994] 1 All ER 457 . . . 51

R v Foreign Secretary ex parte World Development Movement [1995] 1 WLR 386 . . . 195

R v Gaming Board ex parte Benaim [1970] 2 QB 417 . . . 186

R v Health Secretary ex parte US Tobacco International Inc [1992] QB 353 . . . 183

R v Hicklin (1868) LR 3 QB 360 . . . 158

R v HM Treasury ex parte Smedley [1985] 1 QB 657 . . . 195

R v Home Secretary ex parte Bentley [1993] 4 All ER 442 . . . 40, 43, 44, 54

R v Home Secretary ex parte Brind [1991] 1 AC 696 . . . 117

R v Home Secretary ex parte Cheblak [1991] 2 All ER 319 . . . 50

R v Home Secretary ex parte Doody [1994] 1 AC 531 . . . 192

R v Home Secretary ex parte Fire Brigades Union [1995] 2 All ER 244 . . . 40, 43, 54

R v Home Secretary ex parte Northumbria Police Authority [1987] 2 WLR 998; [1988] 1 All ER 556 . . . 40, 42, 52, 102

R v Home Secretary ex parte Venables and Thompson [1998] AC 407 . . . 124

R v Horncastle and Others [2010] 2 WLR 47 . . . 125

R v Horseferry Road Magistrate ex parte Siadatan [1991] 1 All ER 324 . . . 136

R v Howell (Erroll) [1982] 2 QB 416 . . . 138, 144, 147

Table of Cases

R v Hull Prison Visitors ex parte St Germain (No. 2) [1979] 1 WLR 1401 . . . 187

R v Inland Revenue Commissioners ex parte National Federation of Self-Employed & Small Businesses [1982] AC 617 . . . 184, 195

R v Jefferson [1994] 1 All ER 270 . . . 137

R v Jones [2006] 2 WLR 772 . . . 50, 142

R v Keogh [2007] 1 WLR 1500 . . . 162, 163

R v London County Council ex parte Corrie [1918] 1 KB 68 . . . 190

R v Longman [1988] 1 WLR 619 . . . 153

R v Maze Prison Visitors ex parte Hone [1988] AC 379 . . . 187

R v Metropolitan Police Commissioner ex parte Parker [1953] 1 WLR 1150 . . . 179

R v Ministry of Defence ex parte Smith [1995] 4 All ER 427 . . . 117

R v North Devon Health Authority ex parte Coughlan [2001] QB 213 . . . 191

R v Northumberland Compensation Appeal Tribunal ex parte Shaw [1952] 1 KB 338, CA . . . 179

R v Odhams Press [1957] 1 QB 73 . . . 159

R v Offen [2000] 1 WLR 253 . . . 117

R v Panel on Takeovers and Mergers ex parte Datafin [1987] QB 815 . . . 194

R v Ponting [1985] Crim LR 318 . . . 161, 162, 166

R v Porter [2006] 1 WLR 2633 . . . 159

R v Rimmington, R v Goldstein [2006] 1 AC 459 . . . 141

R v Rogers (Philip) [2007] 2 AC 62 . . . 136

R v Secker and Warburg [1954] 2 All ER 683 . . . 158

R v Secretary of State for Social Services ex parte Association of Metropolitan Authorities [1986] 1 WLR 1 . . . 198

R v Secretary of State for the Environment ex parte Association of Metropolitan Authorities [1986] 1 WLR 1 . . . 183

R v Secretary of State for the Environment ex parte Greenpeace [1994] 4 All ER 352 . . . 184

R v Secretary of State for the Environment ex parte Nottinghamshire CC [1986] 2 AC 240 . . . 214

R v Secretary of State for the Environment ex parte Notts CC [1986] AC 240 . . . 95

R v Secretary of State for the Environment ex parte Rose Theatre Trust [1990] 1 QB 504 . . . 195

R v Secretary of State for the Home Department ex parte Fire Brigades Unions [1995] 2 AC 513 . . . 107

R v Secretary of State for Transport ex parte Factortame (No. 1) [1990] 2 AC 85 . . . 98

R v Secretary of State for Transport ex parte Factortame Ltd [1991] 1 AC 603 . . . 93, 94, 96, 97

R v Secretary of State for Transport ex parte Factortame Ltd (No. 4) [1996] 2 WLR 506 . . . 98

R v Secretary of State for Transport ex parte Pegasus [1989] 2 All ER 481 . . . 190

R v Shayler [2003] 1 AC 247 . . . 162, 164

R v Sheer Metalcraft [1954] 1 QB 586 . . . 200

R v Sherwood ex parte The Telegraph Group [2001] I WLR 1983 . . . 160

R v Skirving [1985] QB 819 . . . 158

R v Stratford on Avon DC ex parte Jackson [1985] 1 WLR 1319 . . . 195

R v Taylor (1993) 98 Cr App R 361 . . . 160

R v Thames Magistrates' Court ex parte Polemis [1974] 1 WLR 1371 . . . 186

R v Wear Valley DC ex parte Binks [1985] 2 All ER 699 . . . 190

R (Abbasi) v Foreign Secretary (2002) WL 31452052 . . . 54

R (Al Rawi) v Secretary of State for Foreign and Commonwealth Affairs [2006] All ER (D) 46 . . . 44

R (Al Skeini) v Secretary of State for Defence [2007] 3 WLR 33; [2008] 1 AC 153 . . . 51, 124, 209, 210

R (Alconbury Developments Ltd.) v Secretary of State for the Environment [2003] 2 AC 295 . . . 125

R (Amin) v Home Secretary [2004] 1 AC 653 . . . 130

R (Anderson) v Home Secretary [2002] 4 All ER 108; [2003] 1 AC 837 . . . 107, 124, 125, 130, 131

R (Bancoult) v Secretary of State for Foreign and Commonwealth Affairs [2001] 1 QB 1067 . . . 44, 54

R (Bancoult) v Secretary of State for Foreign and Commonwealth Affairs (No. 2) [2006] All ER (D) 149 . . . 44, 54

Table of Cases

R (Begum) v Denbigh High School [2006] 2 All ER 487 . . . 119

R (Bibi) v Newham Borough Council [2002] 1 WLR 237 . . . 191

R (Binyam Mohamed) v Secretary of State for Foreign Affairs [2010] EWCA Civ 65 . . . 113, 124

R (Black) v Secretary of State for Justice [2009] 4 All ER 1 . . . 125, 130

R (C) v Secretary of State for Justice [2009] QB 657 . . . 197, 200

R (Countryside Alliance and Others) v Attorney-General and Another [2008] 3 All ER 1 . . . 128

R (Daly) v Home Secretary [2001] 2 AC 532 . . . 129

R (Eisai) v National Institute for Health and Clinical Excellence [2008] EWCA Civ 438 . . . 183

R (G) v Governors of X School [2010] 2 All ER 555 . . . 187

R (GG) v Secretary of State for the Home Department [2010] 1 All ER 721 . . . 114

R (Gillan) v Commissioner of Police of the Metropolis [2006] 2 WLR 537 . . . 114

R (Greenfield) v Secretary of State for the Home Department [2005] 2 All ER 240 . . . 119, 131

R (Haw) v Secretary of State for the Home Department [2006] All ER (D) 94 . . . 133

R (Jackson) v Attorney-General [2005] UKHL 56 . . . 80, 85

R (Javed) v Home Secretary [2001] 3 WLR 323 . . . 199

R (JL) v Secretary of State for Justice [2009] 2 All ER 521 . . . 130

R (Kay) v Commissioner of Police of the Metropolis [2008] 1 WLR 2723 . . . 138

R (KB) v Mental Health Review Tribunal [2003] 2 All ER 209 . . . 119

R (Laporte) v Chief Constable of Gloucestershire [2007] 2 AC 205, HL . . . 133, 143–5

R (March) v Secretary of State for Health [2010] EWHC 765 . . . 192

R (Niazi) v Secretary of State for the Home Department [2008] EWCA Civ 755 . . . 191

R (Pretty) v DPP [2002] 1 AC 800 . . . 119

R (Pritpal Singh) v Chief Constable of West Midlands [2007] 2 All ER 297 . . . 137

R (Purdy) v DPP [2010] 1 AC 345 . . . 120

R (Quark) v Secretary of State for Foreign and Commonwealth Affairs [2006] 3 All ER 111) . . . 51

R (Smith) v Secretary of State for Defence [2010] 3 WLR 223 . . . 124, 210

R (Spath Holme Ltd) v Secretary of State for the Environment [2001] 2 AC 349 . . . 199

R (Wood) v Metropolitan Police Commissioner [2009] 4 All ER 951 . . . 175

R (on the application of Abbasi and Another v Secretary of State for Foreign Affairs and Secretary of State for the Home Department [2002] WL 3145052 . . . 44

R (on the application of H) v London North and East Mental Health Review Tribunal [2001] QB 1 . . . 118

RB (Algeria) v Secretary of State for the Home Department [2009] 4 All ER 1045 . . . 125

Rai v United Kingdom (1995) 82 ADR 134 . . . 146

Raissi v Metropolitan Police Commissioner [2009] 3 All ER 14 . . . 114

Rassemblement Jurassien et unite Jurassiene v Switzerland (1979) 17 DR 93 . . . 147, 148

Reckley v Minister of Public Safety (No. 2) [1996] 1 All ER 562 . . . 44, 54

Rederiaktiebolaget Amphitrite v R [1921] 3 KB 500 . . . 211

Redknapp v Commissioner of the City of London Police [2009] 1 All ER 229 . . . 153

Redmond-Bate v DPP [2000] HRLR 249 . . . 138, 145, 148

Rehman v SSHD [2001] 3 WLR 877, HL . . . 50, 53

Reynolds v Times Newspapers [2001] 2 AC 127 . . . 156

Ridge v Baldwin [1964] AC 40 . . . 180, 186, 189

Roberts v Hopwood [1925] AC 578 . . . 191, 192

Rogers v Home Secretary [1973] AC 388 . . . 220

Rowe v UK (2000) 30 EHRR 1 . . . 220

Royster v Cavey [1947] KB 204 . . . 209

Ruddock v Vadarlis (2001) 66 ALD 25 . . . 42, 50

S & Marper v UK [2008] ECHR 1581 . . . 124

Scottish Ministers v Scottish Information Commission [2007] SC 330 . . . 168

Secretary of State for Defence v Guardian Newspapers [1984] Ch 156 . . . 163

Secretary of State for Education v Metropolitan Borough of Tameside [1977] AC 1014 . . . 183

Secretary of State for the Home Department v AF (No. 3) [2009] 3 All ER 643 . . . 124

Secretary of State for the Home Department v AP (Nos. 1 & 2) [2010] UKSC 24 . . . 114

Secretary of State for the Home Department v JJ [2008] 1 All ER 613 . . . 124

Secretary of State for the Home Department v MB and Same v AF [2008] 1 AC 440 . . . 114

Secretary of State for the Home Department v Rehman [2003] 1 AC 153 . . . 118

Semayne's Case (1604) 77 Eng Rep 194 . . . 149

Shaaban Bin Hussien v Chong Fook Kam [1970] AC 942 . . . 150

Shaw v DPP [1962] AC 220 . . . 159

Silver v United Kingdom (1981) 3 EHRR 475 . . . 129

Simmonds v Newell [1953] 1 WLR 826 . . . 197, 200

Smith v East Elloe RDC [1956] AC 736, HL . . . 179, 180

Soering v UK (1996) 23 EHRR 413 . . . 123, 130

Spencer v United Kingdom (1998) 25 EHRR CD 105 . . . 173

Steel v UK (1999) 28 HHRR 603 . . . 144, 146

Stovin v Wise [1996] AC 923 . . . 216

Sunday Times v United Kingdom (1979) 2 EHRR 245 . . . 160

Taylor v Thames Valley Chief Constable [2004] 3 All ER 503 . . . 151

Thoburn v Sunderland City Council [2002] EWHC 195 Admin; [2002] 4 All ER 156; [2002] 1 CMLR 50 . . . 88, 91, 98

Three Rivers DC v Bank of England [2000] 3 All ER 1 . . . 205

Trawnik v Lennox [1985] 1 WLR 532 . . . 209

Van Colle v Chief Constable of Hertfordshire Police [2008] 3 All ER 977 . . . 207, 214, 215

Van Duyn v Home Office [1975] Ch 358 . . . 96

Van Gend en Loos v Nederlandse [1963] CMLR 105 . . . 94

Venables & Thompson v News Group Newspapers Ltd [2001] 1 All ER 908 . . . 119

Venables v News Group Newspapers [2001] Fam 430 . . . 124, 173

Von Hannover v Germany (2005) 40 EHRR 1 . . . 174

Wainwright v Home Office [2004] 2 AC 406 . . . 119, 171

Wason v Walter (1868) LR 4 QB 73 . . . 77

Watkins v Home Secretary [2006] 2 All ER 353 . . . 205

Webb v EMO Air Cargo (No. 2) [1995] 4 All ER 577; [1995] 1 WLR 1454 . . . 91, 97

Williams v Home Office [1981] 1 All ER 1151 . . . 206, 219

Woodward v Hutchins [1971] 1 WLR 760 . . . 172, 174

X v Bedfordshire CC [1995] 2 AC 633 . . . 206, 214, 215

Yarl's Wood Immigration Ltd v Bedfordshire Police [2008] EWHC 2207 . . . 119, 130

YL v Birmingham City Council [2008] 1 AC 95 . . . 119

Z v United Kingdom [2001] 2 FLR 612 . . . 215

Table of Statutes

Acquisition of Land Act 1919 . . . 86
Act of Settlement 1700 . . . 9
Acts of Union 1707 . . . 86, 88
Anti-Social Behaviour Act 2003 . . . 132
    s 30 . . . 137
    s 57 . . . 142
Anti-terrorism, Crime and Security Act 2001 . . . 112
    s 23 . . . 113

Bill of Rights 1689 . . . 9, 54, 88, 121, 197
    Art 1 . . . 84
    Art 9 . . . 75, 95

Constitutional Reform Act 2005 . . . 9, 78
    s 3 . . . 107
    s 133 . . . 106
Constitutional Reform and Governance Act 2010 . . . 167, 211
    s 32 . . . 133
Contempt of Court Act 1981
    s 2(2) . . . 159
    s 2(3) . . . 159
    s 5 . . . 159
    s 10 . . . 163
Crime (Sentences) Act 1997
    s 2 . . . 117
Crime and Disorder Act 1998 . . . 132
    s 31 . . . 136
Criminal Damage Act 1971
    s 1(1) . . . 142
Criminal Justice Act 2003 . . . 118
Criminal Justice and Immigration Act 2008 . . . 155
    s 63 . . . 159
Criminal Justice and Police Act 2001
    s 42 . . . 137
Criminal Justice and Public Order Act 1994 . . . 132, 140, 147, 157
    s 60 . . . 141
    s 61 . . . 135
    s 63 . . . 135, 141

    s 68 . . . 142
    s 69 . . . 142
    s 84 . . . 159
    s 90 . . . 159
    s 168 . . . 158
    Sch 9, para 3 . . . 158
Crown Proceedings Act 1947 . . . 102, 208, 213
    s 1 . . . 211
    s 2 . . . 203, 209
    s 2(1) . . . 209
    s 6 . . . 209
    s 10 . . . 210
    s 21 . . . 204
    s 21(1) . . . 212
    s 25(1) . . . 212
    s 40(2)(f) . . . 209
Crown Proceedings (Armed Forces) Act 1987 . . . 210

Declaration of Abdication Act 1936 . . . 87
Deregulation and Contracting Out Act 1994 . . . 102

Equality Act 2006 . . . 121
European Communities Act 1972 . . . 9, 89, 91, 92
    s 2(1) . . . 90, 95
    s 2(4) . . . 96, 97
    s 3(1) . . . 90, 95
European Parliamentary Elections Act 1999 . . . 29

Freedom of Information Act 2000 . . . 68, 117, 156, 165, 167
    s 53 . . . 168

Government of Ireland Act 1920 . . . 17
Government of Wales Act 1998 . . . 8, 18
Government of Wales Act 2006 . . . 8

Health and Social Care Act 2008
    s 145 . . . 119

Highways Act 1980
  s 137 . . . 141, 147
House of Commons Disqualification Act 1975
  Sch 1 . . . 106
House of Lords Act 1999 . . . 78, 79
Housing Act 1925 . . . 86
Human Rights Act 1998 . . . 49, 51, 52, 88, 103, Ch 8, 177
  s 1 . . . 120
  s 2 . . . 119, 120, 122, 125, 128, 140, 159, 170
  s 3 . . . 9, 117, 121, 131, 140, 162
  s 4 . . . 118, 121, 131
  s 6 . . . 119, 120, 130, 160, 173
  s 6(2) . . . 131
  s 7 . . . 119, 120, 130
  s 8 . . . 119, 120
  s 10 . . . 118, 120, 136
  s 12 . . . 164
  s 22(5) . . . 209
  Sch 1 ECHR . . . 9, 49
  Art 1 . . . 123, 124, 210
  Art 2 . . . 112, 124, 127, 174, 215
  Art 3 . . . 112, 123, 126, 127, 174, 200, 210, 215
  Art 5 . . . 103, 114, 117, 124, 127–9, 143, 149
  Art 5(1) . . . 147
  Art 5(1)(c) . . . 114, 129
  Art 6 . . . 103, 107, 114, 117, 124, 125, 127, 129, 160, 162, 185, 187, 210, 215
  Art 6(3)(c) . . . 114
  Art 6(3)(d) . . . 129
  Art 8 . . . 114, 122, 124, 125, 128, 147, 149, 171, 173, 200, 203, 204
  Art 8(1) . . . 170
  Art 8(2) . . . 128
  Art 10 . . . 133, 140, 143, 145, 147, 156, 162, 171, 173
  Art 10(1) . . . 145
  Art 10(2) . . . 145
  Art 11 . . . 127, 128, 133, 134, 136, 140, 141, 144–8
  Art 11(1) . . . 145
  Art 11(2) . . . 128, 140, 145
  Art 15 . . . 115, 127, 129

  Protocol 1, Art 1 . . . 149, 200
Hunting Act 2004 . . . 29, 128
Hunting Act 2009 . . . 126, 131

Ireland Act 1949 . . . 17

Local Government Act 1972 . . . 186

Magna Carta 1215 . . . 9
Merchant Shipping Act 1988 . . . 91

Northern Ireland Act 1998 . . . 8, 19, 87
  s 1 . . . 86
Northern Ireland Act 2000 . . . 19
Northern Ireland (St. Andrews Agreement) Act 2006 . . . 19

Obscene Publications Act 1959 . . . 155
  s 1 . . . 157, 158
  s 4 . . . 158
Official Secrets Act 1911
  s 1 . . . 161, 166
  s 2 . . . 162
  s 2(3) . . . 162
  s 2(4)(b) . . . 162
  s 3(4) . . . 162
Official Secrets Act 1989 . . . 161, 162, 164
  s 5 . . . 163
  s 7 . . . 163
  s 8 . . . 163

Parliament Act 1911 . . . 85
Parliament Acts 1911–1949 . . . 80, 81
Parliament Act 1949 . . . 85
Parliamentary Papers Act 1840 . . . 77
Police and Criminal Evidence Act 1984 . . . 149
  s 8 . . . 153
  s 10 . . . 153
  s 14 . . . 153
  s 17 . . . 150
  s 17(1)(d) . . . 151
  s 17(4) . . . 151
  s 18 . . . 150, 152, 153
  s 19 . . . 150, 153
  s 24 . . . 150

s 28 . . . 151
s 32 . . . 150, 152, 153
s 32(2)(b) . . . 152
s 32(3) . . . 152
s 67(11) . . . 152
s 117 . . . 151
Prevention of Terrorism Act 2000 . . . 118
Prevention of Terrorism Act 2005 . . . 114
Prevention of Terrorism (Temporary Provisions) Act 1984 . . . 113
Protection of Children Act 1978 . . . 157
Public Order Act 1936 . . . 132
Public Order Act 1986 . . . 76, 132, 144
    s 1 . . . 135, 137
    s 2 . . . 135, 137
    s 3 . . . 135, 137
    s 4 . . . 135, 136, 146
    s 4A . . . 135
    s 5 . . . 135, 136, 143, 146
    s 7 . . . 137
    s 8 . . . 137
    s 11 . . . 138
    s 12 . . . 138
    s 13 . . . 146
    s 14 . . . 137, 142
    s 14A . . . 135
    s 16 . . . 135, 141, 142
Public Order Act 1994 . . . 132
Public Records Act 1958 . . . 167

Racial and Religious Hatred Act 2006 . . . 156

Regulation of Investigatory Powers Act 2000 . . . 115, 117

Scotland Act 1998 . . . 8, 18, 19
Serious Organised Crime and Police Act 2005 . . . 150
    ss 132–138 . . . 132
Sex Discrimination Act 1975 . . . 90
Statutory Instruments Act 1946
    s 3(2) . . . 200
Suicide Act 1961 . . . 120
Supreme Court Act 1981
    s 31 . . . 180, 184

Terrorism Act 2000
    s.11 . . . 115
Terrorism Act 2006 . . . 85, 113
    s 1 . . . 111
    s 34 . . . 112
Terrorist Anti-Freezing (Temporary Provisions) Act 2010 . . . 114
Treasure Act 1996 . . . 54

Video Recordings Act 2010 . . . 157, 159

War Damage Act 1965 . . . 85, 102

Youth Justice and Criminal Evidence Act 1999
    s 43(1)(c) . . . 117

1

Introduction

The two authors have considerable experience in teaching constitutional and administrative law and related subjects. We think that this enables us to give some guidance and advice on how to approach this subject and tackle typical coursework and exam assessment questions. What we do not claim to do is to give you the answer to every possible question that might be asked.

One initial point of clarification. On your course, and in this book, some topics, such as Devolution, specifically consider England, Northern Ireland, Scotland and Wales. Some historical reference may be made to 'Great Britain', 'Britain' or 'England'. This apart, we are considering the constitution of the United Kingdom.

Public law is different from the other compulsory law subjects in that it is very wide ranging. Much of it is not really law at all and therefore calls for different skills in the student. To understand public law properly it helps to have some knowledge of current affairs and politics. Students often think that it is unfair to expect them to know things that are not in the textbook or were not in the lecture but there is a reason for this. Public law is a compulsory subject because of the vital importance of having an understanding of the constitution of the country the laws of which you are studying, for itself and for its significance in terms of the values it rests upon and the historical and cultural context it provides in your further study. Politics is all about governance, so an understanding of who exercises political power, how and why is of immense importance in your study of laws that bind us all in everyday life. You will find your study of constitutional and administrative law very much easier, and probably more engaging, if you keep up with current affairs, even if you never let it darken your door again once the course is over!

With this subject there is often no single, right answer; be it a problem or essay question with which you are faced. There is no constitutional rulebook set in stone and covering every eventuality. For instance a problem question about police powers carries with it the factor that a police officer always has discretion, just as the Prime Minister is constantly faced with decisions requiring him to exercise his judgement, and any essay question concerning constitutional reform is all about argument of options and opinions. It is all about studying in depth and detail, reading enough to encounter 'all' sides of an issue, as well as honing key skills including effective research, critical analysis and evaluation.

As the United Kingdom does not have a 'written constitution', the syllabus is accordingly very wide ranging. Different public law courses will include some different topics and syllabuses may emphasise different themes, although there is a universal core of content. In this book we have tried to tackle the most typical subjects. If you study past examination papers at your institution you will see that there is no magic in what comes up. Rote learning of set answers to set questions is absolutely not what to do. What does assist, however, is that within the parameters of your course, there are only so many topics that can be tested, only so many themes and issues to be examined and only so many styles of problem or essay questions that may be put. This presents an opportunity not for 'question spotting' but to marshal pertinent common material and arguments. Plan in advance by thinking roughly what you would do when faced with several varieties of the same sort of question. The examples we give in the book are meant to help here, embracing many 'typical' questions, demonstrating common lines of argument and emphasising key features of the UK constitution that crop up time and again. You do not have to agree with our arguments or conclusions and they are not designed for regurgitation anyhow. Consider how we have used material and constructed argument.

One particular aspect of constitutional and administrative law is the considerable overlap of topics. In reality no country's constitution operates in conveniently separated boxes. So, you must approach your study and assessments in the same way. You must think across topics and make the links in your answers. It will make all of the difference to your understanding of and success in the subject.

In answering essay questions, objective, coherent, cogent, corroborated argument of all sides is key. Preparation and planning are crucial. You must make effective use of appropriate, referenced sources. Use primary sources wherever possible. Read essay questions carefully, they can often be misunderstood. Identify the main topic first. Do not, as one author once did, mistake a question on crown privilege for one on the royal prerogative! They are not at all the same thing. Often rather dense and obscure quotations are used, putting propositions and quandaries, followed by 'Discuss'. Do not worry if you have never seen the quotation before or have never heard of the author. In fact the quotation may contain useful information and help to focus your answer. Refer back to and use the quotation as appropriate. Above all, provided you understand what is being said and are clear about the topic area, do not be put off. For example, a question like the following might seem intimidating, but in reality it is not hard:

> The short explanation of the constitutional conventions is that they provide the flesh which clothes the dry bones of the law; they make the legal constitution work; they keep it in touch with the growth of ideas.
>
> (Sir Ivor Jennings)
> Discuss.

It is obviously about constitutional conventions! It indicates that only a small part of the constitution is law, 'the dry bones'—much of it is convention. Laws are 'dry bones', because if we only looked at the laws we would get a very misleading impression of the constitution. Without conventions the constitution would be unworkable. Give examples. The 'growth of ideas' bit indicates that conventions are flexible and change as politics and society change. Again, give examples.

To some students, problem questions seem more tangible and clear in public law. The essence is to apply the law to the facts. The facts can be very helpful, provided you make full use of them. Again the first thing to do is to identify the main topics upon which the problem focuses; be warned: it is possible to 'disguise' areas quite easily in this subject. Then identify the main legal points raised. They should often trigger cases in your memory. Do not worry if you cannot remember the exact name; still make full use of them in your answer. Make sure that you answer the exact question set, fully. For example, if it says 'Advise the police', don't advise the person arrested. If you have two clients to advise concerning three incidents in which both were involved, then your answer structure must have six sub-answers. The advice to both clients may or may not be the same on each matter, but the important thing is that you answer the question comprehensively by addressing each element.

Whether you are writing an essay or a problem answer it is always best to do a rough plan first, listing the main points that you intend to cover. For a problem you might also include a list of the main cases. For an essay you would need not just cases, but authors' opinions and examples.

If you have done some work and have some basic knowledge, there is nothing to fear. Constitutional and administrative law is not about mathematical formulas; you will not get 100% or 0% depending upon your final conclusion (essay question) or advice (problem). What matters is how you get there: identifying the right topic, issues and arguments; effective, substantiated argument; and effective application to the focus of the nub of the question set. Remember, again, that there is rarely a single, right answer.

If you are asked for your view, give it, but ensure that it is given in addition to and not instead of substantiated, objective argument. Reform of the UK constitution seems ever to gather pace, as the new government's extensive agenda illustrates. Hence, questions upon reform may crop up more and more. Even if the entire question is devoted to 'what would you do' in reforming the constitution or an aspect of it, you must still give an explanation, analysis and evaluation of what currently happens, then turning to an informed, corroborated argument for (and model of) reform. Having put forward a proper argument supported by evidence, may you then give your own *political* viewpoint? If the terms and nature of the question make it necessary or appropriate, yes. A problem question upon public disorder will very likely require strict application of law to facts only, but a discursive essay question upon the same topic may well seek your view. If you think that the Public Order Act 1986 is draconian in its impact upon freedom of expression and protest, or, to give a different illustration, that the UK's membership of the European Union is vital to prevent the growth of nationalism and xenophobia, so be it: provided, as with everything, what you write or say is relevant and material. If you are asked for an opinion on the way in which European Union law has affected the traditional doctrine of the sovereignty of the UK Parliament, do not express the view that you hate all things European and that you dislike the way 'foreigners' are taking over this country! Irrespective of the marker's view of such an opinion, it fails the test of relevance and materiality. It has no bearing upon the legal and political issues concerning the question posed. Instead, what you should do is show that you are aware of the domestic and European Court of Justice case law on this subject, and, in a really good answer, are aware of why the law has evolved in that way.

As in all legal subjects, there are not any real short cuts to success but we hope that this book can convince you that public law is not quite as intimidating as you thought.

2

Constitutions; the Nature and Sources of the United Kingdom Constitution

Introduction

For many, this is the most difficult area of the whole subject. It is rather theoretical and seems to have no beginning and no end. Different lecturers have very different approaches in this area. Some like to include a lot of political theory and others do not. We hope that the Questions and Suggested Answers in this chapter help your understanding of the key ideas and issues.

This area concerns a fairly traditional set of issues.

A good starting point is, why does any country have a constitution at all? The obvious answers are: first, to limit the power of the government so that it cannot do whatever it likes; secondly, to protect the rights or liberties of the individual not just from the government but also from other powerful groups; and a third less obvious reason is legitimacy. Why do 'the people' accept that a particular small group of individuals is entitled to govern and set the laws of the land? This is often a function of a written constitution: such documents often say that the people of the country have decided upon these particular constitutional arrangements. For example, 'We the People of the United States do ordain and establish this constitution for the United States of America.' Many countries with a written constitution have specialist courts to deal with public law issues, separate from the private law courts.

The UK is different: it is one of the few countries in the world without a 'written constitution', and there is no clear-cut distinction between public law and private law.

Some critics, dating back to Thomas Paine in the eighteenth century (*The Rights of Man* (1792)) and continuing into modern times (for instance F. F. Ridley 'There is no British Constitution: A Dangerous Case of the Emperor's Clothes' (1988) 41 Parliamentary Affairs) claim that the UK's arrangements are so defective that there is no constitution at all as none of the key aims (granting legitimacy, limiting government and safeguarding liberties) is achieved. The conventional view, however, as put in for example A. V. Dicey's *Introduction to the Study of the Law of the Constitution* (1885) and Sir Ivor Jennings' *The Law and the Constitution* (1959), is that the UK does have a constitution but not a 'written constitution', that is instead of being set out in one or a limited series of documents, it comes from many different sources such as statutes, cases and crown prerogative.

Much of the UK constitution is now written down, in a whole swathe of statute law. However, a significant element is unwritten and indeed not law, being the Conventions of the constitution, which oil the wheels and plug the gaps. Vitally important matters like the existence of the Prime Minister and the real powers of the Queen are governed by convention.

Some consider 'restraining principles' such as the Rule of Law and the Separation of Powers as sources; we consider these topics later, in the context of restraining the power of the State.

Question 1

A written constitution would make a great improvement to the United Kingdom system of government.
   Discuss.

Commentary

A constitutional law course will often start by considering what a constitution is, including a comparison between so-called 'written' and 'unwritten' constitutions. Many students will be hoping for a question like this to turn up in an examination, but it is not quite as straightforward as it seems to write a *good* answer to a question like this.

The phrase 'written constitution' is really a misnomer. A written constitution need not be contained in one document and the constitution could be a few pages long or hundreds of pages long. Some unwritten constitutional conventions will also operate. By the same token, an 'unwritten constitution' will include some elements that are written down somewhere. A written constitution is one that is largely codified in one document or a limited series of documents and, invariably, has legal status. A particular country's written constitution may be short and vague or long and detailed, and it may or may not have special, higher legal status than the ordinary laws of the land. An unwritten constitution is a constitution that is not codified as described above, instead having many different sources.

The question poses a proposition. The student should not take it for granted as being right and indeed does not have to agree with it. Typical of many public law questions, there is no single, right answer to this kind of question. What is required in answer is cogently to argue all sides, in

Constitutions; the Nature and Sources of the United Kingdom Constitution

essence discussing the arguments for and against a change to a written constitution for the UK and coming to a substantiated conclusion. An effective answer will proffer sufficient examples of points made, including up-to-date illustration.

Answer plan

- What a constitution is for
- Written constitutions are adopted following major upheaval such as independence or revolution
- Written constitutions have legal status, sometimes as higher law with a special amendment procedure
- Written constitutions often contain a Bill of Rights
- The UK constitution comprises many sources including statutes, cases and conventions
- An unwritten constitution is flexible, whereas written constitutions may be rigid
- A written constitution cannot contain or provide for everything.

Suggested answer

Every organised state has a constitution, but it does not necessarily have to be a written one. Even clubs and societies have a constitution, as there have to be some rules and the members need to know who has the power to make decisions or take actions. So what is the purpose of a constitution? A constitution grants legitimacy to the State and its governance, provides for how the State is to be governed, limits the power of those who govern and (in a liberal democracy) protects the individual citizen from them. It is there to ensure that those who run the State do not behave in an *arbitrary* manner. They must act according to the rules and procedures and not persecute or oppress the citizen. For example, a government official could not just say to someone 'I do not like you, you cannot live in this country.' Instead there must be laws about nationality, immigration and fair trial. A constitution provides for these things, but just as importantly it would also state who has the power to do what. Who can make laws, is there a Head of State, is there a Prime Minister and who has the real power to decide?

Nearly every country in the world, apart from the UK, New Zealand and Israel, has a written constitution. Generally, countries adopt a written constitution when there is a dramatic break with the past and there is a need to make a fresh start with a new system of governance. For example, the end of the eighteenth century saw the United States of America obtaining its independence (from the UK) and the French Revolution overthrowing the rule of King Louis XVI, each country consciously embracing a new beginning with a new, written constitution. England was, in fact, one of the first countries to have a written constitution, with Oliver

Cromwell's 'Instrument of Government' in 1653, after he had overthrown and executed Charles I. It only lasted, however, until 1660, when the old system of royal government was restored. Since then the UK system of government has changed out of all recognition, but it has changed gradually and there has never been such a drastic break with the past that required or engendered a general desire from politicians or the people for a 'clean sweep' embodied in a new, written constitution.

The Constitution of the United States 1787 is generally considered a 'classic model' written constitution starting as it does (the **Preamble**) with a declaration of values and principles:

> We the people of the United States, in order to form a more perfect union, establish justice, insure domestic tranquility, provide for the common defense, promote the general welfare, and secure the blessings of liberty to ourselves and our posterity, do ordain and establish this Constitution for the United States of America.
>
> We hold these truths to be self-evident, that all men are created equal, that they are endowed by their Creator with certain unalienable Rights, that among these are Life, Liberty and the pursuit of Happiness.

The UK has no such statement. Instead, writers such as Bagehot and Dicey propound our constitutional values.

A written constitution often lays down a special procedure under which the constitution can be changed. For example, Article V of the US Constitution 1787 stipulates that two-thirds of both Houses of the Congress or two-thirds of the legislatures of the states can propose amendments to the Constitution. The proposed amendment then has to be ratified by the legislatures of three-quarters of the states. In the Republic of Ireland, a Bill passed by both Houses of Parliament, together with a majority of the votes in a referendum and the assent of the President amends the Constitution. In contrast, there is no special procedure to change any part of the UK constitution.

The written constitution of a federal country will tend to detail the federal structure, providing, in detail or not, for the powers of the regions (the States of the US or Provinces of Canada for instance) and the powers of the federal (national) government. The unification of once independent countries to form a new, single, federal state is often the reason for adopting a written constitution and occurred in the United States of America, Canada, Australia, Nigeria, Malaysia and Germany, to give just a few examples. The UK, as the name suggests, is a union of once separate countries, but it is not federal. Instead, the Parliament of the UK, which sits at Westminster, retains full legislative supremacy. It has recently granted varying degrees of self-government to Scotland, in the Scotland Act 1998, to Northern Ireland in the Northern Ireland Act 1998 and to Wales in the Government of Wales Acts of 1998 and 2006. The UK Parliament can, however, repeal those Acts and regain full powers to govern Scotland, Northern Ireland and Wales. There is no written constitution to stop the sovereign Parliament of the UK doing this. The question is whether Westminster would do this, which comes down to political acceptability and consequences.

Many written constitutions contain a list of rights, to which the citizen is entitled. Often, as in the United States and Germany, they are constitutionally protected and cannot easily be taken away by the Executive or Legislature. The UK has a Bill of Rights from 1689, but that was designed more to reduce the power of the King rather than to grant rights to his subjects. The Human Rights Act 1998 now gives domestic force to most of the European Convention on Human Rights 1950. Section 3 of the Act, however, carefully preserves the supremacy of Parliament. UK courts cannot 'strike down' (judicially review) primary legislation even if it is incompatible with human rights, and Acts of Parliament can still restrict human rights.

Most written constitutions contain some sort of 'organisation chart' of government and explain whether there is a President or Prime Minister, or both, and what their powers are, who has the power to legislate, who appoints the judges, and so on. There is no equivalent in the UK, as the system of governance has just evolved over the centuries. The Head of State is the Monarch, which is a matter of ancient common law, and there is no law that says that there has to be a Prime Minister. The existence of a Prime Minister is down to 'convention' or non-legal custom (below).

The UK constitution is to be found in many sources. Acts of Parliament are important and many are of constitutional significance, for example the Act of Settlement 1700 and the European Communities Act 1972. More and more of the UK constitution is now developed by passage of Acts of Parliament. These can be very important changes, for example the Human Rights Act 1998, making positive human rights directly enforceable in UK courts for the first time or the Constitutional Reform Act 2005 in strengthening the separation of powers. This indicates that nothing is permanent in the UK constitution, everything may change.

Case-law also constitutes an important source of the UK constitution; those cases involving a constitutional matter that is. For example, the House of Lords reaffirmed the principle of the supremacy of Parliament in *Pickin v BRB* [1974] AC 765, but a few years later had to moderate it, to take account of membership of the European Union, in *Factortame (No. 2)* [1991] 1 AC 603. We are talking here of the daily case law of the ordinary courts of the land. Unlike many of the countries with a written constitution, the UK does not have a Constitutional Court that rules on constitutional issues and the Supreme Court, newly established under the Constitutional Reform Act 2005, in no way mirrors that of the United States for example. All legal cases, constitutional or not, go through the same court system.

Historic documents, such as the Magna Carta 1215 and the Bill of Rights 1689 are important for establishing constitutional principles, such as the idea that the King or Executive does not have unlimited power, but these documents do not have the special, formal legal status of a written constitution; indeed all law in the UK is ordinary law, be it concerning the constitution or any other matter.

A lot of the UK constitution is not law at all and consists of constitutional conventions, which were defined by Dicey in his *The Law of the Constitution* as:

> understandings, habits or practices which, although they may regulate the conduct of the several members of the sovereign power are not in reality laws at all since they are not enforced by the courts. (p. 24 10th edn 1959).

Much of the most important parts of the constitution can be found in convention, such as the office of Prime Minister, the Cabinet, ministerial responsibility and how the considerable legal powers of the Queen are exercised by ministers in her name. As constitutional conventions are not law, they are not legally enforceable (*Attorney-General v Jonathan Cape Ltd* [1976] QB 752) and whilst in one sense are constant, they may also be said to be constantly changing. For example, whereas in the 1950s a minister would have had to resign if exposed as having an extra-marital affair or for being homosexual, neither of itself commands resignation today.

This is supposed to be the major advantage of an unwritten constitution, its flexibility and its ability to evolve. By contrast, it can be difficult to change a written constitution. On the other hand, if everything can change, as it can with the UK constitution, then the protection of individual liberties is arguably less strong. Also, without the relative certainty of a rigid, written constitution, the citizen and even the politician may find it more difficult to know just where he stands in terms of the true constitutional position.

Some think that Prime Ministers and the governments that they lead have too much power and can take away any right by just using Parliament to pass an Act or by merely changing a convention. However, even in countries with written constitutions, that document is unlikely to reveal the full constitutional position. For instance in the United States, the power of the Supreme Court to strike down legislation for 'unconstitutionality' is not found in the written constitution but in a case, *Marbury v Madison* [1803] 1 Cranch 137. Under *Article II of the US Constitution*, the President needs the consent of the Senate to agree treaties, but a practice or convention has grown up of making 'Executive Agreements' with other countries without Senate approval.

The difference between a written and unwritten constitution is not as great as some suppose. It is not possible to write down everything in a document that will be valid for all time. Much of the UK constitution is in Acts of Parliament anyway and that is increasingly the position today. Every country has different constitutional arrangements and those of the UK just reflect its individual history of being one of the oldest unified states in the world.

Question 2

The main purpose of constitutional conventions is to ensure that the legal framework of the Constitution will be operated in accordance with the prevailing constitutional values or principles of the period.

(*Re Amendment of the Constitution of Canada* [1982] 125 DLR (3d) 1)

Discuss.

Commentary

Nineteenth century writers like Dicey and twentieth century ones like Jennings stressed the importance of conventions in the UK constitution. Arguably they over-stressed their importance and constitutional writers looked for conventions that did not really exist, for instance some in the area of ministerial responsibility. There was a reaction in the 1960s and some writers asserted that there were no such things as conventions. Opinion has now swung back again, as in *Re Canada* (above). Conventions definitely exist and are of significance in the UK constitution. Questions on conventions usually demand familiar territory to be considered: what are conventions, how do they operate, how do they change and how are they enforced? The student is usually expected to be critical, often done most effectively by using specific examples of operation, breach and sanction.

Answer plan

- Habits or practices, or mandatory conduct of those involved in the day-to-day workings of the constitution
- Conventions are not laws and thus not legally enforceable
- Conventions are enforced by peer pressure, public opinion or personal morality
- Conventions evolve over time.

Suggested answer

In all constitutions, even those that are written, like that of Canada, various practices or ways of doing things that are not strictly provided for in the constitution grow up over the years. These practices can harden and become the accepted way of doing things. Then they may be called conventions. In *Re Canada* (above), although the written Canadian constitution did not require it, it was the convention that the consent of the Canadian provinces be obtained before changes were made to the constitution.

In the UK, a country without a written constitution, conventions are particularly important. In the late nineteenth century, Dicey drew attention to the role of conventions in the UK. He believed that most of the UK constitution and many of its most important parts consisted of conventions. This did not mean that there were no rules, merely that a lot of the rules were not legal ones. As he put it in *Introduction to the Study of the Law of the Constitution* (1885):

> The other set of rules consists of conventions, understandings, habits or practices which, though they may regulate the conduct of several members of the sovereign power, of the Ministers, or of other officials, are not in reality laws at all since they are not enforced by the courts. This portion of constitutional law may, for the sake of distinction, be termed 'the conventions of the constitution', or constitutional morality.

If one looks only at the legal rules of the constitution, this gives a seriously misleading impression. Legally, the Queen may refuse the Royal Assent to a parliamentary Bill. However, by convention she always agrees, taking the advice of Her Majesty's government. Legally, the Queen chooses the Prime Minister, but by convention it is always the person who can command a majority in the House of Commons. By law the Queen chooses her own ministers, but by convention they are chosen by the Prime Minister.

Conventions are clearly not the law because, as in the above examples, they sometimes contradict the strict legal position. The courts take judicial notice of the existence of conventions and in considering them where relevant to the case decision, they may influence that decision, but the courts cannot enforce conventions because they are not law. In *Attorney-General v Jonathan Cape* [1976] QB 752 there is an interesting discussion of the various conventions relating to Cabinet secrecy, but the court could not enforce them, only the material law, breach of confidence. In *Madzimbamuto v Lardner-Burke* [1969] AC 645 the court observed that there was a convention that the UK would not legislate for (the then) Rhodesia without that colony's consent. This however did not stop the UK Parliament from legislating in breach of the convention if it chose.

There are many examples of convention. It is probably impossible to make a complete list. The office of Prime Minister and the existence of the Cabinet are conventional only. Ministers are accountable to Parliament and responsible for the actions of their civil servants. Significant parts of the Ministerial Code reflect conventional behaviour; although the Code is written down, it is not of legal status and merely reproduces and fleshes out convention. Parliament meets every year, but the Bill of Rights 1689 says only that it should meet 'frequently'.

Conventions do not just affect politicians and the Monarch, they apply also to the judges, to councillors, to all involved in the workings of the constitution. So, for example, it is by convention that judges, pursuant to the separation of powers and fair trial being seen to be done, do not involve themselves in party politics.

One of the difficulties with conventions is identifying a convention. It can be hard to differentiate between what is convention and what merely the everyday behaviour of, for example, politicians. Whereas some such as Dicey saw conventions as describing what happens, 'habit', 'practice', above, others consider conventions to *prescribe* acceptable conduct. In *The Law and the Constitution* (1959) Jennings recommended a three-stage test. First, what are the precedents; how often and how consistently has this practice been observed before? Secondly, did the actors in the precedent believe themselves to be bound by the rule, obliged to follow the precedent? Thirdly, there must be a reason for the rule. In other words, the convention must fit in with the perceived notion of what should be done and how, according to the accepted principles or values of the constitution like democracy, accountability. This test works well with some of the major conventions, for example the convention that the Royal Assent always be given. The precedents are very strong, no Monarch having refused since 1708. It seems clear that the present Queen considers herself bound by the convention, having strictly followed the precedent throughout her reign of nearly 60 years. The principal reason for the rule is that an hereditary Monarch should abide by the wishes of the democratic government; it would be unacceptable for an unelected Monarch to interfere. Whilst the convention regulating Royal Assent is a strong, well-established example on the Jennings test, it is not so clear-cut with some others, such as when a minister should resign, and this to some gives rise to doubts about conventions generally.

Conventions are continually changing. Up until 1902 a Prime Minister could come from the House of Lords or Commons. Since then they have always had to be members of the Commons. From the 1960s a convention was established that no new hereditary peerages would be created, yet in the 1980s Mrs Thatcher revived the practice. So, whilst the practice has probably lapsed again, is there a convention here and, if so, what is it; it certainly is not strongly established on the Jennings test, being questionable if not falling down on precedent. How conventional behaviour evolves may either add to or lessen stability and certainty in assessing what will or should happen next time, in essence will the convention be followed. Also, of course, new conventions may be established. For example, Tony Blair was the first Prime Minister to attend the Liaison Committee comprising the 'Chairs' of the various select committees and set up to question the incumbent Prime Minister. Gordon Brown followed Mr Blair's precedent and so, whilst there is no legal requirement for attendance, there is now the expectation of this and perhaps an ever-strengthening sense of obligation. One stance is that put in an editorial in *Public Law* in 1963, pp. 401–2:

> so let us delete those pages in constitutional text-books headed conventions, and talk about what happens and why what happened yesterday may not happen tomorrow.

Conventions are called rules but they do not look much like rules. They are often vague and imprecise. In contrast with laws, there is no body or designated procedure for making a convention. In many cases, despite the efforts of writers like Jennings, it is hard to say whether a convention exists or not.

Even if existence and breach of convention is established in a given situation, there may still be difficulty in enforcement. In court, if a law is broken, a binding penalty can follow. But what if, for example, a minister is revealed to have lied to Parliament in clear breach of convention? Whereas the minister may choose to resign or be forced by the Prime Minister to resign, this is not necessarily the case. Whilst Foreign Secretary Lord Carrington and his ministerial team resigned as a matter of honour in 1982 following the Argentinean invasion of the Falklands, such proactive conduct is rare. If one traces through the many ministerial 'lapses in conduct' of the 1980s and 1990s, most were seen to cling to office and try to ride out the media scrutiny and political pressure, usually supported by the Prime Minster of the time. Even leaving aside the lack of independence of the Prime Minister and his motivation (from principle to pragmatism to expediency), is it satisfactory that some resign and others do not? Whilst the inherent flexibility may better suit what is more naturally a political rather than legal realm of constitutional activity, this leaves those unhappy with the outcome with no recourse, with principles, values or morals at stake. The major apologists for conventions had their solutions. Dicey states that if a convention was broken then legal problems would eventuate. His example was that if Parliament did not meet every year, the Budget could not be authorised nor could a standing army, both legal necessities. It is hard to see how this could apply to some conventions like, for instance, ministerial responsibility. Jennings believed that conventions had to be obeyed because 'the system' would break down if they were not and 'political difficulties' would arise. If the Queen refused her Assent there would be a crisis as indeed there could be if the Prime Minister tried to govern without a Commons majority. Again this can only apply to some conventions. When Mrs Thatcher refused Opposition nominations for life peerages hardly anyone noticed.

Re Canada considered the sanctions available. In extreme cases of unconventional behaviour a constitutional superior can dismiss the guilty person. In 1975 the Prime Minister of Australia was dismissed by the Governor-General for trying to govern without an approved Budget. Prime Ministers sometimes dismiss erring ministers. The real enforcement though is reflected in the quotation in the question. Conventions merely reflect 'the prevailing constitutional values or principles of the period'. This recognises that conventions change over time; indeed it may be argued that, far from being the rock of constancy, conventions are constantly changing. It would now be utterly unacceptable for the Queen actively to rule the UK or an unelected Lord to lead the government. It also means that constitutional 'rules' are not like legal rules. As Dicey suggested years ago they are more like moral rules. Politicians, judges and others refrain from breaking constitutional rules because they accept the rule in terms of right and wrong behaviour or perhaps because they fear the disapproval of their peers or the public. As with any moral rule, there are genuine disagreements as to what the rules are and some rules are considered more important than others. There are strong (or normative) conventions such as those that surround the role of the Queen. These will seldom, if ever, be broken. In contrast there are weak (or simple) conventions, for example that judges must abstain from party politics, perhaps more honoured in the breach than the observance.

The UK system, which is based on conventions, can accommodate enormous constitutional change without the need for a revolution or new constitution. That the Queen no longer governs is just one example. The weakness is that the evolution of the constitution cannot be halted and government may be tempted by the lack of legal restraint to take more power for itself. For example, local government was considered a counterbalance to central government but since the Second World War central government has removed much of its powers. This may or may not be 'unconventional' but it is not illegal.

Question 3

The UK is becoming a more federal country.
Discuss.

Commentary

The structure of the UK is dealt with in the early chapters of most public law textbooks. Many students read this quickly, treating it as merely introductory and raising no constitutional issues. Indeed, most English-based students probably think that the undoubted fact that Scotland and Northern Ireland have different legal systems from that of England is of no great interest, because they have already been told that in their degree they are only studying English law. The structure of the UK should not, however, be taken for granted. It is a product of historical, political change over the centuries including significant recent change by devolution of powers to Northern Ireland, Scotland and Wales. The key to answering this question is an understanding of the structure of the UK, which is nothing like as uniform as is sometimes imagined, and an attempt to define the word 'federal'. Anyone can look it up in the dictionary, but, like many words of constitutional significance, its exact meaning remains elusive, with different writers defining it differently.

Answer plan

- The difference between a unitary and a federal state
- The structure of the UK

- Devolution of administration
- The primary legislative powers of the Scottish Parliament
- The delegated legislative powers of the Welsh Assembly
- The restoration of self-government to the Northern Ireland Assembly
- A written constitution for the UK? The conundrum of parliamentary sovereignty
- The definition of a federal state.

Suggested answer

It is usually assumed, without too much discussion, that the UK is a unitary state. Like many other basic ideas in the UK constitution it can be traced back to the nineteenth century writings of A. V. Dicey, where he stated in his *The Law of Constitution* that:

> Unitarianism, in short, means the concentration of the strength of the State in the hands of one visible sovereign power be that Parliament or Czar.

By contrast:

> Federalism means the distribution of the force of the State among a number of co-ordinate bodies each originating in and controlled by the constitution.

Crudely then, unitarianism means a concentration of power at the centre, whilst federalism means a distribution of power between the central authority and, say, regional governments. Some would be satisfied with this rough and ready distinction, but Dicey is saying that there is more to it than that. The sovereignty of Parliament meant that the UK had to be a unitary state because Parliament did not share its supreme legislative authority with any other person or body. Conversely, in a federal state, supreme authority would lie in a written constitutional document, which would divide power between the central authority and the regions, provinces, states or whatever they might be called. So it depends upon what one means by federalism. It is therefore necessary to consider the structure of the UK to establish whether any divisions of authority between different governmental spheres may be identified.

The structure of the UK is not as uniform as is sometimes supposed, because it is a union of several countries that were once separate. Wales was conquered by England in the middle ages, but the two countries were not formally united until an Act of Parliament in 1536. The same legal system operates in both England and Wales, but some of the administration of government was devolved to Wales as long ago as 1964 with the establishment of the Welsh Office, headed by the Secretary of State for Wales, a minister in the UK 'Whitehall' government.

Scotland was never conquered by England, but instead the two countries voluntarily united (though some would say effectively forced by a dominant England).

From 1603 they were ruled by the same king and by the Treaty of Union 1707, the two countries merged to form Great Britain. Their two separate Parliaments became (or were replaced by) one, but in the Treaty care was taken to preserve some distinctly different Scottish institutions. Scottish private law, the courts, the church and universities were all protected from change by the new Parliament of Great Britain. To this day Scottish law, the church, education and local government remain different from their English equivalents. Some of the administration of government was restored to Scotland with the establishment of a Scottish Office and a Secretary of State for Scotland in 1928.

Ireland presents a far more complicated picture. The kings of England had been trying to conquer and subdue that country since the twelfth century. For a short period from 1782 an Irish Parliament with legislative independence existed, until 1800 when there was an attempt to emulate the 1707 union of England and Scotland. The Union with Ireland Act 1800 formed the United Kingdom of Great Britain and Ireland and established one Parliament for the new country. This arrangement did not endure, because of the growth of a 'Home Rule' movement in nineteenth century Ireland which turned into demands for outright independence in the early twentieth century. The southern part of Ireland broke away in 1920 to form an independent country, The Republic of Ireland, which was formally recognised by the UK Parliament by the Ireland Act 1949.

Northern Ireland remained part of the United Kingdom and under the Government of Ireland Act 1920 had its own Parliament, Prime Minister, Cabinet and Civil Service. This Parliament, however, only had limited powers to legislate, no power to raise taxes and it was clear that the Westminster Parliament retained supremacy. The division between 'the two sects or sides' in 'the North' remained. On the one hand, the wish of the catholic/nationalist minority for reunification with the rest of Ireland and to see 'the Brits' out, and on the other the desire of the protestant/unionist majority to stay within the UK. In the late 1960s this flared up into violence in the so called 'troubles' and in 1972 'direct rule' from London replaced the Unionist-dominated 'Stormont Parliament'.

The 'British Islands' present an interesting constitutional anomaly. The Channel Islands are not part of the UK, but instead are possessions of the Monarch. These islands retain their ancient legislatures, governments, courts and legal systems. They have considerable autonomy to make their own laws, even those relating to taxation. It is generally thought that the Westminster Parliament retains legislative supremacy and could override the wishes of the islands, but, by convention, it does not do this and instead seeks the agreement of the island governments. The Isle of Man is another ancient kingdom and it, too, retains its own legislature, Tynwald, its own government and legal system. It is clear that the UK Parliament still has ultimate legislative authority, but again in practice it is not exercised.

So, it can be seen that a number of separate legislatures and governments already exist or have existed within the UK. Because of an increase in support for nationalist political parties in Scotland and Wales, a Royal Commission on the Constitution was established in 1969, reporting in 1973. This 'Kilbrandon Report' came up with the idea of 'devolution':

> the delegation of central government powers without the relinquishment of sovereignty.

Implementation in 1978, however, met with insufficient support expressed in the referendums held in Scotland and Wales. By contrast, in 1998 significant devolution of powers across the Union (save England) was sanctioned by referendums of the electorates of Northern Ireland, Scotland and Wales.

The Scotland Act 1998 meant that, nearly 300 years on, Scotland has a Parliament once more. Elected by the voters of Scotland, this new Parliament is vested with full legislative power except for those matters specifically reserved to the Westminster Parliament. The Scots Parliament also has the power to vary the basic rate of income tax by up to 3% and to determine spending priorities. A Scottish government has been established with ministers and its own 'First Minister'. Indeed, the Scotland Act could almost be regarded as a kind of 'written constitution' for Scotland for it defines many things that are left to convention in the Westminster arrangements. It specifies how the First Minister is to be chosen and requires 'special majorities' of two-thirds, to do things like call an early election or dismiss a Scottish judge.

The new Scottish Parliament is now well established. Reviewing devolution to Scotland 10 years on, the 2009 Calman Commission declared:

> The Scottish Parliament has embedded itself in both the constitution of the United Kingdom and in the consciousness of the Scottish people. It is here to stay.

The Parliament has grown in stature and influence. Classically illustrating how convention and law work together, the 'Sewel convention' has developed: by cooperative agreement, the UK government has agreed that it will not legislate on matters devolved to Scotland, unless the Scottish Parliament consents. The UK coalition government of 2010 has promised to implement in full the Calman Commission recommendations, including replacing the variable Scottish tax regime with a new, specific Scottish income tax rate, together with new borrowing powers for the Scottish Executive.

The Scottish National Party is in government for the first time in Scotland, albeit a minority administration. It has dropped its plan to put independence for Scotland to a referendum of the Scottish electorate in 2010.

Under the Government of Wales Act 1998, Wales now has an elected Assembly and an Executive (government) which is accountable to the Assembly.

The powers of the Welsh Assembly have been extended by the Government of Wales Act 2006, extending the matters upon which the Assembly may legislate. There is also the possibility of the Welsh Assembly gaining full (primary) legislative powers, if the people of Wales agree in a referendum, although the 2006 Act clearly states the UK Parliament retains the ultimate power to legislate for Wales.

After talks spanning the 1990s aimed at ending the violent conflict in Northern Ireland, a 'home rule' structure embracing forced cooperation through mandatory power-sharing between the two communities was finally agreed. The Northern Ireland Act 1998 restored devolved government in Northern Ireland and established an elected Assembly with legislative powers. It, however, has considerably less power than the Scottish Parliament, as it is unable to legislate on a number of matters reserved to the Westminster Parliament. Unlike the Scotland Act, the Northern Ireland Act makes clear that it does not affect the power of the UK Parliament to make laws for Northern Ireland on any subject. There is a Northern Ireland Executive, however, with ministers accountable to the Assembly. As in the Scotland and Wales Acts, there are provisions distinctly resembling a 'written constitution'. For instance, 'special majorities' are required to elect the First Minister and Deputy First Minister. This caused problems with the first elected Assembly of 1999, when the republican Sinn Fein party and the unionist parties could not agree who should be First Minister. Accordingly the Westminster Parliament resumed control under the Northern Ireland Act 2000. Devolved government was restored by another Act of the UK Parliament, the Northern Ireland (St. Andrews Agreement) Act 2006. Also, in 2006, control over policing was ceded to the Northern Ireland Assembly and now this has been implemented, supposedly the last piece in the 'jigsaw' of 'home rule'.

So has the UK become a federal state? According to Bradley and Ewings' *Constitutional and Administrative Law* a federal UK would need a written constitution to guarantee that the autonomy granted to Northern Ireland, Scotland and Wales could not legally be removed again by the Westminster Parliament. If (above) Northern Ireland, Scotland and Wales now have de facto written constitutions in the form of the Acts of Parliament establishing their localised governance, neither England or the UK do and crucially of course, even if the 'set' of written constitutions were to be completed, the legal sovereignty of the Westminster Parliament UK would still mean, arguably, that that which is given away may always, ultimately be taken back. As Munro puts it in *Studies in Constitutional Law*:

> the United Kingdom is classed as a unitary, not a federal state. The Parliament at Westminster is omnicompetent.

Not all definitions of federalism are quite so legalistic. For instance, de Smith and Brazier (*Constitutional and Administrative Law*) define it in more practical, political terms:

> The difference between a federal and non-federal constitution will often be clear-cut; sometimes it will only be one of degree; sometimes it will be positively misleading.

So in reality is the UK a federal state? Even though Northern Ireland, Wales and, particularly, Scotland have been granted increasing rights to legislate and govern their own affairs, how much independence do Wales, Northern Ireland, Scotland, the Channel Islands and the Isle of Man really have? Perhaps it comes down to political sovereignty, political reality. More than once, when judged necessary, the Whitehall government and Westminster Parliament have taken powers back from the localised authorities of Northern Ireland. From this, however, one may argue that in the absence of such political extremis as has prevailed in Northern Ireland, it would be a brave UK government and Parliament indeed that dared to take back what it had relinquished, especially when the present evidence is of a hunger for *more*, not less devolved governance.

The more powerful Westminster Parliament and government usually have the means to ensure that their wishes are respected, even without legislation. For instance, Westminster decides how great a share of UK tax revenue each part of the UK receives. However, the Scottish Parliament is the most powerful of the devolved structures and, if the people of Scotland actually voted for full independence, that might call into question how powerful the UK Parliament ultimately is; as a matter of law, it could still abolish the Scottish Parliament, but, as a political reality, this seems highly unlikely.

Further reading

Barnett, H. *Constitutional and Administrative Law*, 7th edn (Cavendish, 2008), chs. 1, 2, 4 and 5.

Bradley, A. and Ewing, K. *Constitutional and Administrative Law*, 14th edn (Longman, 2006), chs. 1, 2, 5 and 6.

Loveland, I. *Constitutional Law, Administrative Law and Human Rights*, 4th edn (OUP, 2006), chs. 1, 3 and 9.

3

Prime Minister and Cabinet

Introduction

This topic will be included in any constitutional law course. Assessment questions in this area are common and often concern the same territory, for instance the relationship between Prime Minister and Cabinet. The sample here also embraces the related topic of Responsible Government, in particular the conventions of individual and collective ministerial responsibility.

The working of the constitution here is governed largely by convention rather than law. At the risk of stating the obvious, it is all about politics.

For both problem and essay questions, strong answers will be distinguished by effective use of examples including current political developments.

Question 1

To what extent is it true to say that the UK has moved from a system of Cabinet government to a system of Prime Ministerial government?

Commentary

This is one of the classic subjects for debate in constitutional law, and there are as many opinions on it as there are commentators. The conclusion you may reach is less important than the quality of the arguments displayed. Because the question addresses change in the constitution over time, how the situation has developed historically, it will be desirable to make comparisons between specific Prime Ministers. Any reference to contemporary developments will impress, though the

Prime Minister and Cabinet

core of the answer should include some key examples of Prime Ministers using their powers, or being prevented from doing so by Cabinet. A distinguished answer will 'bring alive' the practical working of the senior reaches of government, peppered with reference to styles of leadership of specific individuals and the influence of circumstances and events. In essence, government boils down the 'human factor', behaviour and interactions.

Answer plan

- PM's powers derive from convention
- Choosing members of government
- Control of Cabinet and its committees
- Downing Street staff
- Style, circumstances, events

Suggested answer

When Bagehot wrote his classic study of the UK constitution in 1867, he identified the Cabinet as the central controlling institution and principal within the 'efficient' parts of the system. When, however, in 1963 Richard Crossman (a Shadow Cabinet member at the time) provided a new introduction to Bagehot's work, he wrote:

> The post-war epoch has seen the final transformation of Cabinet Government into Prime Ministerial Government.

Many commentators have agreed with Crossman, especially concerning the Prime Ministerships of Margaret Thatcher (1979–90) and of Tony Blair (1997–2007). In the case of Mrs Thatcher, arguably Cabinet government was ultimately reinforced, as a key factor in her being forced from office was that she no longer really had the confidence of her Cabinet.

In the UK constitution, both Cabinet and Prime Minister are creatures of convention. Their functions and powers are not defined by law, but have developed gradually in order to provide a form of government answerable to Parliament rather than to the Monarch. The Cabinet developed from the practice of government ministers meeting in private, in the absence of the Monarch, to agree upon policies to be presented to Parliament. No legal rules defined which minister was to be regarded as most important. The position of First Lord of the Treasury, with responsibility for government finance, inevitably made its office-holder the 'first' or Prime Minister.

Initially, the Prime Minister was described as 'primus inter pares', first among equals. Although by the nineteenth century some Prime Ministers, such as Gladstone, were exercising a dominant influence, others, particularly if they sat in the

House of Lords, were little more than chairmen of the Cabinet. In the twentieth century it became an established convention that the Prime Minister must sit in the House of Commons, giving democratic accountability to the elected House and thence to the people. Since 1945, political practice has come to concentrate intense attention upon the position of Prime Minister, and with the growth of the media in more recent times, ever more upon the individual person.

The Prime Minister's powers derive almost exclusively from convention and the Royal Prerogative, not from statute. Whether such powers are exercised by the Prime Minister alone, or by the Cabinet collectively, may be determined by established convention, but will often be a matter of political practice or expediency. Conventions may change over time. The decision to ask the Monarch to dissolve Parliament and call a general election was at one time taken by the Cabinet, but since 1918 the Prime Minister has made that decision, after such consultation with colleagues as appears desirable, in the Prime Minister's judgement, at the time. (The government now proposes replacing this discretionary timing with fixed-term Parliaments.)

The initial creation of a new government provides the first illustration of the inter-relationship between the Prime Minister's powers and political practice. By convention, the Monarch calls on the leader of the party that can command a majority in the House of Commons to form a government. The new Prime Minister then has the power to select all of the members of the new administration. The Cabinet is therefore of the Prime Minister's own choosing and could be expected to reflect his or her ideas. In practice however, the Prime Minister's choice will be constrained. For example, leading members of the party will expect important posts, preferably those that they shadowed while in Opposition; former political favours may need to be repaid, and an inexperienced incoming Prime Minister may be 'advised and expected' to form a Cabinet embracing the wide spectrum of political leanings within the party umbrella. The longer a Prime Minister remains in office, however, the more opportunity there is for the Cabinet to be reshaped according to his real preferences. When first Prime Minister, inexperienced and lacking a power base, Mrs Thatcher was obliged to include in her 1979 Cabinet many of the 'old guard' from the previous Tory administration, many of whom did not share her brand of Conservatism. By 1983, however, she had around her a hand-picked complement of like-minded colleagues. One possible consequence of such like-mindedness is less effective policy formulation arising from less breadth of debate and challenge to perceived wisdom.

It is now accepted political practice for there to be Cabinet reshuffles at least annually; ministers whose performance is seen as inadequate, or who are not fully in sympathy with the Prime Minister's policies may be removed and promising talents of like mind to the Prime Minister will be brought in to key posts. The dismissal of ministers can, however, weaken a Prime Minister by making enemies, providing a focus for party discontent. The very act of leadership in radical change of personnel, invariably carried out with great speed, may backfire and be perceived as weakness or panic, as Harold Macmillan's so-called 'Night of the Long Knives' in 1962 serves to illustrate. Sacking seven Cabinet colleagues including the Chancellor of the Exchequer and Lord Chancellor, was intended to appear strong and give new direction and vitality to a tired government besmirched with scandal and problems, but was actually perceived—at least as portrayed by the Press—as ruthless and desperate.

Once the government is formed, the Prime Minister has a decisive voice in the processes by which it operates. Because of the increasing complexity of modern government, meetings of the full Cabinet deal with only a fraction of government business. The Prime Minister controls the content and order of the agenda. He may keep controversial items off the agenda, though this will be subject to political constraints. In 1986, Michael Heseltine resigned from the Cabinet—in session—when prevented from raising the 'Westland affair' in the particular meeting.

The Prime Minister, in chairing Cabinet, can lead and order the discussion. Cabinet usually decides policy by consensus rather than by vote. The Prime Minister normally concludes discussion by summing up the sense of the meeting, which will be entered in the 'minutes' (general summary notes). It is a matter of personal style whether the Prime Minister allows a genuine consensus to develop or attempts to dominate the debate. Mrs Thatcher tended to dominate, although vigorous arguments were still had. Perhaps in part as an 'antidote', her successor John Major was particularly collegiate.

A 'presidential' style came with Mr Blair, who conducted most business by sub-committee or one-to-one ministerial discussion, merely reporting matters (post facto) to a Cabinet meeting, which often lasted well under an hour.

Sometimes practice varies according to situation, for example in James Callaghan's Administration of 1976–79, Cabinet meetings could take a day, occasionally more, shaped in no small part by the government having no majority in the Commons as well as party in-fighting between 'left' and 'right' political factions. It may be that the rare and uncertain territory of coalition government in itself will shape considerably the relations between David Cameron and his Cabinet colleagues, from two different parties, especially in troubled waters as all governments meet sooner or later.

One constraint is that a Prime Minister may not be able to control how the debate develops (assuming he allows one), and in any event he cannot insist upon the adoption of a policy against the wishes of the rest of the Cabinet. Ultimately, convention dictates that his position depends upon having the confidence of Cabinet. If it is a key policy then he may not survive in office. Some might say that Mr Blair side-stepped the problem by not involving Cabinet in the decision to go to war with Iraq in 2003; the Butler Report 2004 investigates the workings of government in this matter.

The Cabinet forms the apex of an hierarchy of Cabinet committees, sub-committees and working groups, and most government business will be dealt with outside the full Cabinet. The Prime Minister now has considerable freedom in establishing and staffing such committees, and may, by careful selection, ensure that only those likely to favour his opinion are involved in the taking of the decision. Decisions made in a Cabinet committee are generally as final as those made in the full Cabinet, and all ministers remain bound by collective responsibility even if they were not party to the making of the decision, however significant, illustrated again by the Iraq war decision. Since 1992 the identity and membership of several have been officially revealed. A Prime Minister may even avoid the use of such formal bodies and use wholly informal working groups to take sensitive decisions. Tony Blair is said to have met ministers individually to persuade them to support the invasion of Iraq, before any collective discussion; the Butler Report refers to his 'kitchen cabinet' and 'sofa government' style. This clearly shows how the Prime Minister can exercise a dominating influence over the decision-making process. This may, however, store up trouble. Robin Cook, for example, resigned over the invasion of Iraq and subsequently voiced frequent criticisms of Tony Blair's style of leadership. Mr Cameron has vowed to restore proper Cabinet policy-making; we shall see.

Against the back-drop of exponential growth in the volume and complexity of matters of governance, some delegation is unavoidable. That said, the Prime Minister has a general responsibility for government policy and is therefore entitled to intervene in almost any aspect of the work of any department, subject only to the limits imposed by energy and enthusiasm. All Prime Ministers are expected to take a particular interest in economic and foreign affairs. Diplomacy is now conducted to a great extent by summit meetings, and the regular meetings of the European Council of Ministers are the main focus for developments in the European Union. In other matters, a Prime Minister may allow departmental ministers to develop their own policies within an overall strategy, or may insist on involvement in all developments. Exceptionally, Chancellor Brown shut Prime Minister Blair out, to the detriment of effective governance.

The Prime Minister has the assistance of a range of support services, including a Private Office, staffed by the most promising young civil servants, a Press Office, led by so-called 'spin doctors', and a Political Office staffed by party workers. All recent Prime Ministers have engaged policy advisers from outside the Civil Service, though problems have arisen where these advisers are thought to have had too much influence and have harmed the position of civil servants by at least trying to politicise their role. Some commentators argue that, under Tony Blair, these support services expanded to the point where they could be described as a Prime Minister's Department. Gordon Brown purported to lessen this involvement; we shall see how the new Prime Minister conducts matters. Perhaps the only reason why a Prime Minister's Department has not been created on an official basis is that it would be taken as ultimate proof that a system of Prime Ministerial government had been established.

There can be no doubt that recent years have seen an increasing concentration of media attention on the Prime Minister. 2010 saw the first 'Prime Ministerial' debate, probably to become a regular election feature. *The* high-profile feature of the television broadcasting of Parliament is the weekly Prime Minister's Question Time, perhaps creating a perception that the Prime Minister is the government, whatever may be the reality. Elections are described as if they were a contest between party leaders, and it can be argued that elections give the Prime Minister a personal, not just a party, mandate. This strengthens the hand of a successful Prime Minister, but also increases the likelihood that a party's response to unpopularity will be to replace its leader.

Determining ministerial career paths, ministerial breach of convention and sanction and with a Commons majority, the Prime Minister has enormous power. A return to the days when the Prime Minister was only first among equals is unlikely. Even a Prime Minister who does not wish to dominate the government would find it impossible to reverse the popular perception of the dominant leader. There are very considerable powers available to a Prime Minister who wishes to make full use of them, and such a Prime Minister will overshadow the rest of the government. However, Cabinet remains the forum where fundamental issues have to be decided. No Prime Minister can ignore or evade the objections of a Cabinet majority and in difficult times, the Prime Minister needs his Cabinet. The picture drawn by Bagehot is still recognisable.

Question 2

Estella Remington (ER) became Prime Minister last year when her party won a general election with a majority of 30 seats. She promised, during the election campaign, to provide a massive expansion of higher education. She has now decided that this can only be achieved if a special tax is imposed on graduates. She has discussed this privately with the Chancellor of the Exchequer, who agrees with the scheme. No other ministers have yet been informed, and several of them are likely to be critical of the plan.

What steps may ER take to try to ensure that:

(a) the scheme is adopted as government policy;

(b) the necessary legislation is passed through Parliament; and

(c) the public accepts the need for the new tax?

Prime Minister and Cabinet | 27

Commentary

This question is principally concerned with the powers of the Prime Minister, but related topics come into play. The extent to which material on pressure group activity and policy formation would need to be included would depend on your course coverage. You will be expected to demonstrate a clear understanding of the conventions governing the Cabinet and the legal rules governing the passage of legislation by Parliament. The answer will be greatly enhanced by an awareness of political realities. Too often students' answers read as if this was an abstract theoretical problem, whereas this scenario could arise, possibly under the current government. Obviously, being a problem question, it must be answered as such and not as a discursive essay question.

Answer plan

- Policy adopted by Cabinet or Cabinet committee
- Whips' control of governing party (presently parties) in Commons
- Disputes between Lords and Commons
- Influencing the media 'spin'.

Suggested answer

ER has a considerable range of powers and means of influence available to ensure the adoption of her policies. Indeed, it is arguable that the UK system of government has become one of Prime Ministerial government. There are, however, constraints on the Prime Minister's powers, and even determined Prime Ministers may find that they fail to ensure the adoption of at least some of their preferred policies, even with a clear mandate and Commons majority.

(a) The scheme should be formally proposed as policy in a meeting of the Cabinet. It will be discussed and if agreed, usually by consensus, then it becomes policy. By the convention of Cabinet collective responsibility, all Cabinet and junior ministers are bound by it and to support it in public, specifically in Parliament, irrespective of any dissent in Cabinet or private misgivings. If an individual minister cannot accept and support the policy, then by convention he must resign. It would be most unlikely in practice that any such matter would be raised in Cabinet without extensive prior consultations with the Cabinet ministers directly affected, specifically the Secretaries of State for Business, Innovation and Skills (BIS) (which Department includes the Universities portfolio) and perhaps the Education Secretary. To avoid the possibility of an embarrassing defeat, the Prime Minister is sure to take soundings generally among her colleagues, so that she can take the matter to Cabinet having already satisfied herself of a majority there.

Most issues are not, however, dealt with by the full Cabinet because of pressure of business, but are instead referred to Cabinet committees. There are both permanent and temporary committees and sub-committees. As Prime Minister, ER selects the membership and remit of all of these bodies. It would therefore be possible for her to refer this scheme to a committee, the membership of which she has carefully selected to provide a majority in favour of it. The Chancellor of the Exchequer and the Education and BIS Secretaries of State would need to be members, but ER has a fairly free hand in selecting the other members. It would be to ER's advantage to chair the committee herself, giving extra power to guide the discussion.

It is accepted practice that matters decided by a Cabinet committee are not discussed again by the full Cabinet. Only if there is disagreement within the committee, or the matter proves to be one of extreme sensitivity, will it be referred up to a Cabinet meeting. It is therefore quite likely that this scheme could be adopted as government policy without the involvement of some members of the Cabinet, who will nonetheless remain bound by collective responsibility. This gives rise to the possibility that a minister considering himself to have been bypassed, may resign, thereby revealing splits in the government that the Opposition can exploit. The resignation of Michael Heseltine in 1986 over the 'Westland affair' is an example of this. For many senior ministers this is, however, a reluctant path as it may mean an extended period of political oblivion.

Once adopted as government policy, BIS, Education and Treasury civil servants will be instructed to prepare the necessary legislation and administrative procedures. Normally such a major proposal would be announced in the Queen's Speech at the opening of the next session of Parliament, but the government may propose legislation at any time.

(b) Assuming ER succeeds in having the scheme adopted as policy, the next hurdle is the passage of the necessary legislation through Parliament. As a measure affecting taxation, it will be introduced in the House of Commons. The government has a comfortable Commons majority so ER need not be particularly concerned about the attitude of the opposition parties; indeed, vehement criticism of the Bill by them may well encourage the loyal support of her own backbench MPs.

The task of getting the legislation through lies with the sponsoring minister and the whips. The whips must ensure a disciplined turnout of MPs to vote on the measure. After the formal introduction and First Reading, the Second Reading provides the opportunity for the House of Commons to debate and vote on the principle of the Bill. Defeat at Second Reading will force the withdrawal of the Bill, but this is a rare occurrence. The whips will inform ER in advance of potential revolt and any measure likely to be defeated will be withdrawn for amendment before the government suffers the embarrassment of defeat. After second reading, the Bill will be referred to a Standing Committee for detailed examination. The government will have a majority on this committee proportionate to its overall majority, thus it should have no difficulty in getting the Bill safely through this stage, even if forced to accept amendments from its own side. If the opposition parties attempt to delay the bill by filibustering, the government can ask the House to pass a Programme Motion restricting the time allowed for discussion. Once the Committee Stage has been completed, the government will have to decide whether to accept any amendments made in committee, or to have them reversed by a vote of the whole House. The vote on Third Reading will complete the Bill's passage through the House of Commons.

The whips' careful use of persuasion, cajolery and coercion will normally ensure the passage of all legislation to which the government is committed. Backbench revolts have, however, become more common as it is no longer the convention that any defeat will force the government to resign. Only defeat on a formal Vote of Confidence will force a resignation and general election, as in 1979. It is possible for a Prime Minister to turn a vote on a particular piece of legislation into a matter of confidence in order to demand his party's support, but this may be regarded as a sign of weakness rather than of strength, forcing backbench MPs to choose between their beliefs and their political survival.

The Bill will then be sent to the House of Lords, where a similar pattern of readings will be followed. Voting in the House of Lords is somewhat unpredictable because the Upper House is less shackled by party discipline and there are many cross-bench peers without a fixed party allegiance. This Bill is likely to arouse the keen interest of those peers interested in higher education, and the final result of the votes cannot be foreseen.

The House of Lords has become more willing to reject government legislation and, since the removal of (most of) the hereditary peers, has announced that it will no longer observe the Salisbury convention, under which it would not obstruct legislation intended to fulfil government manifesto commitments. It is therefore possible that the government may have to resort to the Parliament Acts procedure, as was done in passing the European Parliamentary Elections Act 1999 and the Hunting Act 2004.

If the Bill were to contain no provisions except for the 'graduate tax', it would be classified as a Money Bill and the Lords could delay it for only one month. If, as is more likely, it also contains other provisions then the Lords may delay it for one session. On the other hand, the Lords may be satisfied with amending the Bill, which will then have to return to the Commons. The government will then have to decide whether to accept the amendments or to try to persuade the Lords to concede. Only if the Bill has been passed by both Houses in identical form can it proceed to Royal Assent, which by convention presents no challenge, and become law within one session.

(c) In persuading the general public of the scheme, ER's greatest asset is the opportunity to make effective use of the media including trying to influence the opinion of the press. The Prime Minister has a Press Office, which holds regular lobby briefings with journalists. All of the arguments in favour of the scheme will be advanced and opposing arguments rebutted. The press will then report, likely giving a range of slants overall. It is vital for any Prime Minister to cultivate good relations with the media so far as possible, but attempts to manipulate it have been subject to considerable criticism in recent years and may prove counter-productive. Some newspapers are traditionally—but not always—supportive of a party of its chosen political leaning so ER might reasonably expect some favourable coverage, giving momentum and leverage with the public mood. However, as the Community Charge ('Poll Tax') of 1989–90 illustrated, a policy imposing a new tax and perceived as unjust may do lasting damage to a government.

It is likely that this scheme will provoke many individuals to write to their MPs, especially as its effects will likely impact particularly upon the articulate and educated. It will therefore be desirable for all MPs of the government party to be supplied with material suitable for explaining and justifying the scheme to their constituents, thereby perhaps keeping both the MPs and their constituents on-board.

It may be that the scheme will provoke protest and demonstrations from students, but these may most wisely be 'ignored' by government as they are as likely to turn public opinion in favour of the scheme as against it, especially if protesters break laws and become violent. When this happened in the poll tax demonstrations, it inflamed opinion on both sides of the argument. In the last resort, it must be remembered that there are as many as four years to go before the next general election. Even if the tax is unpopular, ER may reasonably believe that it will have ceased to be a matter of major concern by then.

Once a measure has been adopted as government policy, its chances of becoming law are very high. Very little government-sponsored legislation is rejected by Parliament, and public opinion can rarely be mobilised so as to prevent the government pursuing its policies. The greatest problems for the Prime Minister lie in getting the initial agreement of Cabinet colleagues, but even here the influence of a determined Prime Minister may be hard to resist.

Question 3

How does the convention of individual ministerial responsibility operate in relation to departmental error? How has this been affected by recent developments in Parliament and government?

Prime Minister and Cabinet | **31**

Commentary

The first part of this requires not just a statement of the traditional doctrine but also analysis identifying the difficulty in establishing how ministers are supposed to behave. Once again, examples should be used including some drawn from recent practice; the stuff of conventions concerning politicians is politics, behaviour and happenings. The second part of the question gives the student useful hints as to where to look for changes. In Parliament, reform of select committees has made an impact. In government, changes to the structure and organisation of departments are making it increasingly difficult to apply the established doctrine.

Note, as ever, the parameters of the question set: it is specifically confined to departmental ministerial responsibility. Its answer should not drift into detail of the responsibility of civil servants, nor digress into ministerial responsibility for personal conduct, such as financial impropriety or sexual scandal. Finally, detail from the Ministerial Code, whilst likely to be pertinent in answering a problem question, is unnecessary here as the Code essentially reflects the spirit and prevailing values of the convention under consideration.

Answer plan

- Government accountable to Commons
- Questioning ministers
- Questioning civil servants
- Questioning Next Steps agencies.

Suggested answer

Ministerial departments are subject to some legal accountability (for example, *Carltona v Works Commissioners* [1943] 2 All ER 560). Albeit not legally enforceable, the Ministerial Code and Civil Service Code set out in written detail much of what is required or expected in the dealings of departments and of their personnel. However, it is convention, unwritten and non-legal, which still governs much of what may or must be done and thus it is political enforceability and sanctions that regulate departmental and ministerial conduct. Traditional constitutional doctrine states that each minister is responsible to Parliament for the work of her department, giving indirect democratic accountability to the electorate via the Commons as well as being a part of the overall accountability of government to Parliament. The ultimate sanction of the Commons is to force a government to resign by passing a vote of no confidence in it. Similarly, a minister who loses the confidence of the House of Commons has to resign, though in practice, a Prime Minister who knew that a minister was facing defeat in such a vote would require an immediate resignation before any vote occurred. How the doctrine operates in less extreme circumstances is, however, more difficult to ascertain.

The classic instance used to describe the doctrine of ministerial responsibility is the 1954 'Crichel Down affair'. Civil servants in the Ministry of Agriculture refused to honour a promise made to a landowner, when his land was compulsorily purchased for military use, that he or his heirs would be given the opportunity to repurchase the land when it was no longer needed. There was no suggestion of corruption or other gross impropriety; rather it was a plain case of maladministration. The minister was not directly involved, but when a critical report was published, he considered himself obliged to resign, being the person ultimately responsible. This course of action was praised as particularly honourable.

In the 40 years since then, it has become clear that this was not a typical example of the doctrine of ministerial responsibility in operation. Rather, it was the unpopularity of the government's whole agricultural policy that led to the loss of backbench support for the minister in question. There have been extremely few ministerial resignations for departmental error since, one notable exception being that of the Foreign and Commonwealth Secretary Lord Carrington and his junior ministers in 1982 when Argentina invaded the Falkland Islands. The stance taken, as subsequently explained by Lord Carrington was that, even though with hindsight he would not have acted differently in the conduct of matters preceding the invasion, the invasion represented a national humiliation (with very serious consequence) for which he had to take responsibility. He did not engage in line-by-line analysis of the Ministerial Code to assess whether he might survive by the letter of the convention; he resigned on principle and in honour.

What then does the doctrine of ministerial responsibility amount to? Its starting point is the right of MPs to question each minister about the activities of the department and the corresponding duty of the minister to answer. Since all Crown servants other than ministers were excluded from the House of Commons at the beginning of the eighteenth century, the minister was the only person available for questioning. When government activity was much less, it was reasonable to expect ministers to know what was going on in their departments. As government activity has increased, it remained the expectation that the minister should be able and willing, given reasonable notice, to answer questions on any aspect of the department's work. This provided one of the principal means by which an individual could seek redress for grievances, as the complainant in the Crichel Down affair eventually did. Many such grievances would be dealt with without publicity, and even those that did reach the floor of the House of Commons would conclude with an explanation, an apology and a promise of redress from the minister, without the issue of resignation even being raised.

From the 1960s onwards, other means of redress were developed, to supplement or even replace the traditional method. In 1967, the office of Parliamentary Commissioner for Administration, now the Parliamentary and Health Service Ombudsman, was introduced, providing an alternative course of action for an MP whose constituent was aggrieved by an act of maladministration. As the

Ombudsman's reports and recommendations are almost always accepted in full by government, and appropriate redress offered, there is no need to invoke the doctrine of ministerial responsibility, and no question of resignation is raised.

Another development has been the immense growth in use of judicial review, providing legal redress, wholly outside the political process. A finding by the High Court that a government department had acted ultra vires may provoke the Opposition to derision, but is not taken as a ground for threatening the minister's political survival. It is possible to imagine that in extreme circumstances, a judicial ruling could bring the minister's future into question. In the case of *Re M* [1994] 1 AC 377, it was held that government ministers could be held in contempt of court; arguably such a finding should place considerable pressure upon the minister to resign.

It remains one of the bases for the doctrine of ministerial responsibility that only the minister was present in Parliament to be questioned. However, beyond the floor of the House, select committees have the right to call civil servants to give evidence, and the departmental select committees use this right extensively. There can be problems; although the committee can in theory insist on the civil servant's presence, the minister may refuse permission and attend in person instead. In practice, the committee would have to be satisfied with that. Civil servants who do attend are expected to obey Cabinet Office directions restricting the answers they can give on sensitive issues. If they refuse to answer particular questions, the committee cannot force them to do so. In spite of these limitations, it has become common to see civil servants appearing before select committees, and MPs are finding this form of scrutiny in some ways more effective than questioning the minister in the traditional way. No longer is the minister the only person who can be called to account by Parliament. The work and effectiveness of these committees may gain new impetus and vigour now that its Chairmen are elected rather than placed by party, stooge or not.

The 'Next Steps' governmental reorganisation, designed to improve management and efficiency by setting up Agencies to run public services in place of the Civil Service, has impacted upon the doctrine of ministerial responsibility. Headed by a Chief Executive, these Agencies implement government policy. No institutional provision was made for any new form of parliamentary accountability, though new procedures have developed. Ministers answer parliamentary questions about the work of agencies by simply informing MPs that they have passed the matter to the Chief Executive, who answers the MP by letter. These replies are published in Hansard, like written answers from ministers, making them matters of formal record. This however, carries the implication that the minister is not responsible or accountable for the operations conducted by the agency, as he would have been before the re-organisation.

An MP has limited scope for raising a complaint on the matter on the floor of the House but Agency's Chief Executive may be called before a select committee, particularly useful when a large number of complaints are giving cause for concern (and 'hit' the media), as happened for instance with the beleaguered Child Support Agency.

If there is direct accountability of the agency to Parliament by means of the detailed scrutiny by a select committee, the responsibility of the minister becomes almost irrelevant. Major difficulties remain, however, in establishing accountability where matters fall between day-to-day operational matters, with which the minister is not concerned, and matters of high policy for which the minister alone remains accountable.

In conclusion, it is clear that the shouts of 'Resign!' which greet a minister whose department has been at fault are little more than a ritual. Crichel Down, far from setting the precedent of expected behaviour, is in fact unique. It is difficult to imagine any circumstances in which a minister—given Prime Ministerial backing—would heed and act upon an obligation to follow that precedent in the absence of personal fault. It would perhaps be better to improve the means by which Parliament scrutinises the Executive directly, rather than trying to revive a doctrine that took shape in a more leisured age, when the minister read and even wrote his own despatches. The arrival of Executive Agencies may yet provide the opportunity for the development of new means of scrutiny, if Parliament wishes to perform this function more effectively.

Question 4

Consider the following situations in relation to the convention of ministerial responsibility.

(a) In her Budget speech, the Chancellor of the Exchequer announced her intention to impose Value Added Tax (VAT) on books and newspapers. Twenty government backbench MPs have told the whips that they will vote against this proposal, and if necessary against the whole Budget. The government has an overall Commons majority of 15 seats;

(b) Sirah, the Secretary of State for Transport, proposed to the Cabinet that extra safety barriers be erected along all elevated sections of motorways, but her proposal was rejected on grounds of cost. Last week, 40 people died in a motorway crash that the safety barriers would have prevented. Sirah told Jenner, a journalist, about the rejection of her proposal, and he has published an article blaming the rest of the Cabinet for the loss of life;

(c) Lesley, the Foreign and Commonwealth Secretary, informed the House of Commons two years ago that he would be adopting a new, morally sustainable foreign policy. It has now been discovered that the Foreign Office has been negotiating for a year to surrender a small UK colony to a neighbouring dictatorship. No information about this has ever been given to the House of Commons;

(d) Smith, a junior minister in the Department for Transport, crashed his car on the M4 motorway. PCs Ford and Austin attended the accident. Smith was breathalysed, the result negative. Smith was slightly injured as was his passenger Jones, a financier, the financial dealings of whom are currently under investigation by the Department for Business, Innovation and Skills. PCs Ford and Austin completed reports on the accident, but were then told by their superiors that instructions 'from on high' were to remove all record of it.

Commentary

This problem covers various aspects of ministerial responsibility. The student's first task will be to identify and explain the particular facet of the convention that may apply in each case, being careful to describe and illustrate how the convention actually operates in practice. Use of examples (including recent ones), an awareness of political realities, and even a familiarity with the attitudes of the press, will be most useful.

Note that it is only the convention that is to be applied, not any laws that may also be relevant.

Answer plan

- Loss of vote of confidence
- Collective responsibility; 'all saying the same thing'
- Individual responsibility for self and department
- Personal misconduct.

Suggested answer

(a) The convention of ministerial responsibility requires above all that the government must have the confidence of the House of Commons. If it loses that confidence it must resign, either to be replaced by another government in which the House of Commons does have confidence or, more usually, to cause a general election. The issue raised in this problem is to identify the circumstances in which a government defeat in the Commons will be taken as an indication of such a fatal loss of confidence. It was thought at one time that any defeat on a major issue would demonstrate a loss of confidence and force the government's resignation, but over the last 20 years or so this has changed. It is clear, however, that any defeat on a formal vote of confidence, moved as such by government or Opposition, will make the government resign. This last occurred in 1979, when the Labour government lost a vote of confidence (by one vote) and immediately called a general election. Here, this government could adopt the high-risk strategy of making the vote on VAT a vote of confidence, if it judges that this would make the 20 (or at least the crucial six) rebel backbenchers rally to support it. If however the 20 were to persist in their rebellion, then the government would, if defeated, have no choice but to resign.

Defeat on one aspect of the Budget would not in itself force the government to resign; it would merely cause political embarrassment. In recent years, a government was forced to rescind an increase in fuel tax, without any threat to its survival in office. Defeat on the entire Budget, however, presents a more complex problem. Traditionally, the votes on the Queen's Speech and the Budget were seen as being tantamount to votes of confidence, but it is not clear whether this is still the case. However, it can be argued that it is both a political and a legal necessity for a government to have its financial proposals accepted by the House of Commons. A Finance Act must be passed each year. Were the Budget to be rejected, the only way the government could survive would be to propose, and have passed, a vote of confidence, and then to introduce a new Budget acceptable to enough MPs. This would be a political humiliation for the Chancellor of the Exchequer that she could hardly survive, but it would be possible for the government as a whole to claim that it retained the confidence of the House of Commons just enough to enable it to continue in office. In this sense, unlike the formal vote of confidence itself, holding the confidence of the House becomes a 'daily' question of degree. From the facts, it appears that all of the 20 rebels have taken a principled stance upon the particular matter, challenging and presumably expecting its front bench to compromise. However, the high stakes are clear to all concerned and it may be that more than 15 from its own side may trouble the government again in the future, especially if it does back down to win them back in this instance.

(b) As well as the relevant laws (official secrets legislation, Public Records Acts and confidentiality), the convention of collective ministerial responsibility requires all ministers (Cabinet and below) to support government policy once decided and to refrain from revealing discussion had in Cabinet. If a minister has a fundamental disagreement with the rest of the Cabinet, and is not prepared to accept government policy, that minister must resign. Foreign Secretary Robin Cook was considered to have acted in a principled way when, in 2003, he resigned because he could not support the invasion of Iraq without United Nations' approval. There was criticism of Clare Short's failure to resign from the Cabinet when expressing similar opinions; Ms Short belatedly resigned.

In reality, in most governments, differences of opinion between ministers will be publicly known and discussed in the media. This may be tolerated for a time, but eventually the Prime Minister's patience with dissent, and with the 'leaks', will be exhausted. Revealing the story to Jenner is in breach of collective responsibility. Journalists jealously guard the identity of their sources. Jenner will also wish other revelations to follow in the future. Accordingly, Jenner is very likely to maintain the confidentiality of his conversation with Sirah and so, on the face of it, Sirah will not be found out as the source of the disclosure.

It can be argued that it is not justifiable to describe collective ministerial responsibility as a convention, given that ministers do not always adhere strictly to it, whether speaking off the record or expressing their views in carefully coded language. There is nonetheless recognition of the political reality that an openly divided Cabinet cannot hope to survive and few ministers will take a disagreement so far as to resign, or to express dissent so openly that the Prime Minister has no option but to dismiss them.

(c) According to the convention of individual ministerial responsibility, a minister is accountable to Parliament for the activities of his department. This gives Parliament the right to question him and imposes on him an obligation to answer; the Ministerial Code gives specific requirements as to the nature of answers. The minister is the only person available for Parliament to question, at least on the floor of the House of Commons. If the minister cannot satisfy MPs, particularly those from his own party, he may lose the confidence of the House of Commons. In extreme circumstances, the House of Commons could force the resignation of a minister by passing a vote of censure against him.

The Ministerial Code and a Resolution of the House of Commons specify that a minister must give truthful and accurate information and must not knowingly mislead Parliament. If it were to be shown that Lesley had knowingly misinformed Parliament by, for example, denying that any such negotiations were taking place, that would be regarded as a grave offence and it is almost certain that he would have to resign. Giving Parliament misleading information by mistake may, however, be forgiven, if the minister admits the error as soon as it is discovered and apologises. For example, in the 1980s a junior Home Office minister assured the House of Commons that pregnant female prisoners were not kept fettered while in labour, having been given that assurance by civil servants. When it was discovered that the civil servants had been wrong, she apologised immediately to the House and the apology was accepted.

It is now considered acceptable for a minister to deny personal knowledge of and responsibility for purely operational matters within his department. Successive Home Secretaries (now Justice Secretaries), for example, have successfully used this stance to avoid responsibility for prison escapes. Could Lesley deny all knowledge of the negotiations? They were of such importance and sensitivity that the Foreign Secretary either must have known or should have known if he were running his department effectively. His defence in these circumstances may be to assert that he has not actively misled Parliament, but has merely failed to keep MPs informed. The 1996 Scott Inquiry into 'Arms to Iraq' revealed the widespread attitude in government that information should not be disclosed if at all possible, in spite of the implications for parliamentary scrutiny of the Executive. What is particularly interesting about that affair is that those ministers who were found to have misled Parliament were protected by their Prime Minister and the government side of the House. The vote on the Scott Inquiry was treated as a vote of confidence in the whole government. Backbench MPs as usual fell into line behind the three-line whip and the government survived by one vote.

Lesley may claim that he has not really misled Parliament or that his failure to keep MPs informed was due to the delicacy of the negotiations, or that there is no real contradiction with the morally sustainable foreign policy. Whether these arguments will win the day will be determined in practice by the attitude of the Prime Minister and the government side of the House. If the government has a loyal majority in the House of Commons that is prepared to back Lesley, then he may ignore calls for his resignation from the Opposition. If, however, the government considers that public opinion is strong and requires a 'scalp', then whether or not Lesley is merely the scapegoat, he may find himself sacrificed. If a minister becomes 'damaged' by mishap and hints of incompetence, as Education Secretary Michael Gove probably is after repeated departmental blunders in issuing inaccurate lists of schools for which scheduled repair and refurbishment was being summarily cancelled, then again this will not help and may tip the balance against the minister's survival.

(d) Although personal misconduct by government ministers will generally lead to public and media criticism, it is unlikely that the mere fact that Smith has crashed his car would endanger his position, although there is the safety perspective given his Transport portfolio. On the facts, he was not over the drink-drive limit, there is no other suggestion that he is particularly culpable and no one has been seriously injured. Much more serious, however, is the question of why Jones was a passenger in his car. Any suggestion of financial impropriety, perhaps even apparently inappropriate association, is likely to be regarded by the public and media as very reprehensible, and various ministers have been forced to resign for such reasons. Peter Mandelson and George Osborne survived the revelation that each had been in the company of controversial Russian billionaire Oleg Deripaska. However, both were tarnished, whatever the truth of the allegations against each of them in their dealings with Deripaska.

In this problem there is the further suggestion that someone in authority is attempting to conceal what happened. If it were merely shown that the police and the Crown Prosecution Service had decided, in the proper exercise of their lawful discretion, not to prosecute Smith for any offence, there would be no problem. Removing police records, however, is a serious matter and any suggestion that there has been political interference in the legal process breaches the separation of powers, would be constitutionally unacceptable and would provoke public outrage. If this were to become known, Smith and any other minister involved would be forced to resign, and such a scandal might embroil and threaten the whole government. A cover-up is always regarded as unforgivable, however minor the initial offence.

Further reading

Bradley, A. and Ewing, K. *Constitutional and Administrative Law*, 14th edn (Longman, 2007), chs. 7, 13.

Hennessy, P. *The Hidden Wiring* (INDIGO, 1996), chs. 3 and 4.

Loveland, I. *Constitutional Law*, 3rd edn (Butterworths, 2003), ch. 9.

Turpin, C. *British Government and Constitution*, 6th edn (Butterworths, 2007), ch. 6.

Woodhouse, D. *Ministers and Parliament* (OUP, 1994).

4

The Royal Prerogative

Introduction

The title 'royal prerogative' seems rather quaint, ancient and irrelevant to the modern constitution. If the ordinary person has heard of it at all it summons up images of the Queen, ceremonials and obscure customs like the Monarch's right to sturgeons and swans on the river Thames. This gives an extremely misleading impression. The royal prerogative in fact contains some of the most important powers of government, in foreign affairs, defence and justice. Munro defined it as:

> those attributes peculiar to the Crown which are derived from common law, not statute and which still survive.
> (*Studies in Constitutional Law* (1999) 159)

Despite the 'royal' reference, the Queen is not in fact the person who takes the decisions. Although in law powers under the prerogative belong to the Queen, by convention they are actually exercised by Her Majesty's government, often by the Prime Minister personally. The main concerns for the constitutional lawyer are control of and accountability for exercise of these Crown powers, reflected in the preponderance of (usually essay type) questions on this subject.

Commonly questions focus upon judicial control, specifically judicial review of the exercise of prerogative power. The most important case is *Council of Civil Service Unions v Minister for the Civil Service* [1985] AC 374. Students often make the mistake of just learning this one case and then are stumped for anything else to talk about. There are other cases! There are not many of them, but it is important to know them well in order to answer questions on this area. They would include *Attorney-General v De Keyser* [1920] AC 508, *Burmah Oil v Lord Advocate* [1965] AC 75, *Blackburn v Attorney-General* [1971] 2 All ER 1380, *R v Home Secretary ex parte Northumbria Police Authority* [1987] 2 WLR 998, *R v Home Secretary ex parte Bentley* [1993] 4 All ER 442 and *R v Home Secretary ex parte Fire Brigades Union* [1995] 2 All ER 244.

More broadly framed questions may also embrace parliamentary accountability and control over prerogative acts (**Chapter 5**).

An interesting constitutional quandary is: in what if any circumstances might the Queen resume her legal powers and take prerogative decisions? This can also be seen as an issue of control. If a government was behaving 'unconstitutionally' by abusing the Queen's prerogative powers, it is thought that the Queen might be able to or even have a duty to dismiss that government. More topic overlap is thus illustrated (Conventions, **Chapter 2** and the position of the Prime Minister, **Chapter 3**).

One of the widest prerogatives, and arguably the most significant, is the Crown's power to conduct foreign affairs, including committing the UK to war. The Crown's decisions in this area are usually unchallengeable as are some of its actions. Whilst there was a parliamentary debate and vote upon whether the UK should go to war with Iraq in 2003, prerogative decision of the government or even of the Prime Minister is legally sufficient. Arguably, a convention of involvement of—if not approving vote by—the House of Commons is being established. In any event, in light of the problems and controversies arising from the last Iraq war what was the Prime Ministerial prerogative of 'war and peace' is now to be a decision of Parliament or more accurately the House of Commons.

Question 1

As De Keyser's case shows, the courts will enquire into whether a particular prerogative power exists or not, and, if it does exist, into its extent. But once the existence and the extent of a power are established to the satisfaction of the court, the court cannot enquire into the propriety of its exercise.

(Lord Fraser in *Council of Civil Service Unions v Minister for the Civil Service* [1985] AC 374)

Discuss.

Commentary

This is the most common question on the royal prerogative and a quite well-used quotation. Note, in particular, that the question does not confine itself to *Council of Civil Service Unions* (the '*GCHQ*' case). The 'twist' in the quotation is that Lord Fraser is explaining what the law was *before* the *GCHQ* case. A good knowledge of this key case would make this apparent but even if you do not recognise this, adequate study of the topic should produce an accurate answer in any event.

Answer plan

- Prerogative is the common law power of the Crown
- The courts may decide the existence and the extent of a prerogative power
- The exercise of some prerogative powers may be judicially reviewed: *GCHQ*

- High policy is not judicially reviewable
- Exercise of prerogative power affecting the rights of the individual may be reviewable.

Suggested answer

The royal prerogative is the remains of royal power. Munro describes it as:

> those attributes peculiar to the Crown which are derived from common law, not statute, and which still survive . . .
> (*Studies in Constitutional Law* (1999) 159)

As they are the powers of the Crown it was thought for a long time that they enjoyed the same legal immunities as the Queen and could not be reviewed by the courts. The House of Lords had made this clear in cases like *Chandler v DPP* [1964] AC 763 and *Gouriet v UPW* [1978] AC 435. This was despite trail-blazing dissents by Lord Denning, notably in *Laker Airways v Department of Trade* [1977] QB 643 and even Lord Devlin in *Chandler* had expressed some doubt. To Lord Denning, prerogative powers were government powers just like statutory powers and if they were abused they should be controlled.

The courts had always been able to exercise some sort of control over prerogative. Since as early as the *Case of Proclamations* (1611) 12 Co Rep 74, the courts have asserted entitlement to decide whether there was adequate precedent for the prerogative claimed to exist. This gives the courts more power than is commonly realised because the precedents are often unclear. For instance in both *A-G v De Keyser's Hotel* [1920] AC 508 and *Burmah Oil v Lord Advocate* [1965] AC 75 the court decided that, although the government could seize and even destroy a person's property in order to defend the realm, compensation must be paid. This had not been clearly established in earlier cases. As late as 1987, the courts recognised that there was a prerogative of maintaining the peace of the realm; *R v Home Secretary ex parte Northumbria Police Authority* [1987] 1 WLR 998. In 2001 the Australian courts established in *Ruddock v Vadarlis* (2001) 66 ALD 252001 that there was still a prerogative power to expel aliens. What is certain, however, is that the courts will not recognise a 'new' prerogative for which there is no historic precedent. As Diplock LJ said in *BBC v Johns* [1965] Ch 32 at 79:

> It is 350 years and a civil war too late for the Queen's courts to broaden the prerogative.

A-G v De Keyser's Hotel [1920] AC 508 recognised that if the government had a prerogative power and a statutory power to do the same thing, the government should act under the statutory power, thus giving the citizen greater protection and respecting the wishes of Parliament. This principle also applies to an Act of Parliament that has not been brought into force; the prerogative must not be used in preference to the statute, *R v Home Secretary ex parte Fire Brigades Union* [1995] 2 All ER 244.

Judicial review of the prerogative was finally allowed in the GCHQ case. Lord Fraser gave a number of reasons for this significant change of tack, chiefly that the Queen was not personally involved in the use of the prerogative and so the court would not be involved in questioning her legal immunity. He also noted that there had already been judicial review of decisions of a Tribunal (in *R v Criminal Injuries Compensation Board ex parte Lain* [1967] 2 QB 864) and of a Coroner's Court (*A-G of Duchy of Lancaster v Overton Farms Ltd* [1982] Ch 277). With the development of judicial review in the last thirty years there was no longer any reason to distinguish between statutory and prerogative powers.

All five House of Lords judges agreed that *some* prerogative powers could be judicially reviewed. It is unclear though *which* prerogative powers would be subject to judicial review. All their lordships agreed that a 'minor' use of the prerogative, here concerning the conditions of service of civil servants, could be reviewed. Lords Fraser and Brightman thought that this was possible because it was only a delegated use of the prerogative. An Order in Council gave the minister for the Civil Service power to alter civil servants' conditions of service. The Order in Council itself could not be reviewed but the minister's decision under it could be. Prerogatives like control of the Armed Forces and foreign policy 'were unsuitable for discussion or review in the law courts' (Lord Fraser, 398).

The other three judges, Lords Scarman, Diplock and Roskill were of the opinion that whether a prerogative could be reviewed depended upon its subject matter. Only the lower level, non-political uses of the prerogative could be considered by the courts. Decisions upon matters like national security, also involved in this case, had to be left to the government: only it had the information upon which to make a decision. Lord Roskill supplied a handy list of prerogatives that were unreviewable and had to be left to government: entering into treaties; defence; grant of mercy; award of honours; dissolution of Parliament and the appointment of government ministers. Lord Diplock thought that the prerogative should also be reviewable when its exercise affected private rights and expectations of citizens.

Judicial reviews of the prerogative resulting in success for the applicant are still rare, notwithstanding the GCHQ case. *R v Foreign Secretary ex parte Everett* [1989] AC 1014 concerned the refusal to renew Everett's passport. The court followed the reasoning of Scarman, Diplock and Roskill in GCHQ and stated that they could not review the prerogative when it concerned matters of 'high policy'. This case did not concern weighty questions of foreign policy and also affected the rights of the individual. It was therefore susceptible to judicial review, but on the facts the court concluded that there had not been a breach of natural justice.

In *R v Home Secretary ex parte Bentley* [1993] 4 All ER 442 the court was prepared to ignore previous case law including the obiter dicta of Lord Roskill in GCHQ, and permit judicial review of the prerogative of mercy. The Home

Secretary had misunderstood his legal powers when taking his decision and, although no formal order was made, he was asked to reconsider. In contrast the Privy Council declined to follow *Bentley* in *Reckley v Minister of Public Safety (No. 2)* [1996] 1 All ER 562.

The court looked at foreign affairs in *R (on the application of Abbasi and Another v Secretary of State for Foreign Affairs and Secretary of State for the Home Department* [2002] WL 3145052. Abbasi, a UK national held at Guantanamo Bay post '9/11', argued that the Foreign Office had a duty to intervene on his behalf with the US government. The court declined to interfere but conceded that judicial review would be available if the Foreign Office decision was irrational or defeated legitimate expectations.

Residents of the UK who do not hold UK nationality, also detained at Guantanamo Bay, have also sought similar judicial review. The claim in *R (Al Rawi) v Secretary of State for Foreign and Commonwealth Affairs* [2006] All ER (D) 46 met with even less success, the courts refusing to intervene in whether the UK government made representations on their behalf or not.

Legislation for the UK's overseas territories is made under the authority of Orders in Council. In *R (Bancoult) v Secretary of State for Foreign and Commonwealth Affairs* [2001] 1 QB 1067, the court ruled that a law ordering islanders to leave Diego Garcia was ultra vires the relevant Order in Council. This is similar to the *GCHQ* case itself, where a delegated power under the prerogative could be reviewed. The courts went further in *R (Bancoult) v Secretary of State for Foreign and Commonwealth Affairs (No. 2)* [2006] All ER (D) 149 where a new Order in Council had been issued, refusing to allow the Diego Garcians to return. It was held that the Crown had no prerogative power to exclude UK subjects from the territory and that this new Order was irrational.

It does seem, therefore, that the courts have become more willing to review prerogative acts when they affect individual rights, embracing matters once considered out of bounds, 'non-justiciable'. *Bancoult*, for example, touched upon important foreign policy considerations; Diego Garcia had been emptied of people in order to make it available as a military base for the United States.

Question 2

The principal convention of the UK constitution is that the Queen shall exercise her formal legal powers only upon and in accordance with the advice of her ministers, save in a few exceptional situations.

(de Smith and Brazier *Constitutional and Administrative Law*)

Discuss.

The Royal Prerogative

Commentary

This is the sort of question that many students of constitutional law dislike! At first glance it is unclear what area(s) of the syllabus it concerns. The student who looks a little longer might think that it is about convention. It is, in a way, only about a very specific group of conventions: those that surround the role of the Queen and her perogative powers. The nub is that the Queen nearly always acts on the advice of her ministers, but it is thought that there are some exceptional situations when the Queen could exercise power and say 'No' to her ministers. In answering this question it is essential to use actual examples. The other aspect of the question is the issue of constitutional control: should the Queen take a more active role in controlling the excesses of 'her' government?

Answer plan

- Does the Queen still have the right to make a personal choice?
- The Queen has the right to be consulted, the right to encourage and the right to warn
- In a 'hung Parliament' the Queen can become involved in establishing who is to govern
- If the Prime Minister acts unconstitutionally, the Queen may dismiss him.

Suggested answer

Old cases like *The Case of Proclamations* (1611) 12 Co Rep 74 made a distinction between the ordinary and absolute prerogatives. The ordinary prerogatives were areas in which the Queen had no personal discretion. Nowadays she would merely act on the advice of her ministers. The absolute prerogative covers areas where the Queen has a choice. Usually this is thought to involve only the award of some honours such as the Order of the Garter. It is possible, though, that in some other, more substantively important constitutional situations the Queen still might have a choice.

It is accepted that the Queen does have the right to express a view to her ministers upon how her prerogatives are used. Bagehot put it that the Queen has:

the right to be consulted, the right to encourage, the right to warn.

(*The Law of the Constitution* (1867))

More recently, these principles were restated in a letter to *The Times* on 27 July 1986 by the Queen's Press Secretary, Sir William Heseltine. There had been press coverage claiming that the Queen disapproved of some of the policies of the then Prime Minister, Margaret Thatcher. The letter said that the Queen 'was entitled to have opinions on government policy and to express them to her chief Minister'. However, the Queen was 'bound to accept and act on the advice of her Ministers'. Importantly the letter concluded with the constitutional reminder that discussions between the Queen and her ministers are confidential. It is difficult therefore to know for certain whether the Queen, or any previous Monarch, has ever gone beyond expressing a forceful opinion. That is allowed as long as the government has the final say.

Some examples are clear. The Sovereign has not refused assent to an Act of Parliament since 1708 and even then it was on the advice of Queen Anne's ministers who did not like what Parliament was proposing. George V expressed the view that he could refuse assent to the Irish Home Rule Bill in 1914. He said that he would do this to 'avert a national disaster' but that there was 'no such evidence'.

Conventionally, the Prime Minister chooses his government. In 1945, George VI is recorded as having expressed a preference in who was appointed to certain ministerial positions. He also expressed opinion on matters such as whether the prerogative of mercy should be extended to persons sentenced to death. There is nothing 'unconstitutional' about such 'advice' to ministers. However, when the Callaghan government (1976–79) made proposals for devolution, the Queen's public broadside that she could not forget that she had been crowned Queen of the United Kingdom was met with some controversy and criticism for being an interference or attempt to influence the elected decision-makers. Times change and the Queen gave no sign of resistance or reluctance when the (more significant) measures of devolution were passed in 1998.

If the Queen actually made a personal choice as to who should become Prime Minister, this would be highly controversial. She would be accused of political favouritism. Usually there is no decision for the Queen to make. There is a clear result from a general election and the leader of the majority party is invited as the person entitled to form a government. If, however, a 'hung Parliament' results, namely no single party having an overall majority of seats in the Commons, matters are by no means so clear. Until 2010 the most recent and thus informative examples were confined to the first half of the last century.

In 1916 the country was ruled by a coalition of parties led by the Liberal leader, Asquith. The war was going badly and he resigned. The King sent for Bonar Law, leader of the second largest party, the Conservatives. Bonar Law could not form a government. This put the King in a difficult position. Would he have to make a personal choice? Instead George V hosted a conference of the party leaders and Lloyd George, another Liberal, emerged as the Prime Minister.

In 1931 the first Labour government, led by Prime Minister Ramsay MacDonald, faced a national economic crisis. MacDonald was convinced that it was essential in the national interest to reduce public expenditure, in particular unemployment benefit. His party could not accept this. The leaders of the other parties agreed with MacDonald. He offered his resignation but the King declined it. Instead George V consulted the leaders of the other parties. They advised that MacDonald should remain as Prime Minister and form a 'National government', a coalition of parties. MacDonald took this advice and won a resounding victory at a general election later in the year. Ironically he ended up as the Labour Prime

Minister of a largely Conservative government. Subsequently George V has been criticised for playing too active a part in the choice of Prime Minister. Presumably the King did what he did on the advice of the other party leaders and because he thought that it was in the national interest. The electorate seems to have approved.

In 1974, amidst considerable economic difficulty and industrial strife, there were two general elections. The first, February 1974, resulted in a hung Parliament. The incumbent governing party, the Conservatives led by Prime Minister Edward Heath, polled the most votes of any single party. Labour, led by Harold Wilson, won the most seats but not an overall majority of seats. Seats counting rather than votes, Heath and his party could not claim to have won the confidence of the Commons. Nonetheless, Heath did not offer his resignation as Prime Minister and instead spent several days in negotiations with the Liberal party trying to form a new, coalition government whilst Wilson waited in the wings claiming legitimacy and authority to form a minority Labour government. During this period it was not clear who would govern and the Queen might have had to become involved. After several days the talks broke down without agreement, Heath resigned and the Queen was advised to send for the Labour leader, Harold Wilson, to form a new Administration.

It had been Heath's duty to remain as Prime Minister until the position became clear but his drawn-out attempt to form a new government was contentious. The unwritten constitution and the nature of convention afforded him some flexibility of action and he was generally adjudged not to have acted unconstitutionally.

The general election of May 2010 bore a hung parliament and, roughly sixty years on from the last, the UK has a coalition government once more. (The 'Lib-Lab Pact' of 1977–78 between the minority Callaghan Labour government and the Liberal party was a collaboration by which the Liberals did not join the government but supported it on key votes and so kept it in office). In February 2010, with the approach of the election and predicted hung parliament, the Cabinet Office consulted and then drafted a chapter for its Cabinet Manual setting out the constitutional position and appropriate conduct to establish a government. A prime objective was to provide maximum certainty and clarity and so avoid the Queen having to become or even appear involved. Symbolic of this 'appropriate distance', during the five days of negotiations (assisted by Civil Servants) between the Liberal Democrats and Tories the Queen's private secretary observed but did not participate and the Queen only came up to London once it was clear that a government-in-waiting had emerged.

It is similarly thought that the Sovereign could refuse the Prime Minister's request for a general election. In a letter to *The Times* on 2 May 1950 the King's Private Secretary said that refusal could be justified if three conditions were satisfied. First, the existing Parliament was able to carry on, secondly a general election would be detrimental to the national economy and thirdly another Prime Minister with a working majority could be found. Following on from the latter condition, the position of the Monarch would be aided if supported by some ministers. Although there are Commonwealth examples, in Canada in 1926 and South Africa in 1939, there are no modern UK examples. The crucial element which might justify the Monarch's refusal would again seem to be the national interest.

The current government is committed to ending a Prime Minister's discretion as to the timing of a general election. If the Fixed-term Parliaments Bill is passed, this will limit the scope of this prerogative power in any event.

The most spectacular example of the Sovereign resuming an active role would be the dismissal of the Prime Minister. This last occurred in 1834 when William IV dismissed Lord Melbourne. In 1975, however, the Governor-General of Australia (the Queen's representative as Head of State) dismissed the Australian Prime Minister, Gough Whitlam. The Senate was refusing to agree to his budget because of illegal ministerial misbehaviour in procuring overseas loans. The Prime Minister recommended that there should be an election for seats in the Senate only. The Governor-General refused and dismissed him from office. A Governor-General acts in the name of the Queen and exercises her powers. It is not thought that the Governor-General consulted the Queen. Whilst it is a myth that he acted without soundings and some influential support and urging across the political party divide, the Governor-General was criticised and there was political 'fall-out' though he had acted within his constitutional powers. The Gough Whitlam affair shows that, at least 'in the name of the Queen', there exists the power to dismiss a Prime Minister for behaving 'unconstitutionally'. The problem in the UK, with its unwritten constitution, is: what is unconstitutional? Trying to evade the correct parliamentary procedure and to continue governing without a majority to pass legislation were the apparent 'crimes' of Whitlam.

In conclusion, there is a rather varied series of incidents, in the UK and the Commonwealth. It does seem that the Monarch claims the right to protect the national interest even if it is against the wishes of the majority party. A difficulty with this, however, is that opinions as to what best serves the national interest may vary. The rarity of incidents of royal interference indicates that Kings and Queens have, rightly, been very cautious about when it is appropriate to interfere. Perhaps it is the *possibility* of this reserve position being invoked that is the key in, for example, deterring inappropriate behaviour and in maintaining responsible governance by those entrusted, by election, to wield political power.

Question 3

The UK and the Republic of Fantasia (Fantasia) are in dispute about possession of an island called Lackland, which has been sovereign UK territory for the last 200 years. Fantasian troops

The Royal Prerogative | **49**

invade and take control of Lackland. UK Armed Forces are deployed to remove them. No formal declaration of war is made, but the Crown takes a number of actions. It withdraws the passports of some UK citizens resident in Fantasia thought to be helping the Fantasian invasion forces; Fantasian citizens resident in UK are arrested and expelled; a number of UK-owned and registered ships are requisitioned, without compensation, for military use; and UK troops occupy and destroy properties belonging to both Fantasian and UK citizens.

The UK action is successful and a peace treaty is concluded between the UK and Fantasia. Among other provisions, it stipulates that neither country accepts liability for loss or damage inflicted during the hostilities. No UK legislation is enacted to give effect to the treaty within the UK, as it is not thought necessary.

A number of UK and Fantasian citizens are aggrieved by the actions taken against them by the UK during the hostilities and each seeks a legal remedy.

Advise them.

Commentary

The actions in question were taken by the UK government by exercise of royal prerogative powers concerning foreign affairs. The Crown has wide powers at its disposal, which in the older cases tended to be challenged without success in the courts. In more recent cases, the courts have been more inclined to intervene to protect the rights of the individual.

Close attention to the facts of the question reveals the prerogatives, and thus the related cases, to be considered: war and the deployment of troops, issuing passports, expulsion of aliens and the confiscation of property at home and abroad. The relationship between treaties upon domestic law should be fairly straightforward, now that we are familiar with European Community law and the **Human Rights Act 1998** giving effect to the **European Convention on Human Rights and Fundamental Freedoms 1950**. Act of State is lurking in there somewhere. To most students it is a nightmare, but it is important to realise that it is not at all clear from the cases what it is.

Depending upon the nature of the particular problem question, it may be best to tackle it line-by-line as the scenario unfolds. This tactic is certainly best in this example.

Answer plan

- The war prerogative is unchallengeable in the courts
- The prerogative to issue passports is reviewable
- Aliens may be expelled under the prerogative
- The prerogative allows the requisition of property, with compensation
- Act of State is unchallengeable in the courts
- So too the treaty-making prerogative.

Suggested answer

The declaration and conduct of war is one of the established royal prerogatives. Whilst there is no formal declaration here, such conflict and troop deployment are covered. It is most unlikely that a court would entertain any challenge as to whether war was justified or troops should be sent: *Chandler v DPP* [1964] AC 763. This was confirmed by *CCSU v Minister for the Civil Service* [1985] AC 374 (the *GCHQ* case) where, in particular, Lord Roskill included war as one of the prerogatives that was beyond the control of judicial review. An indirect challenge to the legality to the 2003 Iraq war was also not allowed in *R v Jones* [2006] 2 WLR 772. This does not, however, mean that the Crown can do as it pleases (below).

It was once thought that the prerogative to grant, replace or withdraw passports was unchallengeable. After the *GCHQ* case this changed. In *R v Foreign Secretary ex parte Everett* [1989] AC 1014 the Court of Appeal held that the Foreign Secretary's refusal to renew a passport was subject to judicial review for Everett had a right to natural justice. Here, however, the facts may be distinguished. Taylor LJ stated that matters of high policy were not justiciable. War is a matter of high policy, so it is possible that the courts might refuse to intervene here. In *GCHQ* itself, a similar matter of high policy, namely national security, overrode the requirement of natural justice. Also, as in *Everett*, whilst the court might find the Applicants' cases reviewable, it might, in its discretion, award no remedy.

The expulsion of enemy aliens has been held to be an unchallengeable prerogative matter; *Netz v Chuter Ede* [1946] Ch 224. In the famous case of *R v Bottrill ex parte Kuechenmeister* [1947] KB 41 it was held that the Home Secretary could intern an enemy alien. What is more, only the Home Secretary could decide when the war was over, that too being a matter of royal prerogative. Even in peacetime the courts of Australia upheld a prerogative power to expel aliens in *Ruddock v Vadarlis* (2001) 66 ALD 25. In the problem presented, war is not formally declared and the Home Secretary would probably act under related (immigration) legislation rather than the royal prerogative. At the time of the first (1991) Gulf War some Iraqi nationals were threatened with deportation. The courts were at least willing to look at their cases, although they decided that they could not investigate an issue of national security; *R v Home Secretary ex parte Cheblak* [1991] 2 All ER 319. Subsequently, the European Court of Human Rights ruled in *Chahal v UK* (1997) 23 EHRR 413 that the courts should be able to review such government decisions based on national security. However, in *Rehman v SSHD* [2001] 3 WLR 877 the House of Lords kept to the view that they were unwilling to question the Secretary of State's decision to deport a foreign national on grounds of national security.

The requisitioning of a UK subject's property is certainly allowed in wartime. Compensation, however, must be paid: *Attorney-General v De Keyser's Royal Hotel* [1920] AC 508.

According to *Burmah Oil v Lord Advocate* [1965] AC 75, when UK-owned property abroad is destroyed for wartime purposes, compensation must be paid. This seems to be confirmed by *Nissan v Attorney-General* [1970] AC 179, when UK forces requisitioned and damaged an hotel in Cyprus. The House of Lords confirmed that this action did not qualify as an Act of State and therefore Nissan might have a remedy. Act of State was here defined as an action of government policy that should not be considered by the courts ('non-justiciable'). The case law seems to make a distinction based upon the nationality of the victim. Act of State cannot be committed against a UK citizen. Nissan was a UK subject and so had his remedy in a UK court. Actions in Fantasia which harm Fantasian citizens almost certainly qualify as Acts of the State, as held in *Buron v Denman* [1848] 2 Ex 167, where the Royal Navy destroyed Spanish property in Africa, acting upon clear government policy to stamp out the slave trade. This can be contrasted with *Johnstone v Pedlar* [1921] 2 AC 262 where the property of a US citizen was confiscated within the UK. This was not an Act of State. The true ratio of this case is hard to define. May an Act of State be committed in the UK? It seems that it cannot be committed against the citizen of a friendly country, here the USA. However *Johnstone* is interpreted, it certainly does not apply to the citizens of a country with which the UK is at war and against which the UK commits acts in that foreign country.

It is clear that the conclusion of a treaty is an unchallengeable act in the UK courts; *Blackburn v Attorney-General* [1971] 2 All ER 1780 confirmed in *R v Foreign Secretary ex parte Rees-Mogg* [1994] 1 All ER 457. However, it is also clear that the treaty cannot affect legal rights within the UK unless it is given statutory force. Statutory rights are unaffected; *Laker Airways v Department of Trade* [1977] QB 643. So too are common law rights, such as trespass and negligence; *The Parlement Belge* [1879] 4 PD 129, confirmed in *Littrell v USA (No. 2)* [1994] 3 All ER 203.

In conclusion, the UK citizen affected by these 'wartime actions' has a fairly good chance of some kind of legal remedy. The removal of passports may, however, be more difficult to challenge. *Rehman* suggests that the Human Rights Act 1998 has not made a significant difference to how the prerogative is interpreted by the courts. Assuming, as would be likely, the government to have extended the territorial coverage of the Human Rights Act to include Lackland (*R (Quark) v Secretary of State for Foreign and Commonwealth Affairs* [2006] 3 All ER 111), the difficult issue then becomes whether the Act would apply to UK troops deployed there; *R (Al-Skeini) v Secretary of State for Defence* [2008] 1 AC 153, concerning the claim that UK forces deployed in Iraq had killed civilians without justification. In this case the court decided that the Act did not apply as the UK forces were not in effective control of the country. Instead, Iraqi law applied as did the First Geneva Convention 1949 on the protection of civilian persons in time of war. It is probable that the Geneva Conventions apply to what happened in Lackland but not the *Human Rights Act,* the latter being intended for time of peace.

Question 4

Behind the phrase 'royal prerogative' lie hidden some issues of great constitutional importance which are insufficiently recognised.
   (Munro *Studies in Constitutional Law*)

Consider whether you agree with this statement.

Commentary

Many students tend not to warm to this sort of question, hence we have included it! It is obviously about the royal prerogative but to answer it properly requires, as is common, knowledge and application of other public law topics including the nature of the constitution (**Chapter 2**) and accountability to Parliament (**Chapters 3** and **5**). Be warned, it is extremely dangerous to revise for a constitutional examination just by looking at, say, four topics and hoping that they will come up. Many constitutional questions spread across several areas.

This particular question draws upon elements of Questions 1 and 2 in this chapter and is really about the large amount of government power hidden behind the prerogative and the lack of adequate legal and political controls over its exercise. The answer is an example of a fairly one-sided argument. The 'lack of recognition' aspect is perhaps of more significance than may at first appear: arguably the very 'mystique' of these ancient powers is a part of the problems of transparency, accountability and control.

Answer plan

- Prerogative powers are used by the government of the day
- These include some of the most important powers of government
- Many of these powers are ill-defined
- Judicial review of some prerogative powers is now possible: *GCHQ* case
- Judicial review of matters of high policy is not possible
- Parliament has limited control over the use of prerogative powers.

Suggested answer

The royal prerogative concerns 'those inherent legal attributes which are unique to the Crown' (De Smith *Constitutional and Administrative Law* (1998)). Whilst some of these do still remain vested in the Monarch in person, by convention most (in volume and significance) are now exercisable only by ministers of the Crown. It is true that by convention again the Queen must be consulted and as Bagehot put it, she has 'the right to be consulted, the right to encourage, the right to warn' (*The Law of the Constitution* (1867)) but in reality the royal prerogative now amounts to powers of Her Majesty's elected government.

Many of the central and most important government powers lie within the royal prerogative. They include the conduct of foreign affairs, defence and national security, claims to territory, maintaining the peace, the running of the Civil Service, mercy and pardon, some aspects of immigration and the grant of honours.

A problem with these ancient powers is that it is often unclear what exactly they allow the government to do. Occasional legal challenges require the courts to attempt to clarify which powers still exist. For instance, in *Attorney-General v De Keyser* [1920] AC 508 historical research was needed to discover the circumstances in which the Crown could requisition property in wartime. No really clear answer was obtained, so that when a similar point came up again in *Burmah Oil v Lord Advocate* [1965] AC 75 there was still doubt. As late as 1987 a 'new' prerogative power emerged in *R v Home Secretary ex parte Northumbria Police Authority* [1987] 2 All ER 282, which stated that the government has the power to maintain peace in the kingdom. This amounted to a significant, very wide and vague tool, in addition to the extensive statutory Executive powers effectively at the disposal of the police. The '*Northumbria*' case related to policing of the miners' strike (1984–85), a long-running industrial dispute of considerable controversy including criticism of the conduct of miners and of the police. In the context of such a 'battle' of high national stakes and much violence, could the government for instance imprison people without trial if it claimed that it was keeping the peace of the realm? To take a roughly similar example, the government has a duty to uphold and maintain national security, as recognised in the *GCHQ* case [1985] AC 374. What exactly is national security and what is government allowed to do to preserve it? There are no clear answers to these two questions. The attitude of the courts has always been to leave to government judgments upon what constitutes a perceived or actual threat to national security and it is therefore perhaps no surprise that in cases such as *Chandler v DPP* [1964] AC 763, and *Rehman v SSHD* [2001] 3 WLR 877 courts have been satisfied upon very little evidence and refuse to 'second guess' government when it invokes national security as its reason for what it does.

In the *GCHQ* case the House of Lords declared that it could control how the royal prerogative was used, by means of judicial review although grounds for control such as illegality, irrationality and procedural impropriety are quite limited in scope and all of their lordships agreed that some government prerogative powers lay outside the control of the courts. Lords Fraser and Brightman considered that only delegated exercise of the prerogative could be reviewed, that is the decision of the minister but not the Order in Council itself. The politically controversial prerogatives had to be left to government. Lord Roskill identified these as treaties, defence, mercy, honours, dissolution of Parliament and the appointment of government ministers.

Cases before and since *GCHQ* show that the courts tend to be very reluctant to interfere with government prerogative decisions. In *Chandler* [1964] the deployment and armament of troops was outside the control of the courts. A decision by the Attorney-General to take legal action or not was unchallengeable, *Gouriet v UPW* [1977] 2 WLR 310. The decision not to renew a passport was, in theory, reviewable *R v Foreign Secretary ex parte Everett* [1989] AC 1014, but in reality the courts agreed with the government's policy not to renew the passports of 'wanted' criminals. Taylor LJ considered that the courts should not look at 'high policy' Executive decisions, but could review lower level decisions affecting the rights of individuals. The court continued this approach in *R (Abbasi) v Foreign Secretary* (2002) WL 31452052. Abbasi, detained by the USA at Guantanamo Bay, wished the UK government to intervene on his behalf. The court refused to tell the government what to do, but maintained that such ministerial decisions were potentially reviewable. Somewhat a contrast is *R v Home Secretary ex parte Bentley* [1994] 4 All ER 442. Here the court, whilst considering itself unable to tell the Home Secretary what to do and not making an Order, did find the manner of exercise of the grant of pardon reviewable and invited the Home Secretary to re-consider the decision not to grant Bentley a posthumous pardon. This, however, was not followed in *Reckley v Minister of Public Safety (No. 2)* [1996] 1 All ER 562. The two *Bancoult* cases, *R (Bancoult) v Secretary of State for Foreign and Commonwealth Affairs* [2001] QB 1067 and *(No. 2)* [2006] All ER (D) 149, may be signs of a new direction: the courts refused to accept the removal of the right of the inhabitants of Diego Garcia to return to their island. Arguably, recognition and protection of human rights have been enhanced by the *Human Rights Act 1998*.

The courts have often justified their approach by saying, in cases like *Chandler* and *Gouriet*, that the proper body to control the use of these highly political powers is Parliament. It is true that Parliament may remove prerogatives as in the *Bill of Rights 1689* and the *Treasure Act 1996*. Where both statutory provision and prerogative apply, government must use the statutory power rather than the prerogative; *De Keyser*. The courts have also held that the government must not ignore the will of Parliament when statutory powers have replaced a prerogative but have not yet been brought into force; *R v Home Secretary ex parte Fire Brigade Union* [1995] 2 All ER 244. However, a government with a

Commons majority usually controls what Parliament does and it is inconceivable that the Legislature would be allowed to remove or restrict an important prerogative power against the government's wishes.

By convention, ministers are accountable for their actions to Parliament. Whilst in principle this includes actions under the prerogative, by long-standing practices many prerogative areas are hidden from the view of Parliament. Since 1955 successive governments have refused to answer MPs' questions concerning the Prime Minister's advice to the Queen, the grant of honours, mercy in death sentences and senior appointments such as to the Privy Council. Similarly, governments may refuse to answer questions on many defence issues such as arms sales, issues of national security and confidential relations with foreign states. The Parliamentary Commissioner for Administration is also prevented from investigating many of the same areas and also personnel matters concerning the Civil Service.

Legally, the Queen decides upon military action, using her prerogative. By convention, the Prime Minister actually takes the decision, perhaps first consulting Cabinet or selected senior ministers. On the back of the controversy surrounding the basis of the decision to go to war with Iraq in 2003, and how matters subsequently turned out, all parties agree that the Prime Ministerial prerogative to commit the country to war should end (save in urgent circumstances) and make it a decision for debate and vote by the House of Commons. The coalition government has promised to implement this change.

It can be seen that the royal prerogative gives the government of the day great power. This power is subject only to limited accountability, not amounting to control. Some change is afoot though there will always be a temptation for those in power jealously to guard that power.

Further reading

Barnett, H. *Constitutional and Administrative Law*, 7th edn (Cavendish, 2008), ch. 5.

Bradley, A. and Ewing, K. *Constitutional and Administrative Law*, 14th edn (Longman, 2007), ch. 12.

Loveland, I. *Constitutional Law, Administrative Law and Human Rights*, 4th edn (OUP, 2006), ch. 4.

Munro, C. *Studies in Constitutional Law*, 2nd edn (Butterworths, 1998), ch. 8.

5

Parliament

Introduction

In any constitutional law course, the subject of Parliament is likely to be central. Courses vary, however, in the balance struck between the political and legal aspects. In a course where political issues are given prominence, one would expect to find examination questions on the likes of the defects of the electoral system, the powers of backbench MPs and reform of the House of Lords. More strictly legal topics would cover parliamentary privilege or the legislative process for example. The sample here spans the range.

Questions addressing possible reforms will be popular with examiners. To answer such questions well, whether you have strong personal opinion, none or are indifferent, you must of course marshal and articulate with cogency the arguments on all sides of the issue.

Question 1

Explain how the following voting systems work and consider their respective advantages and disadvantages as methods of electing a national Parliament:

(a) First Past the Post
(b) Party List
(c) Additional Member System.

Commentary

This is a pretty straightforward question. For a start, your answer must accurately describe the systems, highlighting the differences between them. A good answer would then, as required, go on to evaluate the strengths and weaknesses of each system, of itself and relative to other systems.

Your argument of all sides will be all the more cogent for being substantiated by examples of what each system could produce. Whilst the UK now uses a variety of electoral systems including the three stipulated, comparative analysis from other countries may also be made. In fact, the question is not limited to the UK (or to the General Election) but unless you have particular knowledge of other countries' use of these systems, it seems sensible to major upon the UK, the focus of your study. Having decided and planned your approach, state clearly in the introductory paragraph how you intend to interpret the question. Inevitably, a matter of particular importance is what system should be used for the General Election to the lower House of the UK legislature, the Commons which in turn produces the national government. It is upon this theme that our suggested answer concentrates, accordingly also recognising the underlying issue of what reform may be appropriate. Useful detail on the various systems is to be found in the 1998 Jenkins Commission (October 1998, Cm 4090).

Your conclusion, as well as drawing strands together, might point to priorities for reform and the likelihood of any such reform, or spell out which system appears best overall and why, perhaps because your chosen system best achieves what you consider to be the most important principle. For instance, one might argue that First Past the Post is best as it is most likely to secure strong, stable government or you might prefer the Party List system as the best way of securing representation for all groups in society. The choice is yours as there are few 'right' answers in public law.

Answer plan

- Under First Past the Post a minority vote can elect a government
- First Past the Post often secures a government with a House of Commons majority
- Party List secures proportional representation
- Under Party List there are no constituency MPs
- The Additional Member System combines features of Party List and First Past the Post
- Additional Member and Party List may secure better representation for minority parties
- Additional Member and Party List may lead to coalition government.

Suggested answer

Any liberal democracy will have a system of elections which recognises universal suffrage, the right of all adult men and women to vote in a choice of who is to govern them. Relative to its 'thousand year' history, a fully established franchise without restriction by sex, race, class or wealth is a recent development in the UK. Apart from possibly lowering the minimum age from 18 to 16 years, the focus of debate and reform has become how the various systems in use, in particular the First Past the Post system for the UK national, General Election, works, especially in terms of increasing voter engagement and better reflecting the wishes of the electorate. This in turn requires consideration of the type of legislature and government that each of the three different systems would likely produce. For example, how far an individual vote actually counts and the extent of representation of, for instance, minority groupings, may differ depending upon the electoral process used. Similarly, one system may be much more likely to produce a government with a House of Commons majority, and thus a government that can act, govern, as opposed to one that is emasculated and cannot.

First Past the Post, the 'majoritarian' system, is used to elect MPs to the House of Commons. The UK is divided up into 650 separate constituencies, each with a roughly equal electorate of around 70,000 voters. Each elector in each constituency has one vote, which he casts by writing an 'X' next to the name of his chosen candidate on the ballot paper.

The winner is the candidate who receives more votes than any other single candidate. The candidate does not need an absolute majority over all the other candidates combined, just one more than the runner up. Accordingly, the winning candidate may very well be elected on a minority of the total constituency vote, with more electors having voted for candidates other than the successful one. Those other votes are discarded, 'wasted'. Therein lies a significant problem with this electoral system. Although the winning candidate represents all constituents including those who did not vote for him or at all, those who voted for a different candidate—perhaps a significant majority of voters in the constituency—have no direct representation of their voting preference. Nationally, this equates to millions of voters.

It is very difficult for smaller or new parties to achieve many seats under First Past the Post as even though they may poll a significant share of the vote in a given constituency, they may well not gain enough votes to win the seat. Thus, nationally too they may do creditably in terms of votes but relatively very poorly on seats. The experience of the Green Party illustrates this although they achieved their first constituency success in the 2010 general election, a single seat. Similarly, the so-called 'third party', the Liberal Democrats, tends to be squeezed under the system by the Conservatives and Labour. Usually it gains lots of votes in many constituencies but relatively few seats. In many constituencies, the Liberals will come a good second or close third but of course those votes do not then count either for that constituency or nationally. Highly unusually though the 2010 election has put them into government as the junior partner with the Conservatives, their first direct taste of government since the 1920s. The 2010 election shook the kaleidoscope and the pieces have yet settled. It may change some things 'for ever' but no-one can judge yet. It will be very interesting to see its various medium and long-term ramifications including its impact upon the future fortunes of the Liberal Democratic Party.

Often a general election result can seem a distortion of the true wishes of the electorate. In 2001, for example, the Labour Party won 42% of the vote nationwide, but secured 412 MPs, 63% of the total. In 2005 Labour obtained only 35.2% of the vote, but still won 355 seats, 55% of the total, while the Conservative

Party, only slightly behind with 32.4% of the vote, won only 198 seats. This also shows that a party can win a constituency, and nationally, with less than half of the national vote. The party with most votes nationwide may lose the election, as happened to the Labour Party in 1951 and the Conservatives in February 1974.

First Past the Post also often sees very little change from election to election. It is characterised by 'safe seats' that rarely change hands, staying with the established party of that constituency election-on-election. Only about 20 or so seats change party most elections and one of the two main parties, Labour and Conservative, has always formed the government since 1945, until 2010 that is.

A principal argument of those who support First Past the Post is that it very usually results in a clear majority for one party, thus providing a strong, stable government able to implement the policies it promised to the electorate in its manifesto. Another advantage is that 'the count' (of votes in each constituency) is straightforward and reasonably quick. An important asset is its simplicity, involving no complicated choices for the voter to make: a complex system carries the risk of effectively disenfranchising a voter. Another key strength is the constituency link: the outcome is a single constituency MP with whom the local electorate can identify and to whom they can—and do—take their grievances.

Party List is a very different system. There is no specific constituency-based vote. The electors' choice is between parties, not individuals. Each party puts forward a list of candidates, hence the name, and seats are allocated in accordance with the number of votes nationally. For example, if a party wins 40% of the vote, it gains 40% of the seats nationally, the party allocating its seats, as it chooses, to the candidates on its list. This *'proportional* representation', reflecting voter preference, is the main advantage of this system.

One list for the whole country would be unusual, except in small countries, so commonly the country is divided into regions and the parties present lists of candidates for each region. That was the system used in the UK 2004 and 2009 elections to the European Parliament. Proportional systems such as the List system tend to help smaller parties, for instance in the 2009 'Euro' election the United Kingdom Independence Party won 13 seats in the EU Parliament and the British National Party (BNP) 2 seats, neither of which have any representation in the UK Parliament.

Opponents of Party List argue that a multiplicity of small parties is a bad thing. It might enable extremist groups to gain representation (though that is democracy), influence and some power, as with the BNP. It may also mean that government would have to be formed from a coalition of two or more parties. Others see coalition as potentially beneficial, in securing wider representation of views and in the tempering effect of parties having to compromise in order to reach policy decisions. To the contrary, critics argue that coalition governments are inherently unstable; that as the government parties have to negotiate decisions and actions, either nothing gets done or all policies are so diluted that the wishes of the electorate—or any part of it—are not put into effect, satisfying no one; and that small—perhaps extremist—parties may hold disproportionate influence, even the balance of power. Lastly, the individual constituency MP disappears under Party List so the electors no longer choose their candidate and have no obvious person to whom they can take their grievances.

The Additional Member System seems to be a happy compromise between First Past the Post and Party List. The idea is very simple: some MPs are elected to represent individual constituencies under First Past the Post and other MPs are elected under Party List and do not represent a constituency. So, the elector has two votes, one for a candidate and one for a party. This system is used for elections to the Scottish Parliament and Welsh Assembly, and is effective in reducing the distortion caused by First Past the Post. In the 2007 election to the Scottish Parliament, the Conservative Party won only four constituency seats (with 334,743 votes), but won a further 13 seats (and 284,005 votes) from the Party List element of the system. On the First Past the Post element alone, Labour won 37 seats (648,227 votes), a majority of 16 seats over the Scottish National Party (SNP) (with 21 seats, 648,374 votes); but taking into account the proportional element ('List' seats), the final tally had the SNP on 47 seats (1,297,628 votes) and Labour on 46 seats (1,243,789 votes) in total, the SNP forming a minority government, with support from the Scottish Green Party upon certain matters. The 2003 Scottish election gave Labour the strongest showing but without an overall majority; coalition government with the Scottish Liberal Democrats resulted. That no system is perfect is also illustrated here. There are pro and con arguments for coalition government (above). Also, controversially perhaps the SNP was not included in the 2003 Scottish government. Coalition being the 'choice' of the strongest party that did not do quite well enough not to need other parties, Labour was not going to embrace the SNP—its main rival in Scotland—if it could avoid it. In 2007 the SNP did likewise. This distorts representation.

The two different types of MP, some with constituencies and some without may also one day cause disputes about relative workloads.

Different electoral systems are used in the many UK elections to different forums. Election to the national 'power house', the House of Commons, has however doggedly remained by First Past the Post despite its inequities and ardent critics.

The 2010 general election gave no single party an overall Commons majority. The largest party, the Conservatives, did not get close enough to the crucial 326 seats to enable it to form a viable minority government and so it opted for the only real alternative, coalition with the Liberal Democrat party. A criticism of coalition is that the electors are cheated in what the government does as opposed to what electors thought that they were voting for. A 'grubby' private deal in a 'smoke-filled room' has to be done: the parties carve out an agreement. Who gets which jobs, a compromised principle here and a watered down manifesto policy promise there, so as to arrive at a 'package deal' enabling the two parties to sit together at Cabinet, whether or not they may comfortably look their respective party members and electors in the eye. Liberal Democrat supporters for instance, did not vote for an increase in the regressive tax VAT but that has been one of the first measures taken. Pertinent to discussion here, Tory voters did not vote for a change from First Past the Post to the Alternative Vote system (AV) for general elections. Nonetheless, the referendum (above) was extracted by the Liberal Democrats as part of the coalition agreement (Clause 24, 'The Coalition: Our Programme for Government', 20 May 2010). Parliament is being asked to pass the Parliamentary Voting Systems and Constituencies Bill 2010–11 with a view to the referendum going ahead on 5 May 2011. AV is broadly similar to First Past the Post in not being proportional and in maintaining single-member constituencies. Voters rank the various candidates in preference order. Unless a candidate wins overall on the first count, voter preferences are re-distributed pursuant to detailed rules until a winner emerges. A principal advantage of AV is that the winning candidate must have over 50% of the constituency vote.

In the last edition of this book we asked if political leaders with a vested interest in attaining and keeping power would ever give up the First Past the Post system which tended to 'guarantee' them power on a regular basis, à la 'Buggin's turn'. Well, a cynic might say that a no less ignominious motivation lurked not far from the public scene in May 2010, political expediency; others would strongly reject such outrageous slings and arrows. Whatever, negotiation certainly entails calculation and the smart money is presently on a 'No' in the referendum which might then result in maintaining the status quo, First Past the Post for the foreseeable future. We shall see.

Question 2

What changes have been made in recent years to modernise the procedures and operation of the House of Commons? Have these reforms made the House of Commons more effective? Are there other changes that you consider desirable?

Commentary

The main element in your answer to this question will be a description of the changes made since the 1997 election in accordance with the recommendations of the Modernisation of the House of Commons Select Committee (now replaced by the Political and Constitutional Reform Committee), though where a question uses a vague expression like 'in recent years' you may reasonably justify bringing in material from a longer period. What will make a good answer will be your assessment of the effectiveness of the House of Commons in the performance of its principal tasks, legislating and scrutinising the Executive. As to other, future changes there is a kind of limbo as the 'old' may be dropped and the new has barely got off the ground. It seems appropriate still to make some reference to the 'undone agenda' of the former Modernisation Committee as well as to the new government's proposals set out in 'The Coalition: Our Programme for Government' (May 2010) and any ideas of your own, all the better if grounded upon specifically identified and illustrated defects.

'Procedures and operation' suggests political processes rather than matters over-lapping with law reform such as parliamentary privilege.

Remember, your concern is the Commons, not the Lords or Parliament. In any event an answer to this Question can only cover some of the many issues raised.

Answer plan

- MPs' working conditions and sitting times
- Publishing legislation in draft
- Programme motions
- Carrying over legislation between sessions
- Prime Minister's Question Time
- Back-bench powers
- Public petition.

Suggested answer

The UK is known for its traditions, pageantry and ceremony. To many, the way in which the House of Commons does its business is a prime example, steeped in history from its building to its procedures and language, as if relics of a past age—from voting by herding through an 'Aye' or 'No' lobby (instead of pressing a button), to addressing each other as the 'Honourable' or 'Right Honourable' Member, to the entitlement to take snuff upon entering the Chamber. The structure seems even to be class-ridden, the Lords and the Commons. This is of course a product of continuity in development over a long period of time, although some might say 'without the development'. The influence of history lies perhaps in the atmosphere of the place, originally to all intents a Gentleman's Club where nothing changes and how it has always been done is the rule. Does this incline the House of Commons to be backward-looking and 'conservative'? It is perhaps symbolic that when the Houses of Parliament had to be rebuilt in the nineteenth century, the architectural style chosen was medieval. In recent years however, there have seen some significant changes to the way the House of Commons operates. These have been intended to improve working conditions for MPs as well as enabling it to perform its principal functions, legislating and scrutinising the executive, more effectively and efficiently. Much of the impetus for changes to the legislative process comes from governments, which are always trying to get substantial amounts of (its) legislation through Parliament as smoothly as possible. Governments are, however, likely to be less enthusiastic about measures to improve scrutiny of the Executive. Some long-standing criticisms of parliamentary procedures, such as the ineffective scrutiny of delegated legislation remain to be addressed.

The first aspect that will be examined relates to the working conditions of MPs. Until relatively recently, the work of MPs was seriously hampered by a shortage of office accommodation. Many had to share offices, some had no office space at all. Now, with the opening in 2000 of Portcullis House, all MPs have an office usually with a room for a secretary and research assistant nearby; and further improvement work is in progress. This is of particular value in dealing with the substantial volume of correspondence (including email) from constituents that MPs now receive. MPs are paid a substantial allowance, towards their office costs. This payment and how some have utilised it has caused great controversy recently, with calls for a flat salary only. However, the fact remains that as matters stand appropriate assistance remains necessary for MPs if they are to perform their functions effectively. The expenses scandal and the resulting changes are really outside the remit of the Question though it is noteworthy that the House of Commons, which jealously guards its self-regulation and independence, was effectively forced to hand over the MP expenses portfolio to an outside body.

The change that has probably had the greatest impact on MPs' working conditions concerns the sitting hours of the House of Commons. Traditionally, Commons proceedings began at 2.30 p.m., except on Fridays when sittings began at 9.30 a.m. and ended by 3 p.m. to allow MPs to travel back to their constituencies for the weekend. Debates on legislation would not normally begin until 5 p.m., normally continuing until 10 p.m. and sometimes well into the night. These hours were designed for the convenience of those MPs who had another occupation. Until well into the twentieth century, it was common for an MP to carry on a business or practise a profession, such as law, being in effect only a part-time MP. This became less common as politics developed into a full-time occupation which could thus no longer be combined with another job. A constituency demanded the exclusive attention of its MP and the amount of constituency business increased. In any case, meetings of select and standing committees were normally scheduled for mornings, and more MPs were involved in these.

As well as being outdated, these sitting hours seriously disrupted the private lives of MPs; it was impossible to enjoy a normal family life if one frequently had to be at the House of Commons until 10 p.m. or later. Particular difficulty was caused to women with young children, and it was widely believed that these hours contributed to the reluctance of women to stand for Parliament. For particular reasons the 1997 election saw the first significant increase in the number of women elected, albeit only to 120, and this increased the pressure for a change in the sitting hours. From 1999, Thursday sittings were brought forward to the morning and afternoon only, with Commons business ending at 6 p.m. From January 2003 further reform meant that Commons' business started at 11.30 a.m. on Tuesdays and Wednesdays, ending at 7 p.m. MPs' opinions on this reform varied; those with homes and families in easy reach found them preferable, but others objected to spending isolated and unproductive evenings in rented accommodation. Some considered that the vitality of debate in the Chamber was diminished, by lesser overall attendance and a lack of 'atmosphere' that settling in for an open-ended evening debate engendered. In 2005 therefore, as a compromise, Tuesday sitting hours reverted to 2.30 p.m. to 10.30 p.m. and there is some evidence already of more late night sittings in the chamber with the 'in a hurry' pace so far set by the coalition government.

There have also been adjustments to the arrangement of the yearly sessions, again partly to help MPs with family commitments. For example, there are now half-term breaks in February and May, to coincide with school holidays. The summer recess has been shortened, which should produce a more rational spread of parliamentary business across the year.

Turning to the legislative process, there has long been criticism of the way in which the House of Commons examines legislation, or fails to do so. Even important laws may be rushed through without adequate scrutiny. The Anti-Terrorism, Crime and Security Act 2001 for example had only 16 hours scrutiny in the House of Commons and was not amended at all in that time. It is true that the House of Lords, as is often the case, subjected that Act to much more thorough scrutiny and forced the government to accept significant amendments, but it should be for the elected House to take the lead in questioning legislation of such significance.

There have, however, been some welcome developments in the legislative process. It is now the practice of the government to publish proposed legislation in draft form well in advance of its formal introduction to Parliament, allowing earlier consideration and comment by expert and other interested parties and the public at large, then being subjected to the new procedural stage of pre-legislative parliamentary scrutiny by committee, for example a Joint Committee specifically formed to examine a specific Bill. It is generally agreed that this early scrutiny is desirable and its use should be extended.

The timetable for passing legislation is always contentious. Successive governments have refused to address the effective stranglehold that government has upon what legislation is considered and in turn passed. The vast bulk of Bills are government Bills and government of course wishes to get its way, specifically in getting its mandated legislative programme through. Opposition parties argue that it is to the good of the effectiveness of Parliament, in checking government generally, that it has more of a say over its own business, critically what gets debated and examined, when, and for how long. The current government has promised to establish a new Back-bench Business Committee and House Business Committee, which may wrest back significant control; as with the introduction of the select committee system in the first weeks of the Thatcher government of 1979, it is often the early measures of an in-coming government which (a) get done and (b) have lasting impact.

Governments also object to delays that they attribute to Opposition obstruction. The Opposition and backbenchers generally do not wish their examination of Bills curtailed. The former practice was that discussion of Bills could only be curtailed by an Allocation of Time Order, a 'guillotine'. This Order could be made only after a Bill had suffered delay in Committee, and would itself need a substantial and often acrimonious debate. Since 2000, Programme Motions are generally used. These give the Standing Committee considering a Bill a date by which it should complete its deliberations, but additionally enables it to allocate the time available for each of the various clauses of the Bill. The use of these motions has led to a more rational and less contentious timetabling of legislative scrutiny, and it seems likely that they will replace the 'guillotine' completely.

One of the main reasons for the pressure on the parliamentary timetable is the rule that Public Bills must complete their passage through both Houses within one session. Any Bill not so passed falls and must start again from scratch next session. The Modernisation Committee recommended in 1998 that it should be possible for Bills to be carried over from one session to the next. This would encourage governments to allow more thorough scrutiny and also spread the work of legislating more evenly across the session. This proposal was accepted, in spite of misgivings that it might make life too easy for the government of the day. So far it has been used in respect of complex technical legislation and has generally been regarded as a useful innovation.

There have been other changes to parliamentary procedures. Soon after the 1997 election, Prime Minister's Question Time was moved from the traditional 3 p.m. 15-minute Tuesday and Thursday afternoon slots, to 30 minutes every Wednesday (noon—12.30 p.m.). The intention was to allow for more extended and sober questioning, rather than the short and noisy performance of the past, but there is little noticeable difference. Whilst the trade-off of frequency for depth may be acceptable, a detraction of the single weekly session is that it lessens the immediacy, and thus the element of surprise in the matters of the moment upon which the Prime Minster may be tested by cross-questioning. A further innovation has been the introduction of a parallel chamber for simultaneous debates, using a room in Westminster Hall. This enables backbenchers to raise more issues and provides the opportunity to debate select committee reports. This has again generally been well-received as a valuable innovation.

The idea of enhanced public engagement and involvement by means of public petition has never really taken off. The coalition has stated its intent that any petition attracting at least 100,000 signatures shall be formally debated. Also, a new

'Public Reading' stage is to be added to the passage of Bills, enabling the public to comment online, those comments to be considered in debate by the committee scrutinising the particular Bill.

Although many of the changes discussed, and the removal of other arcane, if harmless rules (like having to wear a hat to raise a point of order during a division!) have been largely welcomed, there remain many areas where further reform could be achieved. For instance, many outside Parliament consider that the slow process of voting by walking through the division lobbies should be replaced by instant electronic voting. However MPs, who value the voting process as an opportunity to buttonhole a government minister, have rejected this. Whatever the merit, perhaps this illustrates the inherent conservatism of an institution that has existed for centuries?

Question 3

At the recent UK general election, 10 seats in the House of Commons were unexpectedly won by the Save the National Health Service Party (SNHS). These 'first-time' MPs seek your advice as to the means available to them to try to influence government policy, especially on health issues.

Advise them.

Commentary

This question touches on a wide range of issues relating to the powers of backbench MPs. Your answer should span more than just the legislative processes and the work of select committees.

The issue, health is of no particular significance in terms of your answer and no specialised knowledge of it is required.

As well as a good knowledge of the House of Commons' activities, an awareness of political realities will enhance the answer.

Note that although the question is not expressly confined to what the MPs can do in Parliament, this is the intended thrust (and there is likely to be little they can do outside Parliament given the absence of specific facts in the question suggesting, for example, a public campaign). Whilst the question is about the Commons, it does not preclude passing reference to the possibility of encouraging the House of Lords to assist.

Answer plan

- Scrutiny of primary and secondary legislation
- Private Member's Bill

- Raising constituents' issues, asking PQs
- Select committees
- Lobbying.

Suggested answer

The most important factor in determining the extent to which the new MPs may influence the government will be the size of the government's majority. A government with a substantial majority, as long as its own supporters remain loyal, need not worry about the attitude of Opposition parties. At the other extreme, a minority government will be dependent on the votes of other parties, which may therefore be able to exact a high price in policy terms, even to the extent of insisting upon places in a coalition government. However, even where a government has a comfortable working majority, parliamentary procedures offer Opposition and backbench MPs a variety of opportunities for the exercise of influence, and a skilful use of such procedures will maximise their effect. Although government business generally has priority, the new SNHS MPs will find opportunities to make their presence felt in Parliament.

The largest single item in the House of Commons' timetable is the consideration of government legislation. The government is bound to introduce Bills on health matters. The SNHS MPs may seek to speak in the Second Reading debate, but the Party's greatest opportunity for influence will be achieved by getting one or two of its MPs on to the Standing Committees that subject Bills to detailed scrutiny. They may then propose amendments, though these will only succeed if they attract the support of some government MPs on the committee in question; the government, provided that it has an overall majority in the House of Commons, will have a majority on each standing committee. Any amendments agreed to in committee can be reversed by the House of Commons Chamber at the Report Stage, but it may be that the government will accept reasoned amendments in order to avoid delay in passing the legislation.

Other forms of legislation may provide opportunities for intervention. If a Health Authority was to promote a Private Bill then that would give opportunities for backbench MPs to call for debates on the floor of the House as well as participating in the quasi-judicial committee stages.

There are various methods by which an MP may propose legislation, but most of these provide no real likelihood of success. The best way to try to have a Private Member's Bill debated and even enacted is for the MPs to enter the annual ballot to promote a Bill on one of the Fridays reserved for that purpose. Competition is very great; most backbenchers enter the ballot, whether or not they have a Bill ready to propose. If one of the SNHS MPs were to be successful in gaining a high place in the ballot, that would give an excellent opportunity to change the law. One important limitation must, however, be noted. Any Bill requiring public expenditure, or the imposition of a tax, cannot be passed unless a Money Resolution is agreed, usually after the Second Reading. Only a government minister can move such a resolution, in which case there would be no real likelihood of the SNHS procuring an increase in spending against the wishes of the government. In any case, all successful Private Members Bills need at least the benevolent neutrality of government and preferably its tacit support. A modest measure, not involving public expenditure, would seem the most promising option for the SNHS MPs.

Some matters of health policy will also be dealt with by secondary legislation, but the opportunities for MPs to scrutinise this are not great. Although the most important Statutory Instruments may require the approval of the House of Commons, most do not and will become law unless a Negative Resolution is proposed and passed. The Joint Committee on Statutory Instruments examines all instruments laid before Parliament and has the power to draw matters of concern to the attention of the House, though not in respect of the substantive content of the instrument.

Apart from legislation, much of the House of Commons time is spent on various forms of debate. Although most debate is at the government's initiative, there are a certain number of Opposition days, when it can choose the subject for debate. Most of these are used by the largest Opposition party, but, by agreement, the SNHS may be allocated a half day to debate a subject of their choice. There have always been daily adjournment debates, with MPs' right to choose the topic being allocated by ballot. The opportunity for these debates has been greatly increased with the recent introduction of the parallel chamber in Westminster Hall. On Tuesdays and Wednesdays, ten slots are available for backbench MPs to debate issues, again chosen by ballot.

One of the most obvious ways for the SNHS MPs to raise health matters is by asking parliamentary questions. To obtain maximum publicity, questions should be set for oral answer, often in an oblique form in the hope of surprising the minister with an embarrassing supplementary question. MPs are, however, subject to restrictions on the number of questions they may table, because of the likelihood of the system becoming clogged and, question time being strictly limited, only some 10 to 20 questions may be dealt with on any given day. Any questions not reached are instead answered in writing, as are all questions where a written answer is requested. This procedure, while not attracting such immediate publicity as Question Time, is extremely useful as a means of obtaining information about the government's actions and policies. Application under the **Freedom of Information Act 2000** also holds potential.

In recent years, the departmentally related select committees have provided MPs with enhanced opportunities for scrutiny of the Executive; the SNHS MPs will hope, having made known their interest and any expertise in the field, to obtain a place on the Health Committee. Competition for places is intense and, while places are formally allocated by the Committee of Selection, in practice the whips of each party have a considerable influence over allocation as between the parties. The government will have a majority on each committee, and the official Opposition party will take the bulk of the remaining places. Determined lobbying by the SNHS MPs might, however, secure them perhaps a single place. Select committees do generally try to operate in a non-partisan way as far as possible, and are more likely to influence government if they do so operate. The opportunities for questioning witnesses in public, and obtaining information from government and other sources tend to make select committees an effective forum. Of particular importance in the health field would be the power of the Health Select Committee to summon and question witnesses including ministers from the Health Department but also departmental civil servants who are more actively involved in implementation of policy and, often most useful, the day-to-day care healthcare providers such as key figures in Health Authorities and Hospital Trusts. The first elections of Chairmen of select committees took place in 2010, another reform of the new government. Replacing the former practice of appointment by party whips, this may further enhance the effectiveness of scrutiny by these committees as well as freeing up backbenchers from pressure to be loyal in votes and debates with the promise of such future patronage.

Given their specific interest, the SNHS MPs are likely themselves to be lobbied on health issues by constituents as well as the various interested parties from the National Health Service (NHS) and private sector alike, for example pharmaceutical companies. Such lobbying is regulated by the Committee on Standards in Public Life established after the 1995 Nolan Committee Report into Standards in Public Life. Restrictions include prohibition of paid advocacy of any cause. Unpaid advocacy and the general making and facilitating of contacts—indeed the whole 'networking' process—are going to be one of the most important tools of the SNHS MPs in the ultimate goal of influencing those with power, government ministers.

In conclusion, there is a range of possible means available to the new SNHS MPs. It may be that events, whether a newsworthy healthcare 'public cause' or a political happening such as the current hung Parliament. Otherwise, it is up to them to use make effective use of the tools described, with political skill and acumen. Their efforts may be frustrated by the dominance of the major parties unless perhaps they win allies within those parties. They should at least be successful in obtaining information, which they would not have had but for their electoral success.

Question 4

What role do departmental select committees play in the scrutiny of the Executive. How effective are they?

Commentary

This is a straightforward question.

The first task is to recognise that *departmental* select committees are confined to the House of Commons.

An answer will first require an account of the committees, their structure, membership and operation. However, a good assessment question will always demand more than mere descriptive narrative. Here, the 'value added' component is the second part of the question, which challenges you to provide critical analysis and evaluation of the effectiveness of such committees since they came into being in 1979. Issues such as government influence on the choice of members, co-operation from witnesses and government reaction to reports will all be relevant. As ever, key will be your cogent, corroborated argument of all sides to the pertinent issues.

Answer plan

- Membership
- Power to summon witnesses and see records
- Non-confrontational style
- Assessing influence.

Suggested answer

As suggested by the Question, the purpose of select committees is to scrutinise the Executive, examining expenditure, administration and policy. They do this by probing investigation, including examining documentary evidence and close questioning of witnesses, work of a nature that cannot be performed adequately in the Commons chamber. Witnesses include civil servants and key personnel of Executive Agencies and other bodies ranging from energy utilities to police forces, all of whom are in any event barred from the Commons chamber pursuant to the Separation of Powers. The end product of a committee's work on a given matter is its Report, including any recommendations for change.

The present system of departmental select committees was established in 1979, when it was agreed that there should be one select committee to examine the work of each Ministry and its associated agencies, boards and 'quangos'. Originally there were 12 such committees, now there are 16 (19 if one still considers the Northern Ireland, Scottish and Welsh Offices as departments). This increase is due to changes in the structure of government and an acceptance that every department should have a committee to examine it. It is therefore now the case that select committees cover the whole range of government activities.

Membership of select committees is in practice confined to backbench MPs. Each committee has between 11 and 16 members. Membership is proportionate to party strength, for example the current Health Select Committee is 11 strong and comprises six government backbenchers and five Opposition (Labour).

Reform under the new government in 2010 has seen Chairmen elected for the first time, some by secret ballot using the Alternative Vote electoral system. This replaces the former practice of allocation by the old Committee of Selection whereby appointments were effectively made by the party whips via a fait accomplice list of nominations to that committee. This change may give enhanced independence and credibility to the committees, bolstering their effectiveness in scrutinising government and other executive bodies. Some of the newly elected chairmen come from the Opposition backbenches, for example Patricia Hodge, chair of the Public Accounts Committee and Keith Vaz who remains chair of the Home Affairs Committee.

A seat on a select committee is a highly sought-after position. For newer MPs, it offers a means of making an impact; for more senior MPs, especially those who know that they will not be offered ministerial office, it offers an alternative career structure. MPs, once appointed, serve on the committee for the whole Parliament unless they choose to resign or are appointed to frontbench posts. MPs may have some relevant expertise to bring to a particular committee. For example the Health Select Committee includes Doctor (of medicine) Sarah Wollaston, a General Practitioner, and its newly elected Chairman is Stephen Dorrell who was Health Secretary in the Conservative government of the 1990s.

Select committees have the power to send for persons, papers and records. Any individual, other than a member of either House of Parliament, may be formally summoned to appear, though in practice committees need do no more than issue an invitation, which will invariably be accepted. Many witnesses will indeed welcome the opportunity to give evidence before such a highly-regarded body. Others may be less cooperative; in 1992 the brothers Kevin and Ian Maxwell declined to answer questions from the Social Security Committee about their late father's fraudulent use of pension funds, because they were facing criminal proceedings. The committees themselves have no coercive powers. All they can do is to refer the matter to the House of Commons, which has the power to punish those found to be in contempt, but is unlikely to be willing to do so except in an extreme case. In 1985 Arthur Scargill (leader, National Union of Mineworkers) was called to the Bar of the House of Commons following his refusal to give evidence to the Energy Select Committee. No attempt was made to punish the Maxwells in this way.

Members of either House, including in particular government ministers, can only be invited, not summoned to appear. The government promised in 1979 that ministers would appear when invited, and very largely this has happened ever since. The House of Commons has the power to compel one of its members to attend a committee, but this power is unlikely in practice to be used against a government minister whilst the government retains its overall majority. It is in any case always possible that the minister who willingly attends the committee meeting may be less than helpful in actually answering the questions.

An interesting issue arises in relation to the appearance of civil servants before select committees. Civil servants are responsible to the government of the day (their departmental minister), which in turn is accountable to Parliament. The select committee system, however, can bypass the departmental minister by calling the civil servants themselves to give evidence, creating an awkward, three-sided relationship between minister, official and committee. Governments have successively issued guidance for officials appearing before committees that, though exhorting officials to be as helpful as possible, reiterates that civil servants remain subject to the instructions of ministers in giving evidence. The guidance suggests that, where issues of the conduct or misconduct of officials are concerned, the official should suggest to the committee that the minister should give evidence instead. Some serious disputes have arisen where ministers have refused to permit particular officials to attend, instead appearing themselves or sending the departmental Permanent Secretary to give evidence. The Defence select committee had difficulty investigating the 1986 'Westland affair' because the relevant officials were not allowed to attend. Ultimately there could be a clash if the committee compels attendance of officials and the minister instructs those officials either not to attend or not to answer any questions put. This might put the committee in an 'impossible' position but the inevitable high-profile (and now 24-hour) media attention to such behaviour concerning such a controversial matter as 'Westland' might just pressure government to reconsider its stance.

The guidance to officials also identifies various classes of material on which no information should be given to the committee without the minister's approval; these include advice given to ministers, confidential personal information, sensitive economic information and matters under international negotiation. While it is acceptable to assert that some matters are too sensitive to be discussed openly in committee, this list appears to cast a wide net, embracing some matters of legitimate concern to an investigating committee and that might be capable of open disclosure and consideration without prejudice to national (rather than government) interests. There is no mechanism for pre-determination: the government's decision is the last word.

Even more complex issues arise in relation to Executive agencies that, while remaining part of government departments, are supposed to operate with a degree of autonomy. Although the creation of these agencies was not intended to alter the arrangements for accountability, their existence has limited the scope for scrutiny through parliamentary questions and has increased the need for other methods of scrutiny to be developed. The government has accepted that, for matters concerning the day-to-day operation of an agency, the head of the agency is the appropriate witness to give evidence to a select committee, though reserving the minister's right to control the answers given.

The most striking feature of these committees is the ability of MPs from different parties to work together, symbolised by the fact that when hearing witnesses they sit together round a table, unlike the confrontational arrangement of the chamber of the House of Commons. Whilst the examination of witnesses may become somewhat adversarial on occasion, the committee itself operates 'as one' so far as possible and tries in reaching its findings to reach a consensus and to issue a unanimous report. Sometimes party divisions prevent this (and so a minority report will also be issued), but not so often as to diminish the effectiveness of the committees. Each committee can choose what topics to examine within its own remit; it will usually conduct one or two major investigations each session, as well as responding quickly to matters of immediate concern, such as the 2007 onwards banking crisis. The government has no direct control over the choice of topics and, while it may try to exert an influence behind the scenes, this has not prevented committees from choosing subjects that have gravely embarrassed the government of the day, such as that concerning the 2003 Iraq war.

Select committees have enhanced the powers of the backbench MP to scrutinise government actions. Just how much impact these committees have had in practice is, however, more difficult to assess. Whilst some of their reports have been followed by statutory reform, other influences have contributed to the pressure upon government to act. Government invariably makes a formal response to select committee reports, whereby it is at least forced to consider and justify its attitude to the issue in question. It is very difficult for a government to dismiss a unanimous select committee report out-of-hand; there is always the risk that the subject will arise again to embarrass the government.

It was never likely that the introduction of these committees would transform the House of Commons into as powerful a legislative chamber as the US Senate, before the committees of which even the most powerful may tremble. The Commons select committees have, however, succeeded in providing backbenchers with a source of detailed information and in encouraging the development of expertise within Parliament. Committee reports have provided insights into the inner workings of government and the televising of committee hearings shows the people that the House of Commons does not amount simply to the bear-garden of the full Chamber in set piece events like Prime Minister's Question Time, but does far more.

The select committees are now an established part of the parliamentary system. Their impact can perhaps best be assessed by trying to imagine the furore that would be caused, both inside and outside Parliament, by any attempt to abolish them.

Question 5

Consider the following situations in the light of the rules on parliamentary privilege.

(a) Giles, a backbench MP, said during a debate in the House of Commons that the directors of the three largest UK fertiliser companies met together regularly to fix prices, in breach of both UK and EU law. The Minister for Agriculture and Food asked Giles to send him further details of the accusation and also suggested that Giles inform the European Commission. Giles wrote to both the minister and the Commission from his parliamentary office. The managing director of one of the companies is threatening to sue Giles for defamation.

(b) A Private Member's Bill to ban the use of chimpanzees in medical research is to be debated next week in the House of Commons. Dr Foster MP is the parliamentary consultant to the British Medical Research Society (BMRS); she is paid £10,000 a year for her services and she has declared this in the Register of Members' Interests. She has been told by BMRS that they will end her consultancy immediately unless she votes against the Bill. Animal rights activists have warned Dr Foster that they will picket her home and her office unless she votes for the Bill.

(c) During a debate in the House of Commons on the decline in moral standards, Pecksniff MP accused Deadlock MP of fathering an illegitimate child. This accusation was false, and Deadlock was so annoyed that he punched Pecksniff in the voting lobby. The following day, the *Daily Bluetop* published a report of the debate, including a mention of Pecksniff's accusation. The *Daily Redtop* published a front page article, under the headline 'Deadlock in Love Child Scandal', not mentioning the rest of the debate.

Commentary

When dealing with questions on parliamentary privilege, it is important to remember that there are two arenas, the court and Parliament and that the perspective of each might not be the same. You must consider the perspective of each forum.

Having revised this topic and it coming up in your assessment, you might be chomping at the bit to show off your up-to-date awareness of political developments and law reform, specifically to talk about the three former MPs and a Peer currently facing criminal prosecution for allegedly 'fiddling' their expenses; the dismissal of their argument (submission of an expenses claim form is a parliamentary proceeding and therefore) that only Parliament, and not the courts, had jurisdiction; the Joint Committee Report on Privilege 1999; and the Draft Parliamentary Privilege Bill just published, 2010. However, whilst this material would be apposite to a discursive essay question including reform, it is not material to answering the problem scenarios posed here: resist straying, stick to solving the problem before you by applying law (and not proposed law) to the facts. Once the prosecutions are decided and (if) the Bill becomes law, then they might well be both relevant and material.

Parliament

Answer plan

- Freedom of speech, absolute within Parliament, qualified outside
- Controls over consultancy
- Reporting parliamentary proceedings
- Procedure for dealing with breach of privilege.

Suggested answer

(a) This problem is concerned with the fundamental privilege of Parliament, freedom of speech. This is protected by **Article 9 of the Bill of Rights 1689**, which states that:

> The freedom of speech and debates in Parliament ought not to be impeached or questioned in any place out of Parliament.

As a consequence, the courts have accepted that words spoken in the course of parliamentary proceedings are absolutely privileged. No action for defamation can be brought in respect of such words, nor can they even be cited in court to support an action for defamation arising from words spoken outside Parliament, as in *Church of Scientology v Johnson-Smith* **[1972] 1 QB 522**. Giles can therefore face no legal action over what he said in the debate.

As for the letter written by Giles to the minister, the position here is less clear. If Giles had given the details orally in the course of the debate, this would be protected as a proceeding in Parliament. Does the writing of a letter count as a proceeding in Parliament? In 1957, the MP G. R. Strauss had written a letter to the minister outlining complaints from a constituent about a public utility. The utility (an Electricity Board) considered the letter defamatory and threatened legal action, which the MP suggested might be a breach of privilege. The Committee of Privileges (now the Committee for Privileges and Conduct) adjudged the MP's letter a proceeding in Parliament that should have the protection of absolute privilege. The House of Commons disagreed and voted to dismiss the complaint of breach of privilege.

Correspondence (including emails) is increasingly used by MPs as the best way of raising issues with a minister, parliamentary questions being reserved as the second line of attack. It may accordingly be argued that the absolute privilege should be extended. Indeed, MPs are now encouraged to deal with the new Executive agencies directly by letter rather than by asking a question of the minister in the House of Commons. An MP's correspondence on official matters will, however, have the protection of qualified privilege and it can be argued that this is sufficient. Why should an MP be immune if maliciously passing false information to a government minister or official? The call for absolute privilege, on the other hand, is that even the unfounded threat of legal action might operate to deter MPs from performing their proper function without fear or favour; arguably, anything that reduces the effectiveness of MPs is undesirable.

As far as the letter to the European Commission is concerned, it would be difficult to argue that this attracts absolute privilege as a proceeding in Parliament: EU institutions are completely separate from UK institutions. Giles would certainly be able to claim qualified privilege, however, so that he will be protected if he has acted without malice.

(b) Provided that Dr Foster has made a full declaration of her agreement with the BMRS, she will not be in breach of any rules by voting on the Bill to ban the use of chimpanzees, whether for or against. Her problem is that two different groups are attempting to force her to vote in particular ways. It is a clear breach of privilege for any outsider to attempt, by bribery or threats, to influence an MP, and any such attempt would be subject to punishment as contempt of Parliament, as well as possibly amounting to a criminal offence. It is, however, not clear how this rule relates to the practice of parliamentary consultancy. This issue was raised in 1947. W. J. Brown, an MP, was appointed by a trade union to further its interests in Parliament, but when political disagreements arose between them, the union threatened to withdraw from the contract, causing Brown financial loss. The Committee of Privileges was concerned mainly with the propriety of the original contract and, having decided that it was proper, found no breach of privilege in the contract being terminated. They also confirmed that any agreement that purported to bind an MP to behave, vote or speak in a particular way would be improper. In some later instances, the threat by a trade union to withdraw sponsorship from an MP has been classed as a breach of privilege. On each occasion the union withdrew the threat as soon as the issue of privilege was raised, and no punitive action was taken.

It therefore seems probable that any express threat from the BMRS, or any subsequent decision to withdraw sponsorship with immediate effect, would be regarded as a breach of privilege, though there would be nothing wrong with a decision to terminate the contract in due course in accordance with its terms. BMRS might be satisfied to reflect that in any case, an MP may still support the causes for which he has accepted a consultancy. Pursuant to the 1994 Nolan Committee Report, Dr Foster would not be able to speak during the debate.

Any physical action taken by the protesters may be a breach of the criminal law; an offence under the **Public Order Act 1986**, assault or criminal damage. Dr Foster's best course of action, if subjected to harassment, may well be to involve the police. It will also be contempt of Parliament to molest or threaten an MP. In the case of the **Daily Graphic HC 27 (1956–7)**, a newspaper was held to be in contempt when it published an MP's telephone number and incited its readers to ring him up to complain about his actions in Parliament. The House of Commons has the power to order an outsider to appear at the Bar of the House to be reprimanded, but this power is rarely used. It is probable that, as happens if people demonstrate in the public gallery, any protesters will be handed to the police to be dealt with.

(c) Because Pecksniff's statement was made during a debate, he is protected by the absolute privilege conferred by the **Bill of Rights**. Deadlock cannot bring any legal action against Pecksniff for defamation, even if Pecksniff knew that the accusation was false; only were Pecksniff to repeat the statement outside Parliament could Deadlock sue him. Deadlock might however argue that Pecksniff is abusing his parliamentary immunity, and may thus refer the matter to the Speaker as a possible breach of privilege; MPs have been reprimanded in such circumstances.

As far as the assault by Deadlock on Pecksniff is concerned, there are various possible consequences. Deadlock has apparently committed a criminal offence. Although MPs were once entitled to freedom from arrest, this no longer applies to criminal proceedings. Deadlock may therefore be arrested, charged and prosecuted just as any other person. It is, however, possible for the House of Commons to exercise its right to regulate its own proceedings. It has from time to time had to deal with disorderly conduct by MPs. It may suspend the MP from the House for a time; the MP is not paid during that time and cannot take part in any business of the House. The ultimate parliamentary sanction available against an MP is expulsion from the House. This has only ever been used in extreme circumstances, such as upon conviction for a grave criminal offence, or following gross contempt of the House. It is unlikely that Deadlock's behaviour would be regarded as justifying such an extreme sanction, though he would certainly be expected to apologise, as was Ron Brown MP in 1988. During an 'overheated' debate, Brown exhibited disrespect for the House by damaging the Mace, the symbol of the authority of the House.

So far as newspapers are concerned, the **Parliamentary Papers Act 1840** provides that absolute privilege only extends to material (such as Hansard) published by or under the authority of either House. A newspaper has qualified privilege for any fair and accurate report of parliamentary proceedings made without malice, as in *Wason v Walter* **(1868) LR 4 QB 73**. The report does not have to be verbatim to be protected. In *Cook v Alexander* **[1974] QB 279**, it was held that a parliamentary sketch, provided it was honest and fair comment, could attract qualified privilege. It therefore appears that the *Daily Bluetop* may be able to claim qualified privilege for its report. The *Daily Redtop*, however appears not to be reporting parliamentary proceedings at all, let alone in a fair and accurate way. It will therefore be susceptible to an action in defamation and cannot plead any privilege as a defence.

Question 6

If it is to fulfil the functions of a second legislative chamber, the House of Lords needs substantial further reform.
Discuss.

Commentary

Reform of the House of Lords remains highly topical. The **House of Lords Act 1999** removed most hereditary peers but was only the first stage of intended further reform. The new government has stated its intention to 'complete' reform by making the Upper House wholly or largely elected.

To answer this question adequately, it is necessary to identify first the principal functions of a second legislative chamber. This will establish the criteria against which the need for further reform may be judged. Whilst you may wish to question what a second chamber should do, the premise of the Question is that it will perform the 'typical' functions of a second chamber and the nub of the Question is reform of its composition and how that is decided upon.

The focus of your answer is of course the House of Lords and its relationship with the Commons, though a strong answer will include some comparative analysis (from other jurisdictions).

There is much useful primary source material, spanning many years. The best and most up-to-date comprehensive consideration is to be found in the Wakeham Commission ('A House for the Future', Royal Commission on the Reform of the House of Lords (January 2000, Cm 4534)) and perhaps the Ministry of Justice White Paper ('The Governance of Britain, An Elected Second Chamber: Further Reform of the House of Lords' (July 2008, Cm 7438)) though this emanates from the last government. This does not preclude embracing other ideas, including your own, radical or otherwise.

Avoid lapsing into too much narrative: a long trawl of the history of Lords' reform will not distinguish your answer.

Remember, the reforms under the **Constitutional Reform Act 2005** are now complete; the Upper House is solely a legislative chamber now so discussion of its former judicial role is neither necessary nor appropriate.

Note that the House of Lords Reform Bill 2010 currently before Parliament is not a government Bill and does not address the broad thrust of salient reform.

Answer plan

- Representation
- Selection or election
- Checking the power of the House of Commons
- Scrutiny of legislation
- Scrutiny of the Executive
- Relationship with the Commons.

Suggested answer

In most liberal democracies, the legislature comprises two chambers. The respective powers of the two chambers will vary according to the constitutional structure of the State in question. In the UK, the House of Lords and House of Commons have developed over the centuries, and, as with much of the UK constitution, their relationship is set by statute and convention.

It is an essential element in any democratic state that the legislature should consist of representatives of the people. Often in a bi-cameral legislature, each chamber represents the people in a different form. Commonly this is by geographical distinction, for instance, in a federal state such as Germany or the United States, the first chamber is representative of the nation as a whole whereas the second chamber specifically represents the constituent parts of the federation, in Germany the 16 Länder and in the United States the 50 States (and 1 District). The US Senate consists of two senators from each State regardless of size. Even in non-federal states, such as France, it is common for the second chamber to consist of representatives of geographic regions.

The principal weakness of the House of Lords is that it lacks legitimacy. This lies at the root of its lack of 'teeth' and why it became merely a revising and delaying chamber, albeit arguably very good at what it does. It is not a democratically representative assembly. All members are there by dint of birth or by appointment, none by direct election by the people. Therefore, it is essential to change the basis of membership of the Lords to give it the legitimacy and acceptability it needs to be able to perform effectively its functions as a second chamber. Whether it has more, less or the same powers, it will have more authority to act if it gains in legitimacy.

The House of Lords Act 1999 removed all but 92 of the hereditary peers, and all major parties agree that the remainder will be removed when the reform of the Upper House is 'completed'. The life peers now form the bulk of members of the House of Lords. Whilst most of these sit and vote on party political lines, with only the minority of 'cross-benchers' being independent, the Lords is less party political, and therefore less adversarial in character than the Commons. Other interests are represented in the Lords; for example the 26 Bishops of the Church of England will represent the stance of the established Church. Of course, every peer—as every MP in the Commons—may exceptionally speak and vote according to individual conscience, most obviously where a 'free vote' is allowed by the parties, for instance upon matters of moral concern such as abortion or stem cell research.

The key 'rule' that prevailed throughout the Wakeham report, the White Papers of 2001 and 2007 and related cross-party discussions was that, however the Lords is reformed, the primacy of the Commons must be maintained. The Commons has—perhaps not surprisingly—endorsed this more than once and it of course will be the decider of the Lords' fate, especially if government allows a free vote on the issue.

Wakeham recommended a wholly or largely appointed second chamber, primarily to avoid rivalry through similarity with the Commons. Following Wakeham and the 2001 White Paper, the Commons voted overwhelmingly for a wholly or largely (80%) elected second chamber whereas the Lords themselves voted convincingly the other way, for a wholly or largely appointed House. The last government came round to the view of the Commons but ran out of steam as the parties failed to reach agreement. The new government has acted swiftly in giving a lead on the issue. It seeks a wholly or largely elected Upper House and is trying to prosecute action with momentum, having set December 2010 as the dead-line for its new cross-party committee to pronounce detailed proposals; however, there is criticism that the committee lacks backbench representation.

The argument for primacy of the Commons is compelling, not only based upon the Lords' democratic deficit but also the **Parliament Acts 1911–1949** ('**Parliament Acts**') and related conventions. There is the clear possibility, however, that an elected House of Lords might one day challenge or even compete with the Commons.

The 2007 White Paper made various proposals to differentiate the two Houses, some derived from Wakeham. It suggested using a different voting system for elections to the Lords, mooting—instead of First Past the Post—the Alternative Vote, Single Transferable Vote or a List system; distinct membership via larger constituencies; a different, non-renewable term (12–15 years); a significantly smaller House (450, 400 or less); and staggered election in tranches of a third so that at no time would the complete Lords' membership be more recent than that of the Commons. The coalition government has already nailed its colours to a proportional voting system and to a long term of office.

It may be that if the Lords becomes a 'hybrid House', with an appointed minority, then as well as there being a marginal democratic deficit as against the Commons, this could retain some of the wealth and diversity of experience and expertise of life peers in particular, in fields such as medicine and science, perceived as a significant asset of the Lords, rather than mirroring the Commons in attracting 'career politicians' only.

A principal role of a second chamber is to act as a check on the first, acting as a safeguard against the concentration of too much power in the hands of one body. The powers of a second chamber vary in different constitutions from a mere power of delay to a complete veto. Under the **Parliament Acts**, the Lords may delay for one year legislation introduced in and passed by the House of Commons. It is significant that the 'Upper House' retains the power to reject any Bill to extend the life of the House of Commons, thus making the Lords a safeguard against any attempt to subvert democracy by postponing elections. In *R (Jackson) v Attorney-General* [2005] UKHL 56, the judicial House of Lords indicated that it would not accept any attempt to use the **Parliament Acts** to remove that safeguard, either directly or indirectly. It is likely that any further reform of the House of Lords will, as Wakeham recommended, restate and clarify relations between the two Houses.

For other legislation, the House of Lords retains some power to act as a check on the House of Commons, because it is still necessary for a Bill to be passed in identical form by each House if it is to become law in a single session. The unrepresentative nature of the Lords as currently composed means that it is usually very reluctant to reject legislation approved by the House of Commons. However, it has done so and when this has happened in the last year of a Parliament then Bills have accordingly fallen. If the second chamber were to be wholly elected, it might justifiably expect greater powers, although a power of veto seems unlikely and might produce legislative 'gridlock'.

A further task performed by a second chamber is to share the onerous work of scrutinising legislation, thus reducing the work burden of the Commons. Modern governments require the enactment of large amounts of increasingly complex legislation. In the UK, some 50 to 70 Acts are passed each year. It is an essential element in the democratic process that all legislation should be scrutinised by the Legislature and that governments should have to justify their proposals in both substance and detail. It is common practice for some legislation, particularly non-controversial measures, to start its passage in the House of Lords where detailed scrutiny can be given, thus saving time in the over-pressed House of Commons.

The House of Lords has been considered to play a very useful role in the scrutiny of legislation. Whereas in the House of Commons the intensity of the party struggle detracts from the technical scrutiny of legislation, members of the House of Lords may be able to take a more detached view, thereby ensuring that legislation, whatever its substantive merits, is well drafted. Were the House of Lords to become a fully elected chamber, it is very possible that its performance of this function would be impaired, as party political strictures would likely be more stringently applied and the quality of relative independence of the Upper House may be sacrificed.

A fourth purpose that can be served by a second chamber is to assist in the scrutiny of the Executive. Whether a government is fully accountable to both chambers will vary from state to state and its arrangements for the separation of powers. It is nonetheless usual for both chambers to play a part in questioning the government and investigating its activities. In the UK, there is fusion of powers between Executive and Legislature. Government is ultimately accountable to the Commons alone through the convention of ministerial responsibility, but some ministers sit in the Lords. So, most government departments will be represented there and members of the House of Lords can ask oral and written questions of them. The House of Lords also uses its power to set up select committees to scrutinise aspects of government behaviour, though there are no departmental select committees like those in the Commons. Were the House of Lords to be wholly elected, its members would likely shed their caution and expect a greater role in the scrutiny of the Executive.

It is as yet unclear if a changed upper chamber would be granted greater or new powers. In the absence of a legally enforceable written constitution and strong separation of powers, and with a government commanding a majority in the House of Commons being thus able to control the legislative programme with arguably little effective restraint, the case for an effective second chamber in the workings of the UK constitution is cogent. The challenge in giving the upper chamber democratic legitimacy is in finding a workable, effective balance between its enhanced role and the maintenance of the primacy of the Commons.

Further reading

Bradley, A. and Ewing, K. *Constitutional and Administrative Law*, 14th edn (Longman, 2007), chs. 9–11; ch. 29D.

Barnett, H. *Constitutional and Administrative Law*, 7th edn (Routledge-Cavendish, 2008), ch. 27.

Loveland, I. *Constitutional Law*, 3rd edn (Butterworths, 2003), chs. 5–8.

6

Parliamentary Sovereignty

Introduction

Parliamentary sovereignty (or supremacy) is central to the workings of the UK constitution. As a concept it generates argument and controversy and many an assessment question. We give an example of a question concentrating on the traditional doctrine and two examples—one essay and one problem—of the more common slant, namely the effect of UK membership of the European Union (EU) upon parliamentary supremacy. One difficulty some students experience is in distinguishing between the approach of EU law, as laid down by the European Court of Justice, and that of English law as shown by the English courts. Only precedents from the English courts should be cited as authority for what English law actually is. Whether this complies with EU law is a separate issue, and may not always be relevant, depending on the terms of the question asked.

It is a truism that to understand the standing and operation of parliamentary sovereignty today requires full cognisance of its historical development, that is, how it came to be over time.

Question 1

What is meant by the term parliamentary supremacy? What are its implications in matters other than those raised by the UK's membership of the European Union?

Commentary

This question requires the student to demonstrate a general understanding of the theoretical basis of parliamentary supremacy and its effects. Because it specifically excludes the problems arising from membership of the EU, the student can concentrate on some of the other issues that have attracted attention such as the ability of Parliament to impose special procedures for the passage of later legislation. Without the express exclusion of the EU dimension, you should include it.

Answer plan

- Parliament may make or unmake any law on any subject
- An Act of Parliament will be obeyed by the courts
- Parliament can repeal, amend or simply ignore any current legislation
- Where there is inconsistency between Acts, the more recent Act will impliedly repeal the older Act to the extent of the inconsistency
- But this may not apply to 'constitutional statutes'.

Suggested answer

In most states, the validity of any law can be traced back to a written constitution, which forms the basis of the organisation of the State. In the UK, however, once the origin of a legal rule is traced back to an Act of Parliament there is no further document by which the validity of that Act can be determined. Instead, the lawyer is forced simply to assert the proposition that an Act of Parliament is law, because Parliament has the power to enact laws. Why Parliament has that power is an interesting historical and political question, but the lawyer is generally happy to accept the existence of Parliament's power as very much established and thus unquestioned and unquestionable.

The historical origins of parliamentary supremacy lie in the gradual development of the accepted practice that changes to the law required not merely the personal decision of the Monarch but also the 'advice and consent' of the representatives of Lords and Commons, formally assembled in the two Houses of Parliament. This understanding was challenged in the seventeenth century, but was confirmed once and for all by the **Bill of Rights 1689, Article 1**:

> . . . the pretended power of suspending of laws, or the execution of laws by regal authority without consent of Parliament is illegal.

From this point, the creation of new law has been a power possessed by Parliament alone. What was not clear, however, was whether there were any limits upon that power. During the seventeenth century there were suggestions that any Act of Parliament that was unreasonable, repugnant or impossible would be declared invalid by the courts. These suggestions were heavily influenced by the philosophy of natural law, by which human law is judged against the standards set by an ideal, God-given law. With the decline of this philosophy and the growth of positivism, the expression of such sentiments waned and as Parliament was not in any case interested in enacting unreasonable legislation, the courts were content to accept the validity of any Act passed by traditional parliamentary procedure.

Parliament was thus established and treated as the supreme law-maker and parliamentary sovereignty as a common law rule.

The most celebrated statement of parliamentary supremacy is that of Dicey:

> Parliament has the right to make or unmake any law whatever; and further that no person or body is recognised by the law of England as having a right to override or set aside the legislation of Parliament.

It received judicial confirmation in *Madzimbamuto v Lardner-Burke* [1969] 1 AC 645, where Lord Reid remarked:

> It is often said that it would be unconstitutional for the UK Parliament to do certain things, meaning that the moral, political and other reasons against doing them are so strong that most people would regard it as highly improper if Parliament did these things. But that does not mean that it is beyond the power of Parliament to do such things. If Parliament chose to do any of them, the courts could not hold the Act of Parliament invalid.

It is clear that Parliament can do, and has done many things that in other countries might be regarded as unconstitutional. It may, for instance, break international law, *Mortensen v Peters* (1906) 8F(J) 93; legislate retrospectively, War Damage Act 1965; provide for detention without trial, Terrorism Act 2006.

It is virtually impossible to imagine any circumstances (other than a breach of EU law) where the UK courts would refuse to accept the validity of an Act of Parliament properly passed and 'enrolled'. Further, the courts will not involve themselves in questions relating to the way in which the legislation was passed. In *British Railways Board v Pickin* [1974] AC 765, the Respondent alleged that a private Act of Parliament had been passed only after Parliament had been misled by the Appellant. The court upheld the validity of the Act, stating that it would be for Parliament itself to investigate any defects in the procedure.

An interesting exception, where the court was prepared to consider Parliament's legislative procedure in relation to the court's interpretive role is *R (Jackson) v Attorney-General* [2005] UKHL 56, where it was argued that the Parliament Act 1949 was invalid as an Act because, in amending the Parliament Act 1911 procedure it was itself passed under the 1911 Act procedure. The court, though it accepted that the 1949 Act was an Act of Parliament and not delegated legislation nevertheless held that the interpretation of the 1911 Act, and hence the validity of the 1949 Act was a justiciable issue. The court distinguished between its role in interpreting the law passed by Parliament on the one hand, and issues relating to the parliamentary process on the other, matters for Parliament.

There remains one disputed area. Can Parliament bind its successors? The orthodox view is that it cannot. The Parliament that is supreme is the current Parliament, so it has the power to amend or repeal the legislation of any previous Parliament. Normally, such repeal is expressed in the later Act. However, if through inadvertence or caution Parliament simply enacts something inconsistent with an earlier Act the courts will treat this as an implied repeal of the earlier Act by the later. In *Ellen St Estates Ltd v Minister of Health* [1934] 1 KB 590, the Court of Appeal rejected an attempt to argue that the Housing Act 1925 should be read subject to inconsistent provisions in the Acquisition of Land Act 1919. The 1925 Act impliedly repealed those earlier provisions.

What is the origin of this rule that Parliament cannot bind its successors? If it is regarded as a rule of common law, then logic would suggest that alike all other rules of common law it would be subject to alteration by Act of Parliament. However, Wade argued in his 1955 article, 'The Basis of Legal Sovereignty' (CLJ 172) that if the rule is regarded as the rule of recognition, on which the whole basis of constitutional legality rests then it is not like other common law rules and nothing short of a legal revolution could change it. Any attempt by an Act of Parliament to change the basis on which Acts of Parliament are treated as law is doomed to failure. Yet, in various contexts the issue of Parliament's ability to bind its successors has arisen and given rise to legal and academic debate.

The first concerns grants of independence to former colonies, which are given legal effect by an Act of Parliament stating that Parliament will no longer legislate for the country in question. Could such an Act be repealed by the Westminster Parliament? Legal theory suggests that it could, but, as was pointed out in *British Coal Corporation v R* [1935] AC 500, that has no relation to realities. The independent State would simply take no notice of any attempt to revoke its independence without its consent. There would likely also be considerable political fall-out in terms of international criticism, condemnation and diplomatic pressure. It appears that the UK courts would consider themselves bound to obey the express terms of the UK statute but such legislation is most unlikely even to be tabled.

There have been some differences of opinion between Scottish and English lawyers over the status of the Acts of Union 1707, various provisions of which are deemed to be unalterable. It is argued that as the Acts were the work of the then separate English and Scottish Parliaments, they could not be repealed by the UK Parliament that replaced them and that it owes its very existence to those Acts. In fact, some of the 'unalterable' provisions have been altered without successful legal challenge in Scotland or England. It is conceivable that any attempt to alter such fundamental matters as the status of Scots law or the nature of the Church of Scotland would be rejected, at least by the *Scottish* courts. Again, however, such change is highly unlikely given the political unacceptability of such a measure.

The question that has given rise to most debate is whether Parliament could prescribe special procedures for the passing of future legislation that might then bind a future Parliament (or the same Parliament) so that that Parliament would have to use the special procedure even if only to pass an Act to get rid of it. There is nothing to prevent Parliament creating special procedures; for example the Northern Ireland Act 1998, s. 1 requires an approving referendum before any legislation changing the constitutional status of Northern Ireland can be passed. However, this so-called constitutional guarantee derives its validity from the 1998 Act which could itself be repealed without a referendum. Would it be possible to prevent this by stating in an Act that the Act itself could not be repealed without a referendum? This would in any event not prevent Parliament simply ignoring the 'mandatory' prerequisite of the referendum and simply change the constitutional status of Northern Ireland by Act of Parliament alone: it might be extremely controversial politically but it would be the law, the *Act* having been properly passed (by Commons, Lords and Assent).

There is a school of thought that Parliament may be bound by such special provision regulating the 'manner and form' of future legislation, providing partial entrenchment by the likes of a referendum or special majorities in each House for amendment or repeal. However, the only authority for this contention is Commonwealth cases such as *Attorney-General for New South Wales v Trethowan* [1932] AC 526, *Harris v Minister of the Interior* 1952 (2) SA 428, and *Bribery Commissioner v Ranasinghe* [1965] AC 172. Significantly, in all of these cases the requirements as to the manner and form of future legislation were contained in the original statutes emanating from the Westminster Parliament by which independence was granted. Accordingly, these 'entrenching' provisions could not be changed by the other legislatures in question. The problem in applying these precedents to the UK Parliament is that it would have to limit itself, rather than being subjected to external constitutional constraints. Whilst successive Parliaments could choose to abide by the limit, none has to: in other words, the real 'problem' is the circular argument that the sovereignty of the Westminster Parliament vests in its membership for the time being. Whilst MPs, peers and monarchs come and go, sovereignty continues.

It can be said that some manner and form changes have bound Parliament, such as His Majesty's Declaration of Abdication Act 1936. The abdication of Edward VIII changed the line of succession for good, altering who gives Assent and so changing the procedure by which the sovereign Legislature passes Acts.

The coalition government's Fixed-term Parliaments Bill (2010–11) has met with controversy. Rather than being hailed as noble work in the national interest and clipping the wings of (its own and future) Prime Ministerial discretion in deciding—for opportune party political reason—the timing of general elections, it has been roundly criticised by the Opposition and backbenchers on all sides. This is because cl. 2 of the Bill seeks to limit Parliament's sovereignty by setting a 66% special majority threshold for MPs to be able to vote for dissolution and early general election (the special majority does not apply on a confidence motion). Behind this the government stands accused of really trying to preserve itself with this device by effectively making it more difficult for the Commons to dislodge the government itself until the fixed-term expiry, 7 May 2015, but the fettering of Westminster's sovereignty is not lost as the big issue.

In *Thoburn v Sunderland City Council* [2002] EWHC 195 Admin, [2002] 4 All ER 156, Laws LJ confirmed the orthodox view that Parliament 'cannot stipulate as to the manner and form of any subsequent legislation' and could therefore repeal any previous legislation. However, he went on to suggest that the courts had begun to recognise a special category of constitutional statutes, those concerning fundamental constitutional rights or otherwise affecting the social contract between citizen and state. These statutes, he said could not be impliedly repealed. If Parliament wished to repeal them, it would have to use express unambiguous words. Otherwise the courts would assume that Parliament intended the constitutional rights to be protected, even against later statutes. Which statutes are 'constitutional' in this sense? Laws LJ suggested some examples: the **Bill of Rights 1689**, the **Acts of Union 1707** and the **Human Rights Act 1998**.

This interesting suggestion would provide a means by which the courts could retain the traditional theory of parliamentary supremacy while offering some protection to individual rights. It would retain the right of Parliament to deal with war, terrorism or other emergencies unhindered by the courts while ensuring that any such legislation would have to be politically acceptable. It remains to be seen whether this new interpretation of parliamentary supremacy is adopted. The greatest test is always situations of exigency, when government implores Parliament and people that a given measure is 'vital' and would be for use only 'exceptionally' as has been argued post–'9/11' in the attempts to extend detention without charge of suspected terrorists (**Chapter 8**).

Question 2

What impact has UK membership of the European Communities had on the doctrine of parliamentary sovereignty?

Commentary

The issues raised by this question are likely to be central to any constitutional law course. Students must be careful to discuss this question in the light of case law, not the often ill-informed pronouncements of politicians. There have now been enough cases to enable definite answers to be given to most issues, but the exact boundaries to the domestic courts' obedience to EU rather than UK laws remain uncertain and therefore debatable. The student will need to explain the general doctrine of parliamentary supremacy, but there is no need to go into detail about the other complex issues that would arise in a more general question.

Parliamentary Sovereignty

Answer plan

- By EU law, EU law has supremacy over the national law of Member States
- By UK law, the law passed by Parliament has supremacy
- These principles are contradictory, but may be reconciled as follows:
  - Any UK law passed before 1972 can be impliedly repealed by the **ECA 1972**
  - Any UK law passed after 1972 will, if possible be interpreted by UK domestic courts so as to comply with EU law
  - The *Factortame* cases ruled that UK laws passed after 1972 and being inconsistent with EU law will not be enforced by the UK courts
  - The **ECA 1972** can be expressly repealed or amended, but not impliedly repealed or amended.

Suggested answer

When the UK joined what is now the EU, concerns were expressed in many domestic quarters about the constitutional implications for the UK. In particular, how could EU membership be reconciled with the conventional doctrine of parliamentary supremacy? In Member States with a written constitution, it was generally possible to spell out the implications of EU membership by an appropriate constitutional amendment. However, the UK constitution being unwritten no such process was available. All that the UK could do was to pass the **European Communities Act 1972 (ECA 1972)** by the same procedure as for all other statutes, with prima facie the same legal force as all other statutes. This left many unanswered questions.

According to Dicey, 'no person is recognised by the law of England as having a right to over-ride or set aside the legislation of Parliament'. This doctrine forms the very basis of the UK constitution with the effect that the current Parliament can pass any legislation it wishes, including legislation to amend or repeal, expressly or impliedly, prior legislation of that or an earlier Parliament. Although there has been considerable academic debate about possible exceptions to this power and possible methods of entrenching legislation, the orthodox view accepted no limits on Parliament's authority.

Before the UK joined the EU, the European Court of Justice had established in *Costa v ENEL* **Case 6/64 [1964] CMLR 425**, that EU law prevailed over incompatible Member State law. The doctrine of direct effect obliged national courts to give effect to rights arising under EU law, regardless of any national law to the contrary. No doubt, in an ideal world no national law inconsistent with the state's EU obligations would ever be enacted. In the real world however it was all too likely that a state would enact such legislation, whether by inadvertence or perhaps in the hope that the inconsistency would not be noticed or challenged. A particular problem faced by the UK legislators was to find some way to instruct the courts to give effect to EU law in preference to Acts of Parliament whenever passed.

It was straightforward to provide in **s. 2(1) ECA 1972** that all rights arising under the EU Treaties were to be given effect in preference to pre-existing UK law. The orthodox doctrines of express and implied repeal authorised that. However, the real problem concerned legislation passed after 1972 which was inconsistent with EU law. This was dealt with in **s. 2(4)** which provided that legislation passed or to be passed in the future should be construed and have effect subject to the rule laid down in **s. 2(1)**: that effect must be given to EU rights. This was reinforced by **s. 3(1)** which instructed the courts to decide any issues of EU law 'in accordance with the principles laid down by, and any relevant decisions of, the European Court of Justice'. This would include the principle of the supremacy of EU law laid down in *Costa v ENEL*.

The *ECA 1972* therefore appeared to provide the courts with an instruction that they should obey EU law, but left unresolved the question of what would happen if different instructions were provided to the UK courts, in a later Act of Parliament. What if an Act passed after 1972 simply contained provisions inconsistent with EU law? By the conventional methods of interpretation, where provisions in an earlier Act are inconsistent with a later Act the earlier Act is impliedly repealed to the extent of the inconsistency: *Ellen St Estates Ltd v Minister of Health* [1934] 1 KB 590. It could therefore be argued that any Act passed after 1972 could impliedly repeal the *ECA 1972*, so that the phrase 'legislation passed or to be passed' would be read with the proviso 'except this new Act'. This would leave the UK in breach of its obligations under the EU treaties. How could the courts avoid this?

The solution for many cases was found in the long-standing rule of statutory interpretation that where legislation is passed to implement the UK's international obligations then any ambiguity should be construed so as to comply with those obligations rather than conflict with them. This rule, taken with the express wording of **s. 2(4)** of the *ECA 1972* has been treated by the domestic courts as a clear instruction to interpret any UK legislation passed to implement EU law in such a way as to ensure that there is no discrepancy between them. In *Garland v British Rail Engineering* [1983] 2 AC 751, the court preferred the interpretation of the *Sex Discrimination Act 1975* which was consistent with *Article 119 (now 141) of the EU Treaty* to the interpretation that created conflict between them. The courts have been willing to use purposive methods of interpretation rather than traditional literal methods to ensure compliance with EU law. In *Pickstone v Freemans plc* [1989] AC 66 and in *Lister v Forth Dry Dock* [1990] 1 AC 546 the courts went far beyond literal interpretation, even implying extra words into a regulation in order to ensure compliance with EU law. This approach has proved to deal satisfactorily with all cases where UK legislation is passed in order to incorporate EU directives and treaty provisions into UK law.

A different problem was posed by the decision of the European Court of Justice in *Marleasing* C-106/89 [1992] 1 CMLR 305, that all national legislation whenever passed should be interpreted in the light of EU law in order to give effect to rights even if they did not have direct effect. The UK courts had earlier refused, in *Duke v GEC Reliance Ltd* [1988] AC 618 to interpret UK statutes passed in 1970 and 1975 in the light of a 1976 directive on the grounds that that could not possibly have been Parliament's intention; the rules stated in the statutes were unambiguously in conflict with the directive. However, in *Webb v EMO Air Cargo (No. 2)* [1995] 4 All ER 577 the House of Lords without debate interpreted an ambiguous 1975 Act to give effect to a 1976 directive, just as the European Court of Justice decision required. There remains considerable uncertainty in both UK and EU law as to just how far a national court is supposed to go in effectively rewriting existing national laws under the guise of interpretation, but the UK courts seem willing to follow the instruction given by the ECA 1972.

The above cases, being treated as issues of statutory interpretation and the reconciling of apparently contradictory rules, managed to avoid the fundamental problem of a direct clash between EU law and a UK statute passed after 1972. The issue finally arose in an unavoidable form in the *Factortame* litigation, C-213/89 [1990] 3 CMLR 375 and C-221/89, [1991] 3 CMLR 589. These cases concerned an apparent clash between the EU laws forbidding discrimination on grounds of nationality and the Merchant Shipping Act 1988, which imposed discriminatory rules concerning fishing boats. When *Factortame* challenged the application of the 1988 Act, it sought an interim injunction suspending the Act pending a reference to the European Court of Justice. UK law would not permit such a suspension as it would clearly breach the Diceyean formulation of parliamentary supremacy, but the European Court of Justice held that EU law could require it. The House of Lords was therefore faced with the ultimate choice, or dilemma: to obey the 1988 Act as the most recent statement of Parliament's intentions, or to obey the ECA 1972 and enforce EU law. The House of Lords decided to obey the ECA 1972 and awarded the injunction. In effect, the ECA 1972 was held not to be subject to the doctrine of implied repeal. All legislation passed after 1972 thus contains an implicit proviso: 'unless EU law provides otherwise'. The ECA 1972 was treated by the courts as having an exceptional status, but perhaps not a unique one. In *Thoburn v Sunderland City Council* [2002] EWHC 195 Admin, [2002] 4 All ER 156, Laws LJ suggested that other 'constitutional' statutes might share this protection against implied repeal.

The ECA 1972 can of course be expressly amended or repealed pursuant to parliamentary sovereignty, and if that happened then EU law would lose its primacy within the UK in the eyes of the UK courts. Parliament would be specifically and expressly directing the UK the courts, and its supremacy would be restored to its Diceyean form by the change.

It is interesting to consider the effect of an express parliamentary enactment, short of a complete repeal of the ECA 1972, stating that some particular provision in the new Act was to prevail over any EU law to the contrary and expressly instructing the domestic courts, the ECA 1972 notwithstanding, to follow the statutory provision instead of the conflicting EU law. What would the domestic courts do? Would they follow the ECA 1972 and the EU law, or the later statute? In *Macarthys Ltd v Smith* [1981] QB 180 Lord Denning suggested that in such a case, unlikely though it was the UK courts would have to obey the new statute as the expression of the current will of Parliament. Whilst the matter would no doubt reach the European Court of Justice, ultimate resolution of what would be a constitutional crisis would be in the political arena not just domestic but also involving EU bodies and Member States. Whilst the European Court is generally recognised as having provided innovative 'fixes' throughout the legal and political development of the EU and its relations with its Member States, the UK courts are confined purely to interpretation and application of 'the law'. Nonetheless, here they would be between a rock and a hard place; which law to apply, which to breach and with which sovereign law-making entity to clash? Perhaps rather than try to differentiate between ranks, the domestic courts would be bound to obey the last order, the unambiguous and express instruction of the Westminster Parliament. This would then leave it to the politicians to resolve matters somehow. The 'offending' Act would almost inevitably have been a government measure (to have been passed) and so the key question would be begged, just who does or should govern the UK and have the last word in the setting of its laws?

In conclusion, it can be argued that the UK Parliament, through its power expressly to amend or repeal the ECA 1972 or to legislate expressly contrary to it, does retain its *ultimate* supremacy in spite of the fact that in its daily operation it is now restrained (or constrained) by EU law. The domestic courts have in effect taken Parliament at its word as expressed in 1972, and will continue to do so until expressly instructed to the contrary. Any other decision would have led to the courts provoking clashes with EU law. Parliament (essentially the elected House of Commons) chose in 1972 to give up exercise of its domestic sovereignty over some (albeit arguably an unexpectedly wide and growing realm of) matters, unless and until it chooses to take it back. As with devolution, it may be ever more difficult—politically—for Parliament to reclaim what it relinquished. The government intends to pass legislation giving a 'referendum lock' on any further transfer of powers or competencies to EU bodies; that is such a measure would be put to a vote of the UK electorate. The Conservatives, senior partner in the new coalition government, made a manifesto pledge that the UK will not accede to any further transfer of sovereignty to the EU in this Parliament and the junior partner Liberal Democratic party has agreed to go along with this.

It seems legitimate that the ultimate decision as to whether EU law should continue to have force in the UK should rest with the UK Parliament. Contentiously, perhaps even provocatively the coalition is to introduce a Sovereignty Bill to make clear that *ultimate* sovereignty lies with the UK Parliament and not with the EU.

Question 3

In January 2008 the EU Commission issued (fictitious) Directive 1/2008 which provided:

> In the event of property of a European Union citizen being compulsorily acquired into public ownership that citizen shall be entitled to prompt, adequate and effective compensation from the nationalising government.

In 2010, due to the world financial crisis, the government of the UK wishes to obtain powers to take banks, which are struggling financially, into public ownership. The Nationalisation of Banks Bill 2010 is placed before Parliament. This Bill passes through all its stages in the House of Commons and is at its Third Reading in the House of Lords. It contains a controversial clause that stipulates that:

> No compensation shall be payable to any shareholders in any bank, taken into public ownership.

In the Commons debate on the Bill, the Minister for Europe explained that this clause was to prevent anyone making excess profits from the collapse of a bank.

Joan is a major shareholder in Farrows Bank, which is named in the Nationalisation of Banks Bill 2010 as one of the banks that is to be nationalised. She wishes to challenge the legality of this proposed measure.

Advise Joan.

Commentary

The major constitutional question raised by the UK's membership of the European Union (EU) is the effect that EU law may have on the traditional doctrine of parliamentary sovereignty. This question is asked in essay form in Question 2, but it can equally well be asked in problem question form, as illustrated here. The most common mistake that students make in answering such questions is to think that there is an easy, straightforward answer and just give that answer. The European Court of Justice (ECJ) has said that EU law is supreme over national law; the House of Lords has accepted this. Often, a student explains *R v Secretary of State for Transport ex parte Factortame Ltd* [1991] 1 AC 603 and leaves it at that. *Factortame* is a vitally important case and cannot be omitted, but there is much more to the supremacy issue than that. Examiners would expect some explanation of traditional ideas about parliamentary supremacy and case law developments preceding *Factortame* and since. An answer to an essay question will be discursive whereas a problem question will demand application of the material law.

The type of EU law specified in this problem is a Directive. This is the most awkward type of EU law for the courts of an EU Member State to deal with, because for starters the court has to decide whether the directive is even enforceable in the national law of that state. This is called the doctrine of direct effect. If the directive lacks direct effect, no issue of whether the EU law or national law has supremacy even arises because the directive is not enforceable in that state. How direct effect works for directives is explained in the Suggested Answer.

Watch out however if other types of EU law arise in a problem. They work in a different way from directives. A Regulation is directly applicable and there is no need to go into the problems of whether or not it has direct effect. Similarly, Treaty Articles do not cause many problems as the ones that grant individual rights have direct effect, *Van Gend en Loos v Nederlandse* **[1963] CMLR 105**; in contrast with directives this is not limited to vertical direct effect (below).

As discussed in the Introduction to this book (**Chapter 1**), the key with problem questions is to analyse them very closely, use the information supplied to the full, not skip over anything in your planning or writing, and of course to apply the law to the facts. A line-by-line approach may suit unless, for example, you are 'advising' in which case it may be appropriate to group facts or issues for each 'client' being advised. If you adopt the approach of 'doing the law' first and then applying it to the facts, be careful: there is an uncanny knack then to miss out some points at the application stage.

With a complex problem scenario, as here, it is probably best to pick out the main issues and tackle them one by one. These are identified in the bullet points. Where possible it may be best to start with the issues with which you are most confident. This creates a favourable impression with the person marking the piece of work and enables you to gain in self-belief before tackling the more difficult areas.

Whatever the form and style of the question asked, never lose sight of the key issue in questions of this type: how have the UK courts adapted to the supremacy of EU law?

Answer plan

- The traditional principles of parliamentary sovereignty: an Act of Parliament cannot be overridden
- The **European Communities Act 1972 (ECA 1972)**: EU law becomes part of the law of the UK
- *Costa v ENEL*: the ECJ holds that EU law has supremacy over national law
- The three conditions for the direct effect of a Directive
- *Marleasing*: interpret national law in accordance with EU law
- *Factortame*: UK courts accept the supremacy of EU law
- Governments must compensate for breach of EU law
- References to the ECJ
- **ECA 1972** can be expressly repealed or amended.

Suggested answer

A good starting point for the traditional theories of parliamentary sovereignty is the writing of A.V. Dicey:

> The principle of parliamentary sovereignty means neither more nor less than this: namely, that Parliament thus defined has, under the English constitution, the right to make or unmake any law whatever; and, further, that no person or body is recognised by the law of England as having a right to override or set aside the legislation of Parliament.
>
> A.V. Dicey *Introduction to the Study of the Law of the Constitution*, 10th ed. (1885 ed. Macmillan, 1959, p. 39).

According to this theory, Parliament can always change its mind so no Act of Parliament can be protected from being amended or repealed by a later Act of Parliament. Parliament may repeal an Act either by explicitly referring to the previous Act (express repeal) or, if two Acts conflict, by the latter being taken to be the law (implied repeal). Even if an Act was worded so as to prevent repeal, that wording would be ineffective: *Ellen Street Estates Ltd v Minister of Health* [1934] 1 KB 590. So, according to Dicey's view there is nothing to prevent the Nationalisation of Banks Bill 2010 repealing any previous legislation. Similarly an Act of Parliament always overrides any other form of law, and this would include foreign legislation: *Mortensen v Peters* (1906) 8F (J) 93. No person or body can set aside legislation made by Parliament.

So, traditionally, the courts have always rejected any attempt to challenge an Act of Parliament. This was confirmed by the House of Lords in *Pickin v BRB* [1974] AC 765. Once a Bill has been passed by both the House of Commons and the House of Lords and has received Royal Assent, it cannot be questioned. Joan might well argue that she does not wish to challenge an Act, but stop a Bill from becoming an Act. *Pickin* offers her no greater chance of success with this; the Lords stated that they did not have the power to investigate what went on in parliamentary proceedings. Other cases, though on delegated legislation, support the idea that the courts will not make any rulings on parliamentary proceedings: *R v Secretary of State for the Environment ex parte Notts CC* [1986] AC 240. Indeed Article 9 of the Bill of Rights 1689 states that '... proceedings in Parliament ought not to be ... questioned in any court'.

According to traditional views then, Joan has no case at all. Membership of the EU has however changed this, though at first this was not clear. Section 2(1) ECA 1972 stated that all EU law was part of the law of the UK. Section 3(1) stated that the UK courts now had to abide by the decisions of the ECJ. The Act did not clearly state what would happen if EU law conflicted with a UK statute. Under the traditional theory of implied repeal, EU law would take priority over any Act of Parliament enacted before the ECA 1972: *Ellen Street Estates* above. Section 2(4) of the ECA 1972 has attracted attention, although its exact meaning is obscure. It states that:

> . . . any enactment passed or to be passed . . . shall be construed and have effect subject to the foregoing provisions of this section.

This could mean that EU law has supremacy over Acts of Parliament passed after 1972, or it could just mean that such Acts should be interpreted ('construed') so as to try to avoid any conflict with EU law. Both interpretations seem to have found favour with the UK courts.

It is clear that some time before the UK joined the EU, its own court the ECJ had decided that the law of the EU had primacy over incompatible national laws:

> The EEC Treaty created its own legal order which is directly applicable to member States and to their nationals, as a result of the partial transfer of sovereignty from member States to the community. Consequently a subsequent unilateral law which is incompatible with the aim of the Community cannot prevail.
>
> (*Costa v ENEL* [1964] ECR 585 at 593)

The Nationalisation of Banks Bill 2010 seems to be 'subsequent unilateral law which is incompatible' with the 2008 Directive, in that it denies any compensation.

First, however, it must be decided whether the directive is actually applicable, that is can it be enforced in UK law? The UK is obliged under Article 249 of the EU Treaty to give legal effect in its own national legal system to a directive, but appears not to have passed any legislation to do this. The ECJ has ruled that in certain circumstances a directive may have direct effect and be enforceable in the courts of a Member State, despite the lack of national legislation.

The ECJ decided this in two UK cases, *Van Duyn v Home Office* [1975] Ch 358 and *Marshall v Southampton and SW Hants AHA* [1986] QB 402 and this has been accepted by the UK courts.

The directive must meet three conditions to have direct effect. The date for the implementation of the directive must have passed, which is the case here. Secondly, the wording of the directive must be clear, precise and unconditional so that there is something that a court may enforce. Directive 1/2008 grants a clear right to compensation, which Joan should be able to enforce. The third condition is the 'vertical direct effect' condition: the directive can only be enforced against a public body, 'an emanation of the state'. Joan is going to be denied compensation by an Act of Parliament (if passed). She cannot sue the sovereign body, Parliament so she would have to sue the government minister responsible for the legislation as an emanation of the state: *R v Secretary of State for Transport ex parte Factortame* [1991] 1 AC 603. Farrows Bank would also be a possible Defendant, if it becomes nationalised and therefore a 'public body': *Foster v British Gas* [1991] 1 AC 306.

The problem is that Directive 1/2008 seems to be in direct contradiction to the 'no compensation' clause proposed in the Bill. The ECJ held in *Costa v ENEL* that EU law has supremacy, but in *Pickin v BRB* the House of Lords insisted upon the supremacy of Acts of Parliament. The ECJ suggested a solution to this difficulty in *Marleasing SA v La Commercial Internacional de Alimentacion SA* [1990] ECR I-4135, in that the national court is obliged to interpret its own national law 'as far as possible, in the light of the wording and the purpose of the directive'.

The House of Lords accepted this obligation in *Webb v EMO Air Cargo (UK) Ltd* [1995] 1 WLR 1454, but it seems impossible to reconcile a directive that requires compensation to be paid and an Act of Parliament stipulating that it should not.

There appears a clear conflict between the UK Act and the directly effective EU directive. Lord Denning was one of the earliest judges to say, in *Macarthys Ltd v Smith* [1981] QB 180 that the UK courts should accord supremacy to EU law in such a case of conflict. His fellow Court of Appeal judges were not willing to go that far and indorse such a radical break with traditional theory. It was not until *R v Secretary of State for Transport ex parte Factortame* [1991] 1 AC 603 that the House of Lords was willing to accept that EU law now had supremacy. Significantly, the House of Lords did not consider this in any great detail as they would not wish to be seen to be questioning traditional theories too openly. Lord Bridge merely said, at p. 659:

> Under the terms of the Act of 1972, it has always been clear that it was the duty of a United Kingdom court, when delivering final judgment, to override any rule of national law found to be in conflict with any directly enforceable rule of Community law.

This is what s. 2(4) of the ECA 1972 required.

Joan could therefore follow the precedent of *Factortame*, but the exact remedy that the court could grant her is more problematic. In the light of the traditional theories of parliamentary supremacy, it is unthinkable that the UK courts would order Parliament not to legislate or order that an Act of Parliament is of no legal force. In *Factortame* itself, the House of Lords merely issued an interim injunction against the government minister responsible for that piece of legislation, telling him not to enforce the offending Act of Parliament. Joan would probably be obliged to wait for the Bill to become an Act. She could then ask the courts to follow *Factortame* and issue an injunction forbidding the enforcement of the Act and so stopping the confiscation of her shares without compensation. The court might even prefer to issue a lesser remedy, a Declaration, as in *R v Employment Secretary ex parte Equal Opportunities Commission* [1995] 1 AC 1.

The ECJ has also provided another remedy for claimants in Joan's position. If a government or public body breaches EU law and causes loss to the claimant, particularly if acting intentionally and persistently, it must compensate the claimant. The directive here confers upon Joan a right to compensation and this would seem to be a serious breach of EU law: *R v Secretary of State for Transport ex parte Factortame Ltd (No. 4)* [1996] 2 WLR 506. Joan could sue the relevant government minister, for compensation.

If Joan brings legal proceedings they have to commence in a UK court and the final order or ruling must come from a UK court, as indicated in *Factortame* and in *Equal Opportunities Commission*. It is very likely though that at some stage of the proceedings, the UK court would seek a ruling on the meaning of EU law from the ECJ under the *Article 234* procedure. This occurred, for example in *R v Secretary of State for Transport ex parte Factortame (No. 1)* [1990] 2 AC 85. The UK court then applies that ruling.

There is one final possibility that is not favourable to Joan's case. In *Macarthys Ltd v Smith* [1981] QB 180, Lord Denning observed that EU law only had supremacy in the UK because an Act of Parliament says so. Parliament could always change its mind about the *ECA 1972* Act and repeal or amend it. Denning went on to say that the words of the repealing Act would have to be clear, 'express'. This is confirmed by *Thoburn v Sunderland City Council* [2002] 1 CMLR 50 which held that the *ECA 1972* Act was a 'constitutional statute', which could not be impliedly repealed. Only express repeal could remove EU law and replace it with a UK statute. The wording of the Nationalisation of Banks Bill 2010 seems clearly to contradict EU law but the court might consider that it would need to consult the record of parliamentary proceedings (as happened in *Pickstone v Freemans plc* [1989] AC 66) in order to ascertain whether Parliament intended to contradict or implement EU law.

If an Act of Parliament clearly did intend to remove this EU Directive, then the UK courts would be bound to follow the intention of Parliament. The ECJ would assert the supremacy of EU law, so there would be a clash between the two courts. As seen in the *Factortame* litigation, it would probably be the UK that had to back down and remove the offending part of the Act of Parliament. Otherwise, political ramifications would likely ensue, though this goes beyond what is pertinent to Joan's situation.

Further reading

Bradley, A. and Ewing, K. *Constitutional and Administrative Law*, 14th edn (Longman, 2006), chs. 4 and 8.

Bradley, A. 'The Sovereignty of Parliament' in J. Jowell and D. Oliver (eds) *The Changing Constitution*, 5th edn (Oxford University Press, 2004).

Craig, P. 'Britain in the EU', in J. Jowell and D. Oliver (op cit.)

Munro, C. *Studies in Constitutional Law*, 2nd edn (Butterworths, 1999), chs. 5 and 6.

Oliver, D. *Constitutional Reform in the UK* (Oxford University Press, 2003), ch. 4.

7

The Rule of Law; the Separation of Powers

Introduction
Any Constitutional and Administrative Law module will devote time to the Rule of Law and the Separation of Powers, whether considered under Constitutional Sources, Fundamental Principles or otherwise. Here, we consider the conceptual nature and practical application of each in the context of the check they provide upon government and Parliament in particular, having first examined the 'engine' of the UK constitution, Parliamentary Sovereignty.

Question 1

In so far as Dicey's general statement of the rule of law may be taken to involve the existence in the English constitution of certain principles almost amounting to fundamental laws, his doctrine is logically inconsistent with the legislative supremacy of Parliament.
(O. Hood Phillips *Constitutional and Administrative Law* (1987))

Discuss.

Commentary

Students often dislike answering questions on the rule of law because the topic seems too vague. Lots of different ideas and theories are identified as the rule of law, which is what causes the confusion. The student must be familiar with at least some of these theories, be able to criticise them and compare them. A good starting point is Dicey's version of the rule of law. It should be referred to in any question on the rule of law even if, unlike in our question, it is not specifically raised in the question set. Students should also be able to discuss at least one other theory of the rule of law.

Here, the particular slant of the question is how the rule of law sits with the power of the Westminster Parliament.

Answer plan

- There must be lawful authority for government action
- Equality before the law
- The common law protects individual liberty
- The supremacy of Parliament
- The Judiciary and the Executive
- The **Human Rights Act 1998**.

Suggested answer

The idea of the rule of law was not invented by Dicey, but he popularised it in the late nineteenth century. His book, *Introduction to the Study of the Law of the Constitution* (1885) can be seen as a strong defence of the English constitution when compared with the constitutions of other countries, particularly those with written constitutions. De Smith states:

> His ideas . . . were very influential for two generations; today they no longer warrant detailed analysis.
> (*Constitutional and Administrative Law* (1998))

It is true that Dicey's ideas went out of fashion for a time, but they have now come back into favour, particularly with senior members of the Judiciary. Indeed they are now specifically mentioned in sections of the **Constitutional Reform Act 2005**. So, once again, these ideas demand detailed analysis.

It is often said that the UK has an 'unwritten constitution', meaning that it is not codified and much of it has no formal legal status. Dicey argued that, far from being a concern, this presented positive advantage. In the UK there was a long tradition of respect for individual liberty and democracy. This tradition was upheld in the country's constitutional arrangements. For short, it could be called the rule of law. Dicey (referring to the 'English' constitution) summarised it under three main principles.

His first principle concerned the rule of law and discretionary powers. No person could be punished or interfered with by the authorities unless the law authorised it. Put another way, all government actions must be authorised by the law. This contrasted the situation in England with a country where there were no rules.

In the latter, the government could do as it pleased and there would be no legal controls over its activities. Examples would be imprisonment when someone had broken no law, or the lack of any trial before punishment.

Dicey also considered that governments should not possess wide discretionary powers. These ideas were classically illustrated in *Entick v Carrington* (1765) 19 St Tr 1030, where the courts declared that the Secretary of State could not order the search of Entick's house because there was no law authorising such searches. The court would not accept arguments of 'state necessity' or that there was one law for government activities and another for ordinary people.

Dicey's second principle has the resounding title of 'equality before the law', namely that the government and its officials should not have any special exemptions or protections from the law. He did not like the French *Droit Administratif* system where government activities were dealt with by separate administrative courts. These he considered to be too partial to the government, and inferior to ordinary courts of law.

The final principle concerns individual rights. The English constitution respects personal liberty. There is no need for a Bill of Rights because civil liberties are respected anyway. The courts protect them in their decisions by developing the common law in a way that respects individual liberty. Parliament legislates on particular problems. In contrast, Bills of Rights are documents that promise all sorts of rights. These promises are so general and capable of so many meanings that they are meaningless. Also, the Bill of Rights might not be respected by the government and might be unenforceable.

Dicey's theory is open to many objections, some applicable when he wrote, some pertaining to the workings of different constitutions now. Some might say that these ideas are so vague and wide ranging that they have no real meaning. De Smith argues that:

> The concept [the Rule of Law] is one of open texture; it lends itself to an extremely wide range of interpretations [and that] … everyone who tries to redefine it begins with the assumption that it is a good thing, like justice or courage.

Some might say that Dicey's theory is so obvious that it is not worth stating it. Of course the government must obey the law and the courts enforce it in a modern constitutional system. R. F. V. Heuston ('The Rule of Law' from *Essays in Constitutional Law* (1964)) claims that Dicey misunderstood French administrative courts. They are not biased in favour of the government and they do at least as well, if not better, in controlling the government as the 'English' courts. Separate 'public law' or 'constitutional' courts are the normal arrangement in continental Europe. E. Barendt ([1985] Public Law 596) argues that Dicey also misunderstood the nature of written constitutions. Although in 1885 Bills of Rights might just have been pious declarations that no one could enforce, nowadays most countries that have them possess sophisticated enforcement mechanisms.

Of course there is a rule of law in the United Kingdom and arguably the Diceyean model still holds credibility at least in its fundamentals. However, the main criticism is that it fails to deal with the supremacy of Parliament. In passing legislation, Parliament must comply with the procedural strictures of the rule of law. Beyond this however, the sovereignty (or supremacy) of the UK Parliament means that, at least in theory, it may pass whatever laws it wishes. If Parliament legislates contrary to the value-laden principles of the rule of law, it is still the law and there is nothing that the courts can do about it. For example statutes can effectively annul inconvenient court decisions, as with the War Damage Act 1965 which reversed, with retrospective effect, *Burmah Oil v Lord Advocate* [1965] AC 75, where the House of Lords had ordered the government to pay compensation to Burmah Oil for the wartime destruction of its oil installations. Statutes also grant government officials some immunity from legal action, for instance the Crown Proceedings Act 1947. Some Acts of Parliament grant the government wide and uncontrolled discretionary powers, such as the Deregulation and Contracting Out Act 1994. Dicey claimed that Parliament would restrain the government. Perhaps that was true in 1885, but nowadays the government of the day controls Parliament through its Commons majority and can nearly always get its own way.

A key element of Dicey's rule of law was that the government must possess clearly defined legal powers to authorise its actions. Under the UK's unwritten constitution it is in fact difficult to be precise about the legal powers that government possesses. Prerogative powers still exist and it can be difficult to identify those powers accurately. For instance in *R v Home Secretary ex parte Northumbria Police Authority* [1988] 1 All ER 556 the court accepted the existence of a prerogative power, to maintain peace in the realm, which had not previously been identified. Again much of the constitution is convention, not law, for example the powers of the Prime Minister. As they are not law, the courts cannot control these powers. Indeed there must be some doubts about whether the courts are always keen to ensure that the government keeps within its legal powers. In *Malone v Metropolitan Police Commissioner* [1979] Ch 344, Malone's telephone had been 'tapped' by the police. He claimed that there was no law that authorised telephone tapping. These facts have strong similarities to the classic rule of law case, *Entick v Carrington* (above). However, in *Malone* the domestic court came to the opposite conclusion: no law forbade telephone tapping by the police, therefore it must be legal.

Despite these criticisms, the rule of law still has its defenders. T. R. S. Allan ([1985] Cambridge Law Journal 111) stressed that Parliament still has a controlling effect on the government, particularly as the Commons is elected by the people. The government does not always get its way in Parliament and although Parliament can be persuaded to change the law in a way favourable to the government, until that has happened the government must obey the existing law. Judges will ensure that they do. Judges can also minimise the effects of 'unjust' laws by using techniques of statutory interpretation.

Perhaps Dicey never intended his rule of law as an accurate description of the 'English' constitution. Perhaps he was just trying to say that this is the way it should be, not the way it actually was. These were the ideals that government, administrators and judges should endeavour to uphold.

The significant growth in judicial review since the 1980s has subjected ministerial action to the check of the rule of law and has imposed a restraining influence upon excess, notably in areas such as counter-terrorism measures. The rule of law has attracted the attention of many senior judges. In *M v Home Office* [1994] 1 AC 377 the House of Lords confirmed the rule of law in its basic meaning. The government must obey the law. It had no immunity from court orders and government ministers could be held liable for contempt.

More significantly, the courts began showing a keen interest in the rule of law in its wider sense. In *Bennett v Horseferry Road Magistrates* [1993] 3 All ER 138, the defendant had been illegally abducted from South Africa to stand trial in the UK. Despite the fact that no UK laws had been broken, the House of Lords threw the case out on the grounds that it would be an abuse of fair procedure to try Bennett. The courts would not 'turn a blind eye' to the authorities' involvement in law-breaking.

Although Dicey disagreed with the idea of a Bill of Rights, the **Human Rights Act 1998** has increased interest in, and perhaps the standing of, the rule of law. Many of the Articles of the **European Convention on Human Rights 1950**, now domestically enforceable under the **Human Rights Act,** embody values similar to those espoused in the rule of law. For example, detention without trial was disapproved of by Dicey and potentially breaches **Articles 5** (liberty of the person) and **6** (fair trial) for starters. It was considered by the House of Lords in *A v Secretary of State for the Home Department* [2005] 2 AC 68. This involved the detention, without trial, of foreign nationals who were suspected of terrorism. The Lords held that this was contrary to human rights on the narrow ground of unjustifiable racial discrimination: UK nationals were just as likely to be suspected of terrorism. Lord Bingham (at p. 113) quoted Professor Lauterpacht:

> The claim to equality before the law is in a substantial sense the most fundamental of the rights of man.

Equality before the law was of course one of the main elements of Dicey's theory. In the follow-up case, *A v Home Secretary (No. 2)* [2006] 1 All ER 575 the House of Lords rejected the use of evidence obtained by torture, not just because it was forbidden by various international Human Rights Conventions, but because it was contrary to the common law traditions of this country. That is just the sort of argument that Dicey would have used.

Despite the views of the senior judiciary, the greatest problem with the rule of law, as defined by Dicey, is that it gives no protection if Parliament legislates in an unfair or unjust way. The **Human Rights Act** has arguably enhanced the protection of freedoms of the individual, providing positive, enforceable rights and a significantly broadened interpretative remit to the courts (**s. 3** in particular). However, the Act has no effect upon parliamentary supremacy.

An intrinsic aspect of parliamentary sovereignty is that there can be no judicial review of Acts of Parliament. If Parliament wishes to pass 'unconscionable' legislation, it may. Perhaps the best protection against this happening is, however, the political responsibility of those who govern and legislate. MPs' very jobs lie ultimately in the hands of those who may be affected by draconian laws, the electorate.

Question 2

Explain what is meant by the 'Separation of Powers'. To what extent is it an important element in the constitutional arrangements of the UK?

Commentary

Questions on the separation of powers are somewhat easier to approach than questions on other constitutional theories like the rule of law. At least the separation of powers has a clearly defined meaning.

Our example is a pretty typical question on this subject. To answer, the candidate must be able to explain the theory of the separation of powers, ideally illustrated by reference to an example of a constitution based on those principles, such as that of the United States or France. Then it is necessary to show how the UK's constitution does not conform to the theory. The difficulty in questions on separation is in what the question asks you to do next. There being both separation and fusion in the UK constitution, a question might focus on either or both elements. The same basic material can be deployed in answer.

The second part of this question really directs us to consider both sides of this equation, requiring then an evaluation of how significant a part separation plays in how the UK constitution works as a whole.

One point of clarification: you need always to define your terms. In our suggested answer 'the Executive' refers to central government except where otherwise stated.

Answer plan

- The Executive proposes the laws
- The Legislative makes the laws
- The Executive administers and implements the laws
- The Judiciary interprets, applies and enforces laws

- The fusion of the legislative and executive functions in the UK
- The independence of the Judiciary in the UK.

Suggested answer

The separation of powers is an ancient and very simple idea: governance of the State should not be concentrated in the hands of one person or body, otherwise tyranny results. Ancient Greeks, such as Aristotle in his *Politics*, first propounded a version of this theory, but the most famous version is that put forward by Montesquieu in *The Spirit of the Laws* (1748) (A. Cohler, B. Miller and H. Stone (eds), Cambridge, 1989). Montesquieu described three functions of government. The Legislative or law-making function, enacting rules for society. The Executive or law-applying function, covering actions taken to maintain or implement the law, defend the State, conduct external affairs and administer internal policies. Finally, the Judicial or law-enforcing function, the determining of civil disputes and the punishing of criminals by deciding issues of fact and applying the law. His view was that:

> There would be an end to everything, if the same man, or the same body … were to exercise those three powers . . . .

This can be interpreted in several ways, but most likely he meant that the three functions should be carried out by separate organs of state and that each organ should only carry out its own function. For instance, the Legislature should not judge and the Executive should not make laws. The Legislative, Executive and Judicial branches should have equal status so each could control the excessive use of power by another branch.

These theories were adopted and developed by James Madison and incorporated into the **Constitution of the United States 1787**, which still remains a classic example of an attempt to implement the separation of powers. **Article I** declares 'All legislative power herein granted shall be vested in a Congress of the United States', **Article II** that 'The executive power shall be invested in a President of the United States' and **Article III** that 'The judicial power of the United States shall be invested in one Supreme Court and inferior courts as the Congress may from time to time ordain and establish.'

The President is not a member of Congress. Elections for the President and for Congress are separate. There is also an elaborate system of checks and balances between the three branches of governance of the United States. For example, under **Article I, Section 7**, the President may in effect veto legislation passed by the Congress if at least one-third of either House of Congress agrees with him. The Supreme Court has the power to declare the acts of both the President or Congress unconstitutional and illegal, though this power came not directly from the written constitution, but rather case law: *Marbury v Madison* (1803) 1 Cranch 137.

The constitution of the UK is nothing like this. There is no written constitutional document and no formal separation of powers. Historically, the King and his *Curia Regis* embraced all three branches of government. Even today, formally the Queen still appoints all government ministers and all members of the Judiciary from the County Court upwards, she summons Parliament and Assents to all Bills before they become law. The Executive is part of the Legislature, in that ministers must be members of one of the Houses of Parliament, though senior judges are no longer members of the Legislature as the new UK Supreme Court has replaced the judicial House of Lords, Constitutional Reform Act 2005.

This has led many constitutional commentators to dismiss the relevance of the theory of the separation of powers to the UK constitution. Instead they have concentrated on 'checks and balances' such as ministerial accountability to Parliament. More recently, some writers, such as Munro (*Studies in Constitutional Law* 2nd edn (Butterworths, 1999)), have tried to reinterpret these 'checks and balances' as a UK version of the separation of powers. Many senior judges have echoed this (below).

It is argued that although all members of the government are also members of the Legislature, these two groups are not identical. There are just over a hundred government ministers, but they are greatly outnumbered by 'ordinary' members of the Legislature amongst the 650 MPs and 707 or so Peers. The Executive does not have complete control over the Legislature as even MPs of the governing party do not always do as they are told. The Legislature can also hold the Executive to account by means of debate, oral and written questions and the select committees.

The personnel of the Legislature and the Judiciary are also largely separate. Under Sch. 1 of the House of Commons Disqualification Act 1975, judges cannot be members of the House of Commons.

The office of Lord Chancellor, once a classical illustration of fusion of power, has been reformed by the Constitutional Reform Act 2005 so as to enhance judicial independence and separation of powers between the Judiciary and Legislature. The Lord Chancellor is still a Cabinet minister but no longer a judge, head of the Judiciary or 'Speaker' of the legislative House of Lords. The office of Attorney-General has recently attracted much, similar criticism in terms of lack of separation of powers and may ultimately be similarly reformed. Also by virtue of the Constitutional Reform Act, Judges are now selected by a Judicial Appointments Commission; the Lord Chancellor must appoint on recommendation by the Commission, although he does not have to accept their first choice. This replaces the Prime Ministerial patronage of old and so lessens Executive control of the Judiciary.

The Legislature cannot tell the Judiciary how to decide a case and in order to protect judicial independence it is extremely hard for the Legislature to dismiss a judge from office. Under s. 133 of the Constitutional Reform Act, judges of the High Court and above hold office 'during good behaviour' but may be removed on an address by both Houses of Parliament. Thus a judge cannot be removed because a politician does not like her decision in a case.

The courts accept the supremacy of Parliament but assert an entitlement to interpret laws made by Parliament. As Lord Diplock put it in *Duport Steel v Sirs* [1980] 1 All ER 529 at p. 541:

> It cannot be too strongly emphasised that the British constitution, though largely unwritten, is firmly based on the separation of powers: Parliament makes the laws, the judiciary interprets them.

The courts will decide against government ministers if they exceed their legal powers, as seen in *M v Home Office* [1992] QB 270 where the House of Lords held the Home Secretary in contempt for disobeying a court order. The modern Judiciary has asserted the separation of powers as can be seen in *R v Secretary of State for the Home Department ex parte Fire Brigades Unions* [1995] 2 AC 513, where the Law Lords refused to allow the Executive to ignore the legislative will of Parliament. As Lord Mustill put it (at p. 567):

> It is a feature of the peculiarly British conception of the separation of powers that Parliament, the executive and the courts have each their distinct and largely exclusive domain. Parliament has a largely unchallengeable right to make whatever laws it thinks right. The executive carries on the administration of the country in accordance with the powers conferred on it by law. The courts interpret the laws and see that they are obeyed.

Despite these arguments that there is a form of the separation of powers operating in the UK constitution, it has to be reiterated that this is not a formal separation as suggested by Montesquieu or as found in the United States. Since the Human Rights Act 1998 came into force in 2000, this has caused problems. Article 6 provides the right to a fair trial including a hearing 'by an independent and impartial tribunal established by law'. This led the House of Lords to rule in *R (Anderson) v Secretary of State for the Home Department* [2002] 4 All ER 1089, that the Home Secretary should not play a part in setting the minimum custodial tariff to be served by a murderer as this was an aspect of sentencing, a job for the Judiciary and not the Executive. As Lord Steyn put it (at p. 1106):

> Article 6(1) requires effective separation between the courts and the executive, and further requires that what can, in shorthand, be called judicial functions may only be discharged by the courts . . .

Section 3 of the Constitutional Reform Act gives the first statutory guarantee of judicial independence. The Lord Chancellor and other ministers of the Crown 'must uphold the continued independence of the Judiciary' and 'must not seek to influence particular judicial decisions through any special access to the Judiciary'. So it can be seen that the UK is becoming more concerned about the lack of a formal separation of powers in its constitution and is trying to do more to ensure the independence of the Judiciary. A full separation of powers looks unlikely however, as this would be a radical departure from the parliamentary democracy tradition: the Legislature would have to be separate from the Executive, precipitating a totally different way of electing a government, selecting a Prime Minister and holding government to account. Such radical change does not seem imminent or pressing.

Further reading

Barnett, H. *Constitutional and Administrative Law*, 7th edn (Routledge-Cavendish, 2008), chs. 3 and 4.

Bradley, A. and Ewing, K. *Constitutional and Administrative Law*, 14th edn (Longman, 2007), chs. 5, 6.

Loveland, I. *Constitutional Law, Administrative Law, and Human Rights*, 4th edn (Oxford University Press, 2006), ch. 3.

Turpin, C. and Tomkins, A. *British Government and The Constitution*, 6th edn (Cambridge University Press, 2007), ch. 2.

8

The Human Rights Act 1998

Introduction

Although the Labour government that won the 1997 General Election had promised, in its election manifesto, to enact the European Convention on Human Rights into British law, the speed with which this was done took many by surprise. The Human Rights Act 1998 adopted an existing human rights treaty, the European Convention on Human Rights and gave it force in UK law from 2 October 2000. In a sense this was nothing new, since the European Convention on Human Rights had existed since 1951. It was issued by the Council of Europe, *not the European Union*, which is a common mistake made not just by students, but by the media and even some judges as well! The UK was a founder member of the Council that was established, in 1949, to promote democracy, human rights and the rule of law in a Europe devastated by war. Britain played a leading role in drafting the Convention, but it was not then thought necessary to give it legal force in British law as it was considered that the rights protected in the Convention were already respected in this country.

Despite this, it was always possible to enforce the Convention on an international level. Any of the 47 Member States could bring a complaint of breach of human rights against any of the other members, alleging that the State had not respected the rights laid down in the Convention. This procedure is rarely used, but the Convention also allows individual 'victims' the right to bring a complaint against the State that they claim has infringed their human rights. Nowadays these complaints go directly to the European Court of Human Rights, which is an international court staffed by judges from the 47 Member States, sitting in Strasbourg. (Note that this is not to be confused with the quite separate European Court of Justice, which is the court of the European Union and sits in Luxembourg.) The European Court of Human Rights will rule upon whether there has been any infringement of human rights and may order the offending

State to award compensation to the victim. Member States, including the UK, have a very good record for obeying these judgments, which often mean that domestic law has to be changed. Over the years the European Court of Human Rights has decided thousands of cases, which means that there is a lot of guidance upon what the Convention actually means in practice.

All that the Human Rights Act 1998 does is provide that the 'Convention rights' can be enforced in British courts. British legislation must be interpreted in a way that is consistent with the rights granted under the Convention. All public authorities must also act in a way that is compatible with the Convention. As 'public authorities' includes courts, this means that case law must be interpreted to 'take into account' the cases decided by the European Court of Human Rights.

When Gordon Brown became Prime Minister, in 2007, he tried to initiate a debate upon whether the UK should go further and draw up a 'British Bill of Rights and Duties': *The Governance of Britain* (Cm 7170). In 2010, the new Conservative/Liberal Democrat government agreed to investigate these ideas further by setting up 'a Commission to investigate the creation of a British Bill of Rights that incorporates and builds on all our obligations under the European Convention on Human Rights': *The Coalition: our programme for government*.

So what would an examiner expect you to know about all this? At the very least you would need to know what the Human Rights Act actually says. It would also be helpful to know the procedure to make a complaint to the European Court of Human Rights, which has been mentioned above. Even after the Human Rights Act came into force this procedure still exists and someone dissatisfied with the British courts might choose to go there. Even more important, it is essential to have some idea of which rights are actually protected in the 'Articles' of the Convention and some idea of the major cases that tell us what those rights actually mean. A more difficult question is the discussion essay on what difference the Act and/or the Convention has made to the protection of rights in this country. Of course there is no definite answer to this but armed with some *factual* knowledge about the Act, Convention and case law any student should be able to at least offer some sort of answer.

Question 1

The response to terrorism has been at a considerable cost to traditional liberties formally protected by the European Convention on Human Rights and the Human Rights Act ...
(Bradley and Ewing *Constitutional and Administrative Law*, p. 653)

Discuss.

Commentary

This is a discussion question on human rights, which draws attention to a recently controversial area, a common tactic amongst lecturers. When threatened with problems like terrorism, most governments consider it necessary to alter the normal legal rules on how suspected criminals are treated. This can bring the courts into conflict with the government or executive. Judges may not agree with the legal changes and may feel that they unnecessarily threaten human rights or the liberties of the individual.

The question seems straightforward, but the words 'formally protected' may cause some concern. All that they mean is that liberties were traditionally respected by the UK courts, but now they are listed as rights in the **Human Rights Act 1998**. That is the 'formal' part.

There has been a lot of legislation on terrorism. In a relatively short essay for coursework or in an examination, it would be difficult to cover it all. Even if you could it would make for a boring read. Students should not just repeat information but should try to criticise and analyse. It would pay to be selective and just to look at the legislation that you consider most significant. I have taken this a stage further and decided to look at the most important cases. I would hope that this would make for a more interesting read. It is also much easier to remember a few cases than to try to recall hundreds of pages of statute.

Answer plan

- Statutory definition of terrorism
- The right to life
- Torture and inhuman or degrading treatment or punishment
- Detention without trial
- The right to a fair trial
- Reasonable suspicion
- The right to legal assistance
- Public emergency and derogation from the Convention.

Suggested answer

Some people might think that terrorism is a problem that has only affected the United Kingdom since the attack on the Twin Towers in New York on 11 September 2001, but in fact it is not a new problem. If we only consider recent history, there has been a terrorist problem in Northern Ireland since the late 1960s.

Terrorism is defined in **s. 1 of the Terrorism Act 2000** as threatening serious violence against a person, serious damage against property, endangering a person's life, creating a serious risk to the health and safety of the public or seriously interfering with an electronic system. These threats must be designed to influence the government or to intimidate the public. Crucially the threat must be made for the purpose of advancing a political, religious, racial or ideological cause. Threats involving using a noxious substance were added in the **Anti-terrorism, Crime and Security Act 2001** and the **Terrorism Act 2006** added threats against 'an international governmental organisation' in **s. 34**. This is a very wide definition, but even so governments have found it hard to convict terrorists using the normal processes of the criminal law. So a succession of special measures has been introduced, which have sometimes brought the government into conflict with the courts.

Article 2 of the European Convention of Human Rights guarantees the right to life and this has come up in the courts, when alleged terrorists have been shot by the security services. In the notorious 'Death on the Rock' case, *McGann, Farrell and Savage v UK (1995) 21 EHRR 97*, three members of the Provisional IRA were shot dead by plainclothes members of the SAS. The victims were given a command to stop and appeared to reach for remote-control devices in order to detonate a car bomb. They were shot dead before they could do this. Although the soldiers had been told that there was a bomb on Gibraltar, this was not the case and the deceased were not carrying remote-control devices. The European Court of Human Rights concluded that the soldiers honestly believed that the victims were carrying detonators and that it was necessary to kill them. However, the majority of judges concluded that the UK authorities were to blame. They could have arrested the three earlier, when they entered Gibraltar, they wrongly believed that a remotely controlled bomb would be used and maybe the victims could have been wounded rather than killed. In the words of the Convention, the killing was not 'absolutely necessary'.

Jordan v UK (2001) 11 BHRC 1 also involved IRA men shot dead by the SAS and Royal Ulster Constabulary. Again there was a breach of **Article 2**, because there was not an independent and effective investigation into the circumstances of their deaths.

Article 3 outlaws 'torture and inhuman or degrading treatment or punishment'. In *Ireland v UK (1978) 2 EHRR 25* suspected terrorists in Northern Ireland were imprisoned and subjected to harsh interrogation techniques such as beatings, wall-standing, hooding, noise, sleep-deprivation, and deprivation of food and drink. These were not isolated incidents, but were a systematic practice authorised at a high level of the British government. The European Court concluded that the use of these techniques had led to physical and mental suffering, but were not severe enough to amount to torture. They were, however, inhuman and degrading and the UK was in breach of the Convention. Despite this, allegations have been made, at the *Baha Mousa Public Inquiry* (see http://www.bahamousainquiry.org), that similar interrogation techniques have been used by the British army in Iraq.

In *Chahal v UK* (1997) 23 EHRR 413, the British Home Secretary wanted to deport Chahal, an Indian citizen, living in the UK, as a suspected terrorist and threat to national security. This was forbidden by the Court, because there was a real risk that he would be tortured if he was returned to India. So nowadays the UK courts must evaluate whether there is a real risk of ill-treatment before allowing deportation: *RB (Algeria) v Secretary of State for the Home Department* [2009] 4 All ER 1045.

The UK House of Lords considered the history of the use of torture, both within Britain and worldwide in *A v Secretary of State for the Home Department (No. 2)* [2006] 1 All ER 575. They concluded that evidence obtained by torture in other countries was inadmissible in UK legal proceedings. This was the common law rule long before there were Human Rights Conventions. A British resident was allegedly tortured by the US authorities, in collusion with the British MI6, and the courts insisted upon revealing this, against the wishes of the British government in *R (Binyam Mohamed) v Secretary of State for Foreign Affairs* [2010] EWCA Civ 65.

Because it is difficult to prove involvement in terrorism the authorities have often resorted to prolonged detention of suspected terrorists, who have not been convicted of any offence. This can be a form of preventive detention or it can be a way of providing extra time to question suspects. In 1971 hundreds of suspected terrorists in Northern Ireland were indefinitely detained, a practice known as internment. This was questioned in *Ireland v UK* (above), but because of a derogation (see later) the Court accepted the practice. Under the **Prevention of Terrorism (Temporary Provisions) Act 1984**, it was possible for the police to detain arrested persons suspected of terrorism for up to a week for questioning. In *Brogan v UK* (1988) 11 EHRR 117, the European Court of Human Rights condemned the treatment of Brogan, who had been detained for four days. In their view, this length of detention had to be authorised by a judicial authority. In the recent **Terrorism Act 2006**, the government sought the power for the police to detain suspected terrorists that had been arrested, for up to 90 days. The Houses of Parliament refused to accept this and the maximum period was extended to 28 days, but crucially this has to be authorised by a High Court judge.

The government had another problem with suspected terrorists of foreign nationality. The Home Secretary has power to deport foreign nationals, who she considers to be a threat to national security, but under *Chalal*, above, she cannot do so if they are likely to be tortured or ill-treated on their return to their home country. It might also be difficult to prosecute these alleged offenders in the normal way because of a lack of evidence that could be used in court. The solution adopted in **s. 23 of the Anti-terrorism, Crime and Security Act 2001**, was to give the Home Secretary power to detain suspected international terrorists, indefinitely and without trial. The nine detainees challenged their detention in the House of Lords' case *A v Secretary of State for the Home Department*

(No. 1) [2005] 2 AC 68 and succeeded on the very narrow grounds that it was discriminatory to detain foreign nationals, but not UK nationals. Both could be a terrorist threat. After this case the government had to think again and came up with 'control orders' in the Prevention of Terrorism Act 2005, which apply to both UK and foreign terrorist suspects. These are a form of 'house arrest' where the suspect is not put in any form of custody, but allowed to remain in their own home, with severe restrictions upon where they are allowed to go and who they are allowed to contact. The courts have expressed some concern about control orders, in particular that the procedure to make them infringes Article 6, the right to a fair trial. In *Secretary of State for the Home Department v MB and Same v AF* [2008] 1 AC 440, the House of Lords condemned control orders, on the grounds that the person being subjected to the order was not allowed to see the evidence against them, because to reveal that evidence would itself be a threat to national security. In *Secretary of State for the Home Department v AP (Nos. 1 & 2)* [2010] UKSC 24, 26, a control order that confined AP to a flat, far away from his family and friends for a lengthy period of the day, was condemned as being in breach of Article 5, the right to liberty and Article 8, the right to a private life and revealing his identity would be a further breach of Article 8. Control orders do not extend to search of the person: *R (GG) v Secretary of State for the Home Department* [2010] 1 All ER 721.

Much of the anti-terrorism legislation also allows the police to arrest, search or take other action on less evidence than for 'normal' crimes. Normally, the police must have 'reasonable suspicion' before they act, which is supported by Article 5(1)(c) of the European Convention. A series of recent cases have upheld the need for reasonable suspicion, even in cases under anti-terrorist legislation. A police constable did not have reasonable suspicion when he arrested a person merely because he was the close brother of a suspected terrorist and the officer could not just assume that his superiors had reasonable grounds for suspicion: *Raissi v Metropolitan Police Commissioner* [2009] 3 All ER 14. *R (Gillan) v Commissioner of Police of the Metropolis* [2006] 2 WLR 537 involved a power in the Terrorism Act 2000 to stop and search without the need for reasonable suspicion, which was permitted by the House of Lords as it was only a minor infringement of a person's liberty. The European Court of Human Rights disagreed and held it to be a breach of Article 8 in *Gillan and Quinton v United Kingdom* (2010) 50 EHRR 45. The freezing of terrorist assets on the grounds of reasonable suspicion was not permitted in *HM Treasury v Ahmed & Others* [2010] 2 WLR 378, because it was *ultra vires* the terms of a United Nations Security Council Resolution. Emergency legislation had to be passed in the Terrorist Anti-Freezing (Temporary Provisions) Act 2010.

After a person is arrested there is a recognised right for that person to contact a lawyer, under Article 6.3(c) of the Convention and under common law: *R v Chief Constable of South Wales ex parte Merrick* [1994] 2 All ER 560. In terrorist cases, particularly in Northern Ireland, access to a solicitor has often been delayed for up to 48 hours. The European Court of Human Rights has repeatedly condemned this in a whole series of cases such as *Murray v UK* (1996) 22 EHRR 29, *Magee v UK* (2001) 31 EHRR 822 and *Averill v UK* (2001) 31 EHRR 839. Yet the House of Lords held that the clear words of the Regulation of Investigatory Powers Act 2000, allowed the covert surveillance of solicitor/client interviews and overrode both the common law and the Convention: *Re McE* [2009] 4 All ER 335.

It can be very difficult to prove that someone is a terrorist, so some terrorist offences reverse the normal burden of proof. An example is s. 11 of the Terrorism Act 2000, which makes it a criminal offence to belong or profess to belong to a proscribed (terrorist) organisation. The defendant has to prove in his defence that he belonged to the organisation, before it was proscribed and did not take part in its activities. In *Attorney-General's Reference (No. 4 of 2002)* [2005] 1 AC 264, the House of Lords thought this unfair and interpreted the section to mean that, if this defence was raised, the prosecution would need to prove involvement in terrorist activities.

A state may suspend some of the rights guaranteed under the Convention under Article 15 if there is a 'war or other public emergency threatening the life of the nation'. This is a process known as 'derogation' and in its early days, the European Court of Human Rights insisted that they would be the final judge of whether there really was a public emergency and whether the measures taken were justified: *Lawless v Ireland (No. 2)* (1961) 1 EHRR 15. The UK has frequently used derogations to counter the terrorist threat in Northern Ireland. In *Brannigan and McBride v UK* (1993) 17 EHRR 539, the Court accepted that there was evidence of a public emergency caused by terrorism emanating from Northern Ireland and that this justified up to seven days detention without trial for police questioning. In *Ireland v UK* (above) a derogation existed and could perhaps justify detention without trial, but not torture, which is protected by Article 3. Detention without trial was also the issue in *A v Home Secretary (No. 1)* and there the majority of the judges were willing to defer to the government's view on whether there actually was a public emergency. Lord Hoffmann vigorously dissented on the grounds that although lives were threatened this was not the same as 'threatening the life of the nation': 'Whether we would survive Hitler hung in the balance, but there is no doubt that we shall survive Al-Qa'ida.' [2005] 3 All ER 169, 220.

Both the European Court and the UK courts have recognised that terrorism is a serious problem and have been willing to allow some suspension of normal rights in order to combat it. The UK courts have seemed more willing to allow this, perhaps because the problems are closer to home, but the two *A v Home Secretary* cases have indicated that the domestic courts will still insist that the most basic and most important human rights should be respected.

Question 2

What effect has the Human Rights Act 1998 had upon English law? Discuss.

Commentary

Since the Act was passed there has been a torrent of court cases and a welter of academic opinion based on its provisions. A good structure for an answer is to go through the most important provisions of the Act and explain their effect. This is not very difficult to do and this is not a very long Act. A good answer though must refer to some of the case law. No student could possibly be familiar with all the cases, but textbooks and your lecturers will give you some guidance on the best examples. Another approach, but not the one taken by the example below, is to look at the effect of the Act on just one area of the law. One could look at prisoners' rights, criminal trials, privacy, family law or whatever interests you. This is still an evolving area of law, so watch out for important new cases to give your examination answer something different from other students'.

Answer plan

- A tradition of civil liberties in the past
- Legislation must be interpreted in a way that is compatible with human rights
- Courts may make a declaration of incompatibility
- Judicial deference to the legislature and executive
- It is unlawful for a public authority to act in a way that is incompatible with human rights
- The Human Rights Act 1998 may also apply in private disputes.

Suggested answer

The Human Rights Act 1998 came into force on 2 October 2000 and made it far easier to enforce the European Convention of Human Rights in British courts. There have already been a large number of court decisions that refer to the provisions of the Act. As we will see, although there have been inconsistencies, particularly in the lower courts, a trend of cautious application by the judges has begun to appear.

Before this Act Britain had a tradition of civil liberties, popularised by the late nineteenth-century writer, A. V. Dicey. Citizens did not have rights guaranteed by the constitution, but rather they had liberties, they could do anything that the law did not forbid. Judges would prevent governments taking actions for which they did not have legal power, as in the classic case of *Entick v Carrington* (1765) 19 St Tr 1030. If any problems remained Parliament would enact legislation to deal with the matter.

Unfortunately, that is not always what happened. Sometimes judges would decide that public authorities, such as the police, could take action against a person, simply because there was no law to say that they could not, as in the telephone tapping case *Malone v Metropolitan Police Commissioner* [1979] Ch 344. This is the exact opposite of what Dicey said. Similarly, although Parliament sometimes passes Acts that add to the liberties and rights of the people, as in the Freedom of Information Act 2000, they can also legislate in a way that greatly reduces liberties and adds to the power of the police and similar agencies, as in the Regulation of Investigatory Powers Act 2000.

The United Kingdom has been a party to the European Convention of Human Rights since 1951. Even before the Human Rights Act 1998, the courts of this country could refer to the provisions of the Convention to help interpret ambiguous legislation: *R v Home Secretary ex parte Brind* [1991] 1 AC 696. The courts had also said that breaches of the European Convention would encourage them to judicially review a minister's decision and hold it to be unreasonable and therefore illegal: *R v Ministry of Defence ex parte Smith* [1995] 4 All ER 427.

The 1998 Act requires more of the courts. Section 3 states that:

> So far as it is possible to do so, primary legislation and subordinate legislation must be read and given effect in a way which is compatible with the convention rights.

The courts have held that this requires them to go much further than ordinary statutory interpretation, where the court might depart from the ordinary language of the statute to avoid absurd consequences. If necessary the judge could read words into a statute that were not there to ensure compliance with the Convention. As Lord Steyn put it in *R v A (Complainant's sexual history)* [2002] 1 AC 45, 68:

> The techniques to be used would not only involve the reading down of express language in a statute but also the implication of provisions.

Section 43(1)(c) of the Youth Justice and Criminal Evidence Act 1999 forbids the questioning of a rape complainant about her previous sexual history. The court reinterpreted this to mean that the judge could allow such questioning, if to do otherwise would prevent a fair trial. Similarly, in *R v Offen* [2000] 1 WLR 253, the Court of Appeal looked at s. 2 of the Crime (Sentences) Act 1997, which says that a defendant should be given a life sentence if they commit two serious offences, unless there were 'exceptional circumstances'. The court took account of the European Convention and interpreted it to mean that a life sentence should only be imposed if the defendant was a serious risk to the public. So far a lot of the cases on the Human Rights Act have involved a consideration of the fairness or otherwise of criminal and, sometimes, civil trials, which is covered by Articles 5 and 6 of the Convention. If the court concludes that there is no breach of the Convention, as they often do, then the judges do not have to do any 'interpreting' under s. 3 and the existing law remains: *Poplar Housing v Donoghue* [2001] 3 WLR 183.

If there is a clear breach of a Convention Article and the courts cannot interpret the difficulty away under s. 3, the court has no power to declare the Act void. Such a power would conflict with the supremacy of Parliament. Instead, s. 4 allows the courts to make a 'declaration of incompatibility'. The court merely states that the Act of Parliament in question is 'incompatible' with human rights. Only the High Court and above can do this. Then it is up to Parliament to amend or repeal the offending Act, if Parliament chooses to do so. There is a special 'fast-track' procedure to do this under s. 10 of the Human Rights Act 1998, using delegated legislation. This was done after the declaration of incompatibility in *R (on the application of H) v London North and East Mental Health Review Tribunal* [2001] QB 1, where the court held that it was a breach of Article 5 to place the burden of proof on a restricted patient to show that he was no longer suffering from a mental disorder warranting detention. In fact, declarations of incompatibility have not been that common and it has not been unusual for a higher court to overturn the declaration of incompatibility made by a lower court, on the grounds that there is no breach of the Convention. Examples of this would be *Matthews v Ministry of Defence* [2003] 1 All ER 689, where Crown Immunity prevented a sailor suing the government and *Wilson v First County Trust (No. 2)* [2003] 4 All ER 97, where a lender was denied access to the courts. In contrast, the House of Lords made a declaration of incompatibility in *R (Anderson) v Home Secretary* [2002] 4 All ER 108, and said that the Home Secretary could not decide the minimum period that a murderer must stay in prison. This was not a fair trial under Article 6, because a trial should be conducted by a judge, not a politician. The government and Parliament decided upon satisfactory legislation to implement this judgment in the Criminal Justice Act 2003.

In fact the courts have been rather cautious in their application of the Convention. Indeed, Richard Edwards has eloquently argued that a culture of 'judicial deference' has developed, in that judges can be reluctant to interfere with laws enacted by a democratically elected Parliament: (2002) 65 MLR 859. In *R v DPP ex parte Kebilene* [2000] 2 AC 326, 381, a case involving the Prevention of Terrorism Act 2000, the Court of Appeal issued a declaration of incompatibility. The House of Lords disagreed that there was a breach of the Convention and Lord Hope observed that:

> In some circumstances it will be appropriate for the courts to recognise that there is an area of judgment within which the judiciary will defer, on democratic grounds, to the considered opinion of the elected body or person whose act or decision is said to be incompatible with the Convention.

On some questions, the courts will also defer, not only to the legislature, but also to the executive. In *Secretary of State for the Home Department v Rehman* [2003] 1 AC 153, the House of Lords declined to interfere with the Secretary of State's decision to deport Rehman as a possible threat to national security. As Lord Hoffmann said at p. 192:

> On the other hand, the question of whether something is 'in the interests' of national security is not a question of law. It is a matter of judgment and policy. Under the

constitution of the UK and most other countries, decisions as to whether something is or is not in the interests of national security are not a matter for judicial decision. They are entrusted to the executive.

Section 6 of the Human Rights Act 1998 makes it 'unlawful for a public authority to act in a way which is incompatible with a Convention right'. This combined with the succeeding ss. 7 and 8, creates a new right of action and allows the 'victim' of a human rights abuse to sue and recover damages among other remedies. The courts have had some difficulty in deciding what is a public authority, as it is not defined in the Act. In *Yarl's Wood Immigration Ltd. v Bedfordshire Police* [2008] EWHC 2207, the court held that a private company, operating an immigration detention centre under a contract with the Home Office, was a public authority. In contrast, in *YL v Birmingham City Council* [2008] 1 AC 95 the House of Lords held that private care homes that accommodated persons paid for by the local authority were not public authorities. However, this decision was reversed by s. 145 of the Health and Social Care Act 2008.

The European Court of Human Rights can award damages, but sees its function more as to make rulings on the law rather than to compensate victims. In cases like, *R (KB) v Mental Health Review Tribunal* [2003] 2 All ER 209, the UK courts have awarded torts-type damages. In *R (Greenfield) v Secretary of State for the Home Department* [2005] 2 All ER 240, the House of Lords decided that the purpose of the Human Rights Act 1998 was not to give victims better remedies at home than they could recover at Strasbourg. It was more important to ensure 'just satisfaction' and issue an order remedying the breach of rights.

A much-discussed question is whether the Human Rights Act applies to legal disputes between private individuals or just when a public authority infringes a person's human rights. Section 2 would suggest that the Act could apply to any legal dispute, because it states that all courts and tribunals must 'take into account' decisions of the European Court and Commission of Human Rights, whenever a 'Convention' right arises. Also, under s. 6, the courts are themselves public authorities and bound to promote Convention rights. The courts have so far not been willing to recognise completely new rights based on the Convention in disputes between private individuals. In *Wainwright v Home Office* [2004] 2 AC 406, the House of Lords rejected a free-standing right of privacy, but the UK courts have tentatively moved towards using the Convention in private disputes to reinforce claims that already exist in English Law. In *Hello! v Douglas* [2001] 2 All ER 289, *Venables & Thompson v News Group Newspapers Ltd* [2001] 1 All ER 908 and *Campbell v MGN* [2004] 2 AC 457, Convention rights were used to reinforce claims for breach of confidence.

The public maybe has a misleading impression of the Human Rights Act 1998. Some cases generate enormous publicity, such as *R (Pretty) v DPP* [2002] 1 AC 800, on whether the right to die allowed assisted suicide and *R (Begum) v Denbigh*

High School [2006] 2 All ER 487 on the right to wear a particular form of Islamic dress to school. What is lost in all the publicity is that the applicants lost in both cases and English law remained the same.

Most judges, particularly in the higher courts have taken a cautious approach. The assisted suicide issue returned to the House of Lords in *R (Purdy) v DPP* [2010] 1 AC 345. In *Pretty v UK* [2002] 2 FCR 97, Pretty had gone on to win her case in the European Court of Human Rights, on the basis that it was a breach of her right to a private life. The Lords are not bound to follow decisions of the ECHR, but usually do so. The DPP was instructed to publish detailed guidelines upon when a person who assisted a suicide should be prosecuted. This was a satisfactory compromise, as only Parliament can change the law, here by amending the Suicide Act 1961.

Figure 8.1 Procedure under the Human Rights Act 1998

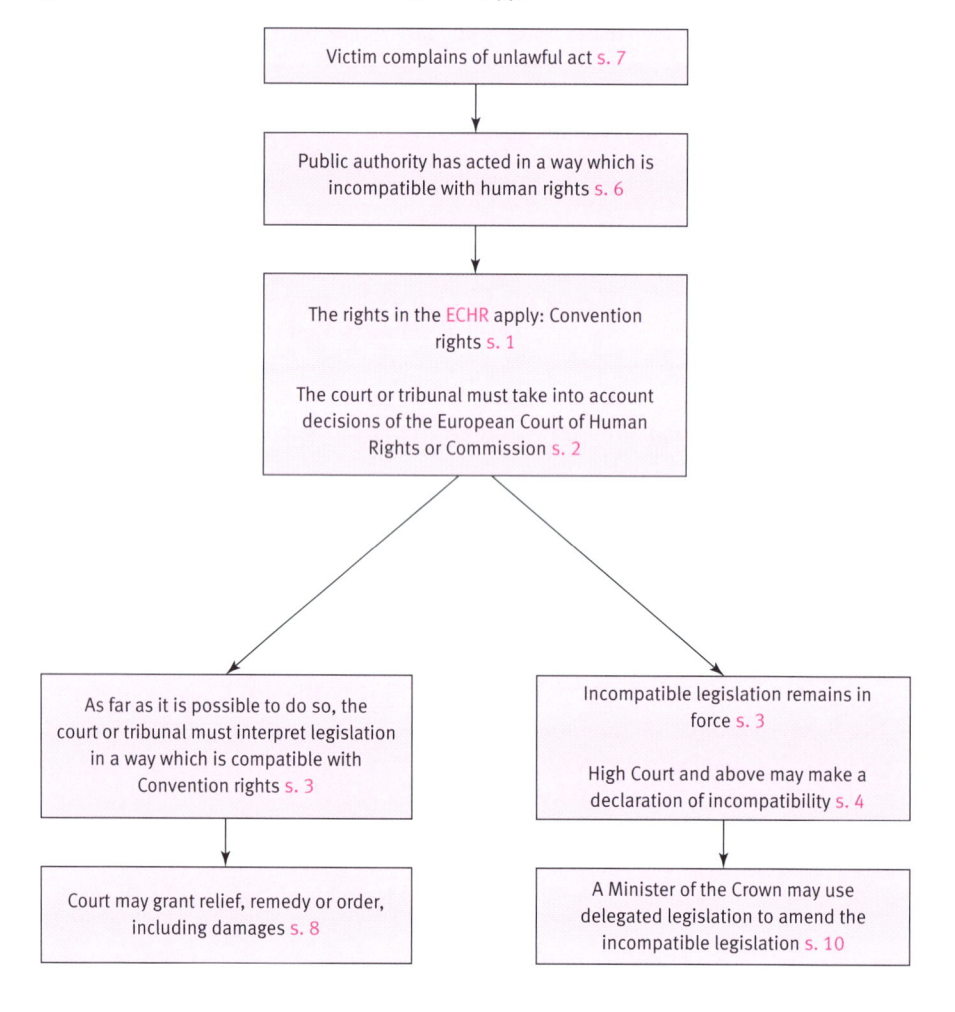

```
Victim complains of unlawful act s. 7
                │
                ▼
Public authority has acted in a way which is
incompatible with human rights s. 6
                │
                ▼
The rights in the ECHR apply: Convention
rights s. 1

The court or tribunal must take into account
decisions of the European Court of Human
Rights or Commission s. 2
           ╱         ╲
          ▼           ▼
```

| As far as it is possible to do so, the court or tribunal must interpret legislation in a way which is compatible with Convention rights s. 3 | Incompatible legislation remains in force s. 3 — High Court and above may make a declaration of incompatibility s. 4 |

| Court may grant relief, remedy or order, including damages s. 8 | A Minister of the Crown may use delegated legislation to amend the incompatible legislation s. 10 |

Question 3

Should the **Human Rights Act 1998** be replaced with a UK Bill of Rights?

Commentary

Before the **Human Rights Act** was passed in 1998, there had been a long debate about whether the UK should have a Bill of Rights or not. Many, if not most, countries in the world have a written constitution and often those countries also have a charter or bill of rights as part of that constitution. The USA is a well-known example. All that a bill of rights would do is list and briefly describe the rights respected in that country and maybe say something about the status of those rights and how they might be enforced. Before 1998 it was quite common to set students an essay question where they could debate the pros and cons of a bill of rights for the UK.

It was sometimes forgotten that England already had a **Bill of Rights**, that of **1689**, but that document, although it acknowledges some individual rights, is not a bill of rights in the modern sense. Instead it acknowledged the transfer of government power from the King to Parliament.

The **Human Rights Act 1998** allows the rights in the **European Convention on Human Rights** to be enforced in UK courts. Yet some still argue that the UK needs a bill of rights.

One camp thinks that the **Human Rights Act 1998** does not go far enough. They consider that more rights should be protected, such as a right to work or a right to social security. For example, the Equality and Human Rights Commission, created by the **Equality Act 2006**, promotes these wider rights, not just those specifically protected by the **Human Rights Act 1998**. Some want human rights to have a protected status in the constitution, so that rights cannot be repealed by Parliament.

The view that has gained more publicity is that the **Human Rights Act** goes too far and has had the effect of giving rights to the undeserving. Some court decisions have been unpopular, preventing government ministers from doing what they want and frustrating newspaper editors from publishing stories.

There are serious arguments against having the **Human Rights Act 1998**. One is that the rights protected are defined only in general terms and leave too much to the interpretation of unelected and unrepresentative judges. Some consider that it is more appropriate for Parliament to change the law on contentious social issues. The ultimate authority on the meaning of the **European Convention on Human Rights** is the European Court of Human Rights. Some resent a 'foreign' court having any sway over British law, but on a less prejudiced level perhaps the judges of that court do not always understand British law. Most continental countries have a written constitution and legal codes based on the civil law tradition, whereas the UK has no easily identifiable constitution and the very different common law system.

So there are a good number of arguments that can be considered in answering this essay question and the answer below attempts to deploy some of them.

Answer plan

- All the major political parties have considered enacting a bill of rights
- The **Human Rights Act 1998** allows the enforcement of Convention rights
- The Council of Europe created the **European Convention on Human Rights**
- Deportation might be inhuman or degrading
- Control Orders breach the right to a fair trial
- A fair trial requires a judge to decide the sentence
- The **ECHR** might apply outside the UK
- **Article 8** protects the privacy of an individual
- Under **s. 2** the UK courts are not bound by European Court of Human Rights decisions
- A Commission will investigate the creation of a British Bill of Rights.

Suggested answer

The Conservative Party Manifesto for the 2010 General Election stated that 'To protect and strengthen our civil liberties, we will—Replace the **Human Rights Act** with a UK Bill of Rights.' This is not such a startling proposition as it might seem, as even the old Labour government, under Gordon Brown, had looked into this issue. The government White Paper, 'Rights and Responsibilities: Developing Our Constitutional Framework' (Cm 7170) of 2007, summarised the arguments for and against a UK Bill of Rights. One suggestion was that 'Duties' should be added to the rights, duties such as the duty to pay taxes.

The politicians of the Conservative and Labour parties are reacting to what they perceive as public concern over the working of the 1998 Act. Some court decisions have aroused unfavourable publicity in the Press and others have been unpopular with government ministers angered to see their policies frustrated by judges.

A brief explanation of the Human Rights Act is called for. The **Human Rights Act 1998** allows the rights in the **European Convention on Human Rights (ECHR)** to be enforced in UK courts. The rights are listed and the main body of the Act explains how they are to be enforced, so it is roughly equivalent to the charter or bill of rights found in many constitutions. The ECHR is not a product of the European Union or a consequence of the UK joining the European Union, as is commonly misunderstood. A different European organisation, the Council of Europe, created the ECHR, which was signed in Rome in 1950 and came into force in 1953. The UK was a founder member of the Council of Europe, which was formed to promote democracy, the rule of law and human rights in a Europe recently devastated by fascism and war. British lawyers, such as the future Lord Chancellor, Lord Kilmuir, played a prominent role in drafting the Convention. It was intended to reflect the basic civil liberties or rights respected for many years in countries such as the UK.

Article 1 of the ECHR requires States that have ratified the treaty 'to secure to everyone within their jurisdiction the rights and freedoms set out in the Convention'. It is worth noting that this does not require Member States to enact or give legal effect to the Convention within their own legal system. The country's laws might already protect human rights, so there might be no need to make the Convention law in that country. That was the position of the UK government for many years, in which the UK was one of the most prominent supporters of the Convention. The UK was the first State to ratify the Convention, in 1951, and led the way in allowing individuals to bring cases to the European Court of Human Rights, in 1966.

The incoming Labour government of 1997 changed their minds about enacting the Convention into UK law, for a number of reasons. As the name of the government paper that advocated this, 'Rights Brought Home: The Human Rights Bill' (Cm 3782) suggests, one motive was to save UK citizens and residents the trouble and expense of taking their case to the European Court of Human Rights in Strasbourg. The UK had also lost a few prominent cases in that court, which was bad publicity in Europe and the wider world. Membership of the European Union also required the UK to respect human rights. As long ago as 1974 the European Court of Justice held in *Internationale Handelsgesellschaft* [1970] ECR 1125, 1135 that 'respect for fundamental rights forms an integral part of the general principles of law protected by the Court of Justice'. In 1997, the Treaty of Amsterdam made clear that Member States must respect human rights and could be penalised by the European Union if they did not. This is made explicit in Article 6.2 of the Treaty of European Union 'The Union shall respect fundamental rights, as guaranteed by the European Convention for the Protection of Human Rights and Fundamental Freedoms signed in Rome on 4 November 1950 and as they result from the constitutional traditions common to the Member States, as general principles of Community law.'

Since 1998 the Human Rights Act has attracted some unfavourable publicity. A number of examples can be given. The European Court of Human Rights held that people who were not British citizens could not be deported if they might face inhuman or degrading treatment or torture (Article 3) in their home State. The UK courts have followed the precedents set for 'ordinary criminals' in *Soering v UK* (1996) 23 EHRR 413 and alleged terrorists in *Chahal v UK* (1996) 23 EHRR 413 and often refused to sanction the government's wish to deport.

Parliament's anti-terrorist laws have been questioned on the basis of human rights. Control Orders allow the government to restrict the movement of suspected, but unconvicted 'terrorists'. The European Court of Human Rights has held, in *A v UK (2009) 49 EHRR 29*, that there is a potential breach of Article 6, the right to a fair trial, in that, because of national security considerations, the suspected terrorist might not be told the evidence against them. The UK House of Lords implemented this in *Secretary of State for the Home Department v AF (No. 3) [2009] 3 All ER 643*. On their own initiative the UK courts have condemned Control Orders that confine the suspect to their home for 16 hours a day in *Secretary of State for the Home Department v JJ [2008] 1 All ER 613*, as a breach of Article 5, the right to liberty and Article 8, the right to a private life.

If we turn to ordinary crime, the UK judiciary has claimed the right, under Article 6 (fair trial), to decide the length of a life sentence rather than allowing the executive to decide. This occurred first in the case of children in *R v Home Secretary ex parte Venables and Thompson [1998] AC 407* and then for adult murderers in *R (Anderson) v Home Secretary [2002] 4 All ER 108*. The Home Secretaries of the time were not pleased and nor were certain elements in the Press, particularly, in the case of Venables and Thompson, when they were also told that they could not reveal their new identities or whereabouts: *Venables v News Group Newspapers Ltd. [2001] Fam 430*.

In the fight against crime, the government has tried to build up a DNA database, of not only those convicted, but also those acquitted or released without charge. This undiscriminating intrusion into the individual's private life is a breach of Article 8, according to *S & Marper v UK [2008] ECHR 1581*. The previous Labour government grappled with how to implement this decision and now its resolution has been left to the new coalition government.

Human rights have also affected the UK's foreign policy in that the ECHR applies wherever the UK has 'jurisdiction' (Article 1). The protections of the Convention extend to Iraqis held and mistreated on a British military base in that country *R (Al Skeini) v Secretary of State for Defence [2007] 3 WLR 33* and the right to life, Article 2, covers British soldiers, when they are on base: *R (Smith) v Secretary of State for Defence [2010] 3 WLR 223*. Intelligence cooperation with the USA was allegedly compromised by a UK court revealing allegations of torture of a British resident at the hands of the CIA in *R (Binyam Mohamed) v Secretary of State for Foreign Affairs [2010] EWCA Civ 65*.

The courts have used a combination of the old equitable action for breach of confidence and the right to a private life in Article 8 to begin to develop a right of privacy in English law: *Campbell v Mirror Group Newspapers [2004] 2 AC 457*. Even the sex life of a public figure might be protected as in *Mosley v News Group Newspapers [2008] EMLR 20* much to the consternation of media that make their money by exposing such activities. Yet no legislation has been passed to make this 'change' in the law.

Under **s. 2 of the Human Rights Act**, the UK courts have been obliged to 'take into account' decisions of the European Court of Human Rights, but are not bound, in the precedent sense, to follow them. The House of Lords has held that the UK courts should normally abide by decisions of the European Court of Human Rights. As Lord Slynn put it in **R (Alconbury Developments Ltd.) v Secretary of State for the Environment [2003] 2 AC 295, 313**: 'In the absence of some special circumstances it seems to me that the court should follow any clear and consistent jurisprudence of the European Court of Human Rights.' The new Supreme Court refused to do so in **R v Horncastle and Others [2010] 2 WLR 47**. The European Court of Human Rights had held, in **Al-Khawaja and Tahery v UK (2009) 49 EHRR 1**, that it was a breach of the right to a fair trial (**Article 6**) for a defendant to be convicted solely on the evidence of an absent witness, who could not be cross-examined. The Supreme Court considered that the European Court judges, who come from a civil law tradition, did not fully understand the common law way of doing things and that the protections in English law guaranteed the defendant a fair trial.

It is not unknown for the UK courts to re-interpret European Court of Human Rights decisions as in the possession proceedings case of **Doherty v Birmingham City Council [2008] 3 WLR 636** which found no breach of **Article 8** (the right to home), unlike the European Court of Human Rights in **McCann v UK [2008] 47 EHRR 40**. To refer back to the examples such as **Chahal v UK** given earlier, the courts do approve deportations if the judge(s) are satisfied, on the evidence, that the deportee will not be ill-treated back home: **RB (Algeria) v Secretary of State for the Home Department [2009] 4 All ER 1045**. In **R (Black) v Secretary of State for Justice [2009] 4 All ER 1**, the courts declined to follow **R (Anderson) v Home Secretary [2002] 4 All ER 108** and accepted that the Home Secretary could have the final say on the release of those who were not life prisoners, but had a fixed sentence. It was hoped at the time of the **Human Rights Act** that 'British judges will be enabled to make a distinctively British contribution to the development of the jurisprudence of human rights in Europe': 'Rights Brought Home: The Human Rights Bill' Cm 3782 para. 1.14. Even the **Treaty of European Union**, which we saw earlier, encourages Member States to develop human rights within their own constitutional traditions.

In May, 2010, the new Conservative-Liberal Democrat government announced its plans for the **Human Rights Act** in 'The Coalition: our programme for government':

'We will establish a Commission to investigate the creation of a British Bill of Rights that incorporates and builds on all our obligations under the **European Convention** on Human Rights, ensures that these rights continue to be enshrined in British law, and protects and extends British liberties. We will seek to promote a better understanding of the true scope of these obligations and liberties.'

A 'better understanding' is a curious phrase. Is this aimed at the general public or the judges? The judiciary are already aware that they do not have to slavishly follow the judgments of the European Court of Human Rights and are already trying to develop human rights in a way that fits in with the constitutional traditions of this country. The executive cannot give instructions to the judiciary upon how to decide a case or they might infringe s. 3 of the Constitutional Reform Act 2005, under which the Lord Chancellor and other government ministers must uphold the independence of the judiciary.

So it is possible that it is planned to add extra rights and duties to the basic rights in the Convention, as was considered by the previous Labour government. Under the doctrine of Parliamentary Supremacy, repeal of the Human Rights Act 1998 is possible, but it would cause the UK international problems. The UK would still be a party to the ECHR and complainants could still petition the European Court of Human Rights. To stop this, the UK would have to resign from the Convention and leave the Council of Europe. For example, Greece did this between 1969 and 1974, but leaving the Council would do nothing for the UK's international reputation. Ignoring human rights might also lead to the UK having to leave the EU, which, although it might please some, would be damaging to the UK's trading interests. The UK is also a permanent member of the United Nations Security Council and the UN Charter also requires Member States to uphold human rights. It is important to remember that the Human Rights Act 1998 does not alter Parliamentary Supremacy (see s. 3) and Parliament can always enact new laws if it finds a judicial decision on human rights unacceptable.

Question 4

Parliament decides to strengthen the law prohibiting the hunting of wild mammals with dogs and enacts the Hunting Act 2009. The Act makes any organisation engaged in hunting an illegal organisation and membership of such an organisation a criminal offence. Members of such an organisation can be arrested and held without trial for a period of up to three months. Under the Act the Home Secretary decides whether a person detained can be released.

Anonymous informers say that Dougie, Karen and Paul are all members of the Borchester Hunt, so the three are arrested and detained at a disused army camp. The camp, which is run for the government by a private security company, lacks any heating and the food and conditions are very poor. Dougie is placed in a cell with another inmate, Boris, who is known to be violent. Boris kills Dougie.

Karen and Paul are denied access to lawyers, but friends of theirs petition the Home Secretary to release them, but he refuses.

Karen, Paul and Dougie's widow, Sharon, are wondering whether any legal action would be worthwhile.

Advise Karen, Paul and Sharon.

Commentary

This question raises various important issues of human rights, but in a problem format, rather than an essay. So you need to be familiar with what is in the **Human Rights Act 1998** and how that Act works. You also need to be acquainted with the different Articles in the **European Convention of Human Rights** and what those Articles actually say. It is also extremely useful to be able to give the extra detail that the leading cases on this area can provide. Unfortunately, there are a huge number of cases on this subject and the number is increasing all the time. So a useful tactic to adopt is to look out for new cases, which often make the headlines in the ordinary media, not just legal journals, and show that you are up to date by including them in your answer. The facts of this problem are fairly unlikely, but they do raise issues on common human rights problems such as unlawful detention and fair trials, which you would probably have studied in your course. Try to spot each human rights issue as it is raised, identify the relevant Article of the **European Convention of Human Rights** and try to establish whether there has been a breach of human rights. This can be done by comparing the facts to the wording of the Article, with the help of any cases that you know of, that have been decided on that point.

Answer plan

- Article 11—freedom of assembly
- Article 5—the right to liberty and security
- Imprisonment without trial
- Article 15—derogation in time of emergency
- Article 6—the right to a fair trial
- Article 3—prohibition of torture
- Article 2—the right to life
- Public authority
- Proceedings under the **Human Rights Act 1998**
- Declaration of incompatibility.

Suggested answer

What has happened to Dougie, Karen and Paul would seem to raise some serious human rights issues. Since the **Human Rights Act 1998** came into force these issues can be raised in an English court, and, if the three fail to gain satisfaction, they could still raise a complaint with the European Court of Human Rights in Strasbourg. First we need to advise them upon whether there are any human rights breaches and then upon who would be liable for those breaches and what remedies the courts might grant.

The real **Hunting Act 2004** made hunting mammals with dogs a criminal offence and was challenged in the courts on a number of grounds, including that it infringed human rights, in *R (Countryside Alliance and Others) v Attorney-General and Another* [2008] 3 All ER 1. Participants in hunting claimed that it was part of their private life and to stop them doing it was a breach of **Article 8**, the right to a private life. The House of Lords disagreed, stating that fox hunting, for instance, was a very public activity carried out in daylight with considerable colour and noise and so could hardly be termed 'private'. **Article 11** guarantees freedom of association and it was argued that this included the right to form and join 'hunts'. The court held that freedom of association was intended to protect political activity and, anyway, according to **Article 11.2** it was permissible to restrict this freedom for a number of reasons, which included 'the protection of morals'. **Article 8.2** also allowed the right to a private life to be restricted for the same reason. The aim of the **Hunting Act 2004** was to prevent or reduce unnecessary suffering to wild animals, but there was also a moral objective: Parliament regarded causing suffering to animals for sport as unethical. The court accepted that there was a difference of opinion on whether hunting animals actually caused excessive suffering, but were willing to defer to the decision of Parliament on this sort of moral issue. So it would seem acceptable to have laws banning hunting, but any law that restricts rights must be proportionate to the aim; it must not restrict rights any more than necessary to stop hunting. In *R (Countryside Alliance and Others) v Attorney-General and Another* [2008] 3 All ER 1, it was acceptable to make hunting illegal, but to make hunting organisations illegal and to imprison their members without trial would not seem to be a proportionate response to the problem and might be a breach of **Article 11**.

Imprisonment without trial has always been regarded as a serious breach of civil liberties (*Liversidge v Anderson* [1942] AC 206) and is now clearly prohibited by **Article 5**, the right to liberty and security. *Brogan v United Kingdom* (1988) 11 EHRR 117 held that detention without trial for only four days was excessive. The detainee must be brought before a judge, who can determine the legality of the detention, but we know from our facts that Karen and Paul's only remedy is to the Home Secretary, an elected politician, and that is unacceptable. *Brogan* is a decision of the European Court of Human Rights, which, under **s. 2** of the Human Rights Act 1998, must be 'taken into account' by any UK court, when deciding upon the meaning of a 'Convention right'. Despite this wording, which would suggest that a UK court is not bound to follow an European Court decision, the House of Lords would nearly always follow such a decision. For example, it is possible for a state to suspend some of the human rights protected by the Convention, such as Article 5, by making a 'derogation' under Article 15. This can only be done if there is a 'war or other public emergency threatening the life of the nation'. In *Lawless v Ireland (No. 3) (1961) 1 EHRR 15*, the European Court of Human Rights was prepared to accept the view of Ireland that IRA activity constituted a public emergency, even though there was not much evidence of a serious threat. The House of Lords was willing to follow this case in *A v Home Secretary (No. 1) [2005] 2 AC 68*, despite at least one judge expressing some scepticism whether there was a terrorist threat serious enough to threaten the life of the nation. Both *Lawless* and *A* involved suspensions of Article 5 and imprisonment without trial, but there is no evidence in the facts of our problem that there is any form of public emergency and no evidence that the UK government has applied for a derogation. Hunting does not threaten the life of the nation.

The trio have been arrested and Article 5.1(c) requires there to be 'reasonable suspicion' that they have committed the offence. The European Court of Human Rights accepted that information from unnamed informants could amount to reasonable suspicion in *Fox, Campbell and Hartley v UK (1991) 13 EHRR 157*, but that was a case involving terrorists and the Court did say that that could justify a lower standard of evidence upon which to reasonably base suspicion. So maybe there is not enough evidence to justify Dougie, Karen and Paul's arrests and the House of Lords held in *R v Davis (Iain) [2008] 3 WLR 125* that it is not permissible to convict anyone, solely on the evidence of anonymous witnesses. This is a breach of common law principles and Article 6; the right to a fair trial, specifically Article 6.3(d), which states that everyone charged with a criminal offence, has the right to examine witnesses.

Dougie, Karen and Paul have clearly not received a fair trial. Legal advice is an essential preparation in making a proper defence and to deny access to a lawyer is a breach of Article 6.3(d): *Golder v United Kingdom (1975) 1 EHRR 524* and *Silver v United Kingdom (1981) 3 EHRR 475*. There is no doubt that the English courts accept that defendants, prisoners and arrested persons must be allowed to communicate with their lawyers without any interference from the authorities, as shown by the prison case *R (Daly) v Home Secretary [2001] 2 AC 532*. The House of Lords accepted that it was a basic right existing in English law, irrespective of anything in the European Convention. The three, in fact, have not received any trial at all, as we are not told that the Home Secretary has held 'a fair and public hearing' as required by Article 6. The hearing must also be held by 'independent and impartial tribunal' and a number of cases have held that a politician, who may be influenced by electoral considerations, should not act as a judge. It was held in *R (Anderson) v Home Secretary* [2003] 1 AC 837 that the Home Secretary should not decide upon the minimum sentence or release date of life prisoners. The Home Secretary is allowed to decide the release date of prisoners serving fixed sentences, according to *R (Black) v Secretary of State for Justice* [2009] 4 All ER 1, but a court must decide the initial sentence. The applicants here have not had a trial from any sort of court at all.

The treatment of Dougie, Karen and Paul, while detained, leaves something to be desired. 'Inhuman or degrading treatment' is prohibited under Article 3 and, although what has happened to the three is not as severe as the beatings and psychological interrogation techniques in *Ireland v United Kingdom* (1978) 2 EHRR 25, sending a prisoner to the harsh conditions of 'death-row' in the United States was a breach in *Soering v United Kingdom* (1989) 11 EHRR 439. So poor prison conditions could be an infringement of human rights, as could allowing a prisoner to be murdered, because, under Article 2, the State has a duty to protect the right to life. *R (Amin) v Home Secretary* [2004] 1 AC 653 has quite similar facts to the killing of Dougie by Boris, for it concerned a young prisoner who was killed by a cell mate, whom the prison authorities knew to be both racist and violent. Article 2 required that there should be full investigation into his death, in which his family could be involved. *R (JL) v Secretary of State for Justice* [2009] 2 All ER 521 stressed that the investigation should be independent and might even involve funding legal representation for the deceased's family. The State is also required to do all that is reasonable to protect a person from a real and immediate risk to their life, if the State has knowledge of that risk. This duty applied when the police failed to protect a boy from the persistent threats of his eventual murderer in *Osman v United Kingdom* (1998) 29 EHRR 245 and so it could also apply to Dougie's death.

The three detainees would clearly seem to have suffered human rights infringements and so would be 'victims' of an unlawful act and able to bring a case against a 'public authority' under ss. 6 and 7 of the Human Rights Act 1998. The Act does not define a public authority, but the Home Secretary clearly is, as seen by the cases against him mentioned earlier in this essay. The private security company that runs the camp might not be so straightforward, as in *YL v Birmingham City Council* [2008] 1 AC 95 it was held that a private care home that took residents placed there by the council, which paid their fees, was not a public authority. In contrast, *Yarl's Wood Immigration Ltd v Bedfordshire Police* [2008] EWHC 2207 decided that a private company, operating an immigration detention centre under a contract with the Home Office, was a public authority, albeit under different legislation. The company exercised the coercive power of the State, as does the company running the detention centre in our problem, so Karen, Dougie's widow and Paul can bring their case. They could seek a judicial review of the decision to detain and not release them and compensation for the harm that they have suffered under *R (Greenfield) v Secretary of State for the Home Department* [2005] 2 All ER 240.

According to s. 6(2) of the Human Rights Act 1998, the court cannot overturn an Act of Parliament, even if it is contrary to human rights, but has to enforce it: *Doherty v Birmingham City Council* [2008] 3 WLR 636. So the court would have to consider making a 'statement of incompatibility' under s. 4 of the Act as they did in the similar cases where the Home Secretary had the statutory power to detain without trial: *R (Anderson) v Home Secretary* [2003] 1 AC 837 and *A v Home Secretary (No. 1)* [2005] 2 AC 68. There seems little likelihood that the Hunting Act 2009 could be interpreted in a human rights friendly way, as courts are required to do by s. 3 of the Human Rights Act 1998.

So Karen, Paul and Sharon might well be granted a declaration of incompatibility by the courts, then it would be up to Parliament to amend or repeal the Hunting Act 2009. If Parliament decides not to do so, or delays excessively, there is nothing to stop the three applying to the European Court of Human Rights itself. In the light of the gross human rights abuses detailed in this answer, that Court would rule in their favour. The UK government might be ordered to pay compensation to the three and would come under pressure, from the Council of Europe, to remedy these breaches of human rights.

Further reading

Barnett, H. *Constitutional and Administrative Law*, 8th edn (Cavendish, 2011), ch 18.

Bradley, A. and Ewing, K. *Constitutional and Administrative Law*, 15th edn (Longman, 2010), ch. 19.

Edwards, R. 'Judicial Deference under the Human Rights Act' (2002) 65 MLR 859.

Loveland, I. *Constitutional Law, Administrative Law and Human Rights: A Critical Introduction*, 5th edn (OUP, 2009), Part V, particularly chs. 21 & 22.

9

Freedom to Protest and Police Powers

Introduction

This is sometimes known as the law of public order. There are a number of criminal offences involved so, occasionally, it is treated as part of a criminal law syllabus. It, however, concerns a very important civil liberty, that of protest against the government or other powerful bodies, so historically it has been an important constitutional law issue. How far may the citizen lawfully go to indicate their dislike of government? According to the British tradition of civil liberties, citizens may protest in any way that they want, as long as they do not break the law.

To study this subject we need to know, fairly accurately, which laws may be broken. Problem questions are common in this area. All that you need to do is to identify which laws may have been broken or offences committed. Many students find essay questions more demanding: you have to have a point of view, argue it and marshal evidence to support it. You may be asked whether you think that there is sufficient liberty to protest or whether you approve of the Criminal Justice and Public Order Act 1994 for example.

There is a lot of duplication in the laws on this area. The old common law such as breach of the peace remains. Added to this was the Public Order Act 1936. Some of that Act still remains although much of it was replaced by the Public Order Act 1986. On top of that the Criminal Justice and Public Order Act 1994 creates additional criminal offences and police powers. Anti-social behaviour orders under the Crime and Disorder Act 1998 and dispersal powers under the Anti-Social Behaviour Act 2003, could also impinge upon freedom to protest. Sections 132–8 of the Serious Organised Crime and Police Act 2005 require that anyone wishing to stage a demonstration in the vicinity of Parliament must obtain prior authorisation. This was aimed at the one-man protest of Brian Haw against government action in Iraq and was considered in *R (Haw) v Secretary of State for the Home Department* [2006] All ER (D) 94. The measure has been seen as heavy handed and oppressive and has been repealed by **s. 32 of the Constitutional Reform and Governance Act 2010**.

We must now also take into consideration the **Human Rights Act 1998**, which introduced **Article 11**, the right of peaceful assembly, and **Article 10**, freedom of expression, into UK law. This has had an influence on how the existing UK law is interpreted. For instance in *DPP v Jones (Margaret)* [1999] 2 AC 240 it was conceded that a right to peaceful assembly on the highway might exist. The House of Lords also accepted in *R (Laporte) v Chief Constable of Gloucestershire* [2007] 2 AC 205 that the police had no power to stop persons travelling to a demonstration unless a breach of the peace was imminent. It was not enough for the police just to act 'reasonably'.

So it can be seen that it is perfectly possible for the same set of facts to give rise to liability under several different laws. The more one looks at a public order problem the more offences one can see. Under examination conditions this is not a problem, time will limit what you can identify. If it is an essay you have to be sensible about what you are going to cover. Select material to support your argument.

If you are considering a problem question only deal with the legal issues raised by the facts. For instance, if you are given a set of facts indicating fairly minor public disturbances it is unlikely that you would be expected to consider riot. A reasonably high level of violence would indicate riot.

Question 1

Twelve members of the 'No Abortion Campaign' are protesting on the pavement outside an abortion clinic on Eastby High Street. They are displaying placards with the words 'No to abortion' and speaking to each woman who enters the clinic asking her to consider whether she is 'doing the right thing'.

The owner of the abortion clinic summons the police and PC Kent arrives. She stands on the pavement observing the 'No Abortion Campaign' members, but takes no action.

Then 12 members of a group in favour of abortion, 'Women's Choice', arrive and start shouting at the 'No Abortion Campaign' members, insulting them with words such as 'religious fanatics go home'. Three of the members of 'Women's Choice' throw stones, breaking the windows of the clinic.

PC Kent asks the 'No Abortion Campaign' members to leave, which they unwillingly do. They slowly walk the half a mile down the High Street to the railway station.

PC Kent, together with other police officers who have joined her, arrest the 12 members of the 'No Abortion Campaign'.

Advise the 'No Abortion Campaign' on whether they have committed any public order offences and whether the police actions are legal.

Freedom to Protest and Police Powers

Commentary

This is a fairly standard sort of problem question on public order law. What you have to do is to identify and discuss possible offences that might have been committed and consider the police's powers to control public protest. The question asks you to confine yourself to public order law, so do not stray off into ordinary criminal law and consider things like criminal damage. Nor is it necessary to consider civil matters such as nuisance. Your answer will be quite long enough and complicated enough just confining yourself to public order law! This area of law has many overlapping provisions and some contradictory case law. A good answer will make sense of this law by applying it to the problem and trying to come to a conclusion. Reasoned conclusions show that you understand the law. There are 12 members of the No Abortion Campaign, 12 members of Women's Choice and three women throw stones. This is not just chance, as numbers of participants are important in public order law and give the student a clue as to which area of law they should be considering.

The **Human Rights Act 1998** means that the **European Convention on Human Rights** is now relevant to this area of law, in particular **Article 10**, which provides for freedom of expression and **Article 11**, which provides for freedom of assembly. This is actually helpful, because court decisions on these Articles are helping to clarify what English law on public order should be.

Answer plan

- The police have discretion
- Wilful obstruction of the highway
- Threatening, abusive or insulting words or behaviour
- Immediate unlawful violence or provocation of immediate unlawful violence
- Conduct likely to cause harassment, alarm or distress
- An assembly of two or more persons in a public place open to the air
- Riot is 12 or more persons present together using or threatening unlawful violence for a common purpose
- Violent disorder is three or more people present together using or threatening unlawful violence
- Breach of the peace is an act or threat of violence against a person or their property in their presence
- The organiser of a procession must give the police six days' notice.

Figure 9.1 The numbers required under public order legislation

---

ONE PERSON

Affray s. 3 Public Order Act 1986
Fear or provocation of violence s. 4 POA 1986
Intentional harassment, alarm or distress s. 4A POA 1986
Harassment, alarm or distress s. 5 POA 1986

TWO PEOPLE

Violent disorder s. 2 POA 1986
Public assembly s. 16 POA 1986
Public procession—no statutory minimum, but must be more than one person.
Power to remove trespassers on land s. 61 Criminal Justice and Public Order Act 1994

THREE PEOPLE

Violent disorder s. 2 POA 1986

TWELVE PEOPLE

Riot s. 1 POA 1986

TWENTY PEOPLE

Trespassory assembly s. 14A POA 1986
A rave s. 63 Criminal Justice and Public Order Act 1994

Suggested answer

There are a number of public order offences that could have been committed by both the 'No Abortion Campaign' and 'Women's Choice' and also a number of powers that PC Kent could have used to control the developing situation. According to *R v Chief Constable of Devon and Cornwall ex parte The Central Electricity Generating Board* [1982] QB 458, the police have discretion on how they use their public order control powers. They are not obliged to arrest for crimes or to use their powers to disperse protesters. The police have a duty to protect the human rights of those affected by protesters. The rights might include Article 2, the right to life and Article 3, protection from inhuman or degrading treatment. As long as the police act reasonably and do not show any bias for one side or the other, the courts will not interfere with police discretion: *Re E (a child)* [2009] 1 All ER 467.

A gathering on the pavement has been held to be obstruction of the highway in *Arrowsmith v Jenkins* [1963] 2 QB 561. It is still the offence of wilful obstruction, even if there was no intention to obstruct and even if no one was actually obstructed. The highway is for passage and repassage and purposes incidental to that movement. However, the European Court of Human Rights has ruled, in *Platform Arzte fur das Leben* (1988) 13 EHRR 204, that there is a right to hold meetings in a public place. Another case more favourable to the 'No Abortion Campaign' is *DPP v Jones (Margaret)* [1999] 2 AC 240, where the House of Lords held that a small protest on a roadside verge, near Stonehenge, was not an obstruction of the highway. Lord Irvine, the Lord Chancellor, thought that a right of peaceful assembly on the highway might exist and that the common law should develop to conform to Article 11 of the European Convention, which gives a right of peaceful assembly. The 'No Abortion Campaign's' protest is certainly peaceful and quite small in number, so it is probably not obstruction of the highway.

They also do not seem to be committing any offences under the Public Order Act 1986. They are not using 'threatening, abusive or insulting words or behaviour' nor are their signs 'threatening, abusive or insulting' and there are no threats of violence, so there is no offence under s. 4 of the Act. Even the lesser offence in s. 5, where it is enough for 'disorderly behaviour' to be likely to cause 'harassment, alarm or distress' is not committed. *DPP v Clarke, Lewis, O'Connell & O'Keefe* [1992] Crim LR 60 also involved a protest outside an abortion clinic, but the protesters had no intent to be threatening, abusive or insulting. All that the defendants did in that case was to show pictures of an aborted foetus to police officers and one passer-by. To commit an offence under s. 5 the protest needs to be more vigorous, as in *DPP v Fidler and Moran* [1992] 1 WLR 91, where there were also shouts and threats against those attending the clinic, in addition to the display of photographs and models of dead foetuses. *Percy v DPP* (2002) 166 JP 93 confirms that the 'No Abortion Campaign' are unlikely to have committed an offence. Even if behaviour is held to be insulting, this must be balanced against the right to freedom of expression under Article 10 of the European Convention of Human Rights.

Women's Choice appear to have committed criminal offences. Unlike the 'No Abortion Campaign', they are using insulting words, which seem intended or likely to cause their opponents to fear immediate personal violence: *R v Horseferry Road Magistrate ex parte Siadatan* [1991] 1 All ER 324. There is a more serious version of this offence, under s. 31 of the Crime and Disorder Act 1998, if it is racially or religiously aggravated. This means that the offender demonstrates hostility based on the victim's membership, or presumed membership, of a racial or religious group. In *R v Rogers (Philip)* [2007] 2 AC 62 the defendant referred to three Spanish women as 'bloody foreigners'. The offence is committed if hostility is shown to foreigners in general as a particular racial group does not have to be identified. So by analogy hostility to religious people in general could also be an offence.

There is also a lesser offence under s. 5 of the Public Order Act 1986. It seems likely that the 'No Abortion Campaign' would experience harassment, alarm or distress, unless the courts decide that by their frequent protesting they will have become used to insulting, threatening and abusive words or behaviour, rather like the police officers in *DPP v Orum* [1988] 3 All ER 449.

It is possible that more serious offences have been committed. **Section 1 of the Public Order Act 1986** defines riot as '12 or more persons who are present together use or threaten violence for a common purpose . . . as would cause a person of reasonable firmness present at the scene to fear for his personal safety'. There are over 12 members of 'Women's Choice' and according to **s. 7** 'violence' can include violence towards property, not just people and would include the throwing of missiles. It would have to be proved, though, that at least 12 of them had a common purpose to violently attack the clinic or their opponents: *R v Jefferson* [1994] 1 All ER 270. This could prove difficult, so **s. 2**, which makes violent disorder an offence, is more likely. This is similar to riot, but only requires three participants and does not require a common purpose. The three window breakers would have committed this offence as the 'No Abortion Campaign', the inmates of the clinic, bystanders and even the police officer would have been put in fear. Affray, under **s. 3**, has not been committed, as under **s. 8**, violence against persons is required.

Section 14 of the Public Order Act 1986 allows the senior police officer on the spot to impose conditions upon a public assembly, if he reasonably believes that it may result in serious public disorder, serious damage to property, intimidation or serious disruption to the life of the community. A public assembly used to require a minimum number of 20 persons, but this was reduced to two by the **Anti-Social Behaviour Act 2003**. PC Kent could give directions as to the place, number of people and duration of the assembly. This would seem to allow her to act against either 'Women's Choice' or the 'No Abortion Campaign'. In addition to these powers, she also has common law and other statutory powers to disperse assemblies.

Section 30 of the Anti-Social Behaviour Act 2003 allows the police to disperse groups of protesters according to *R (Pritpal Singh) v Chief Constable of West Midlands* [2007] 2 All ER 297. Members of the public have to have been 'intimidated, harassed, alarmed or distressed' and then a senior police officer has to give an authorisation allowing dispersal in that locality. An authorisation would only exist if there had been trouble in the area of the abortion clinic before, but the facts suggest that this is not a long-running protest, so it is unlikely that an authorisation is in force. **Section 42 of the Criminal Justice and Police Act 2001** allows the police to disperse persons who are outside a dwelling and 'likely to cause harassment, alarm or distress to the persons living at the residence'. The clinic is not a 'dwelling' though.

PC Kent does, however, have a common law power to take reasonable measures to prevent a breach of the peace. The accepted definition, today, of a breach of the peace is an act or threat of violence against a person or their property in their presence, which puts someone in fear of violence: *R v Howell* [1982] 2 QB 416 and *Percy v DPP* [1995] 3 All ER 124. This power has been used to disperse meetings as in *Duncan v Jones* [1963] 1 KB 218 and to refuse to obey the reasonable instructions of a police constable is the offence of obstruction of a police officer in the execution of his duty: *Duncan v Jones* (ibid.).

On the facts it seems reasonable for PC Kent to assume that violence might break out, but has she acted against the wrong group? The old case of *Beatty v Gillbanks* (1882) 9 QBD 308 held that the Salvation Army should not be forbidden from marching through Weston-super-Mare, just because they might be violently opposed by the rival Skeleton Army. In *Platform Arzte fur das Leben* (above), the European Court of Human Rights has ruled that this is the correct approach and that, in certain circumstances, the State has a duty to protect peaceful protesters from those who would oppose them with violence. In *Redmond-Bate v DPP* [2000] HRLR 249, the defendants were women preaching from the steps of Wakefield Cathedral but, as the listening crowd were becoming hostile, the police stopped the women. Sedley LJ said at 259 that the police were wrong to do this and that 'the common law should seek compatibility with the values of the European Convention on Human Rights'. 'The question for the police officer was whether there was a real threat of violence and if so, from whom it was coming.' So PC Kent should really have taken action against the troublemakers, 'Women's Choice'.

Processions and marches are well regulated by law and under **s. 11 of the Public Order Act 1986**—the organisers must give the police six days' written notice 'unless it is not reasonably practicable to give any advance notice of the procession' or 'the procession is one commonly or customarily held in the police area'. There is no definition of a procession in the Act and even a mass cycle ride held as a protest in London was held to be a procession, but as it was customarily held, once every month, there was no requirement to notify under the Act: *R (Kay) v Commissioner of Police of the Metropolis* [2008] 1 WLR 2723. So possibly walking back to the station could be a procession, if they were still continuing their protest and it certainly could not be said to be 'customary'. It is surely arguable here that it is not reasonable to expect the 'No Abortion Campaign' to notify the police in advance as their march has, in effect, been caused by the police. **Section 12** allows a senior police officer to give directions to the organisers if he 'reasonably believes that' the procession 'may result in serious public disorder, serious damage to property or serious disruption to the life of the community' or the purpose of the march is intimidation. As these directions have to be in writing, they are hardly practical in this situation. The law, in the **Public Order Act 1986**, makes a clear distinction between assemblies and processions, for instance there has never been a minimum number for processions and assemblies do not have to be notified to the police in advance. The facts of this problem illustrate, that there may not be a clear-cut distinction between assemblies and processions, as was shown in *DPP v Jones* [2002] EWHC 110.

In conclusion, PC Kent took legal action against the wrong people, the 'No Abortion Campaign' group, who were merely exercising their peaceful right of protest, a right that PC Kent should have protected as well as their other human rights: *Re E (a child)* [2009] 1 All ER 467. She should have taken action against the violent and threatening 'Women's Choice'.

Question 2

Margaret and her friends oppose the use of British and US troops in Afghanistan. They travel from London to protest outside RAF Blackham, an airfield where both British and US aircraft are based.

She and 10 of her friends set up an encampment on the roadside just outside the main gates of RAF Blackham. This attracts a lot of attention from passing motorists, many of whom slow down, causing a delay to other traffic.

Two of the group, Janet and Steve, climb over the perimeter wall into Blackham and enter a hanger, where they damage an aircraft by hitting it with hammers. Janet also burns the US flag, the 'Stars and Stripes', which distresses the US service personnel standing nearby.

The police arrive, arrest Janet and Steve and the nine others, dismantle their camp and take them all back to London, which takes six hours.

All the protesters say that they have not broken the law. They claim that they have a legal right to protest and that they were trying to prevent the aircraft being used in Afghanistan, which would be an illegal use of force in international law.

Advise them on the law relating to their case.

Commentary

This problem is designed to mirror the modern kind of protest, where a small group has very strong views about government policy and wishes to take action to publicise their views. You may think their actions silly or you may think them justified, depending on your own political views, but leave those aside and try to analyse what the legal decision would be on facts like these. Freedom to protest is a right guaranteed under the **European Convention on Human Rights** and under common law, so that needs to be stated in any answer. Often the inspiration for a problem is an important new case, so it is always worthwhile for the student to take note of new cases, particularly if their lecturers seem interested in them. *Austin v MPC* [2009] 4 All ER 227 is a House of Lords case which accepted the legality of the police tactic of 'kettling' or confining protesters to a small area. This may have inspired the Conservative-Liberal Democrat government promise in their programme for government that 'We will restore rights to non-violent protest.' Part of the problem concerns the ancient legal concept of breach of the peace. There are hundreds of cases on this subject, but you are being pointed towards modern developments. It always pays to keep up to date.

Answer plan

- **Article 11** Right to protest
- Unless it causes disorder or crime
- **Criminal Justice and Public Order Act 1994**—caravans and raves
- Wilful obstruction of the highway
- Public nuisance
- A public assembly of two or more persons in a public place open to the air
- Aggravated trespass—intimidate, disrupt or obstruct a lawful activity
- Lawful activity does not include preventing breaches of international law
- Insulting behaviour causing harassment, alarm or distress
- Reasonable action to prevent a breach of the peace.
- **Article 5,** the right to liberty.

Suggested answer

Article 11 of the European Convention on Human Rights guarantees that 'Everyone has the right to freedom of peaceful assembly and to freedom of association with others . . . ' Freedom of expression is also guaranteed by **Article 10**. Both these 'Convention rights' must be taken into account by courts and tribunals of the UK under **s. 2 of the Human Rights Act 1998**. Under **s. 3**, UK legislation 'must be read and be given effect in a way that is compatible with Convention rights'. Irrespective of this, English common law has long recognised that people are allowed to protest and to hold public meetings, as illustrated by the case of *Beatty v Gillbanks* **(1882) 9 QBD 308**. The Salvation Army should have been allowed to march in Weston-super-Mare, even though they knew that they would be violently opposed by the Skeleton Army. The Salvation Army was acting lawfully and it was not their fault if this caused another organisation to act unlawfully.

Protest can become unlawful though. This is recognised both by English common law and by the **European Convention**. **Article 11(2)** states that the right to freedom of assembly can be restricted 'for the prevention of disorder and crime' . . . 'or for the protection of the rights and freedoms of others'. Let us examine whether Margaret's protest has become unlawful or not.

The encampment by the roadside may be trespass, but that is usually only a civil matter that does not involve the police. The **Criminal Justice and Public Order**

Act 1994 criminalises certain forms of trespass. Under s. 60 there is a power to remove trespassers, but this was aimed at travellers who are trespassing and requires there to be at least one caravan and one vehicle present. None of this seems to be the case here. Under s. 63 of the same Act, there is a police power to disperse raves and seize equipment. This is definitely not a rave as that requires at least 20 persons to be present and requires amplified music to be played during the night. Even if it was a rave, the police have no power to seize camping equipment, so dismantling their camp seems to be illegal.

Obstruction of the highway is an offence under s. 137 of the Highways Act 1980 and can be used by the police to disperse peaceful, non-violent protest. The offence is committed 'if a person without lawful authority or excuse in any way wilfully obstructs the free passage along a highway'. Pavements and grass verges are part of the highway and a person can even be off the highway and yet cause an obstruction on it, as shown by *Nagy v Weston* [1965] 1 All ER 78, where a hot dog van in a lay-by caused the obstruction on the highway. *Arrowsmith v Jenkins* [1963] 2 QB 561 involved a public meeting in the road, which was held to be an obstruction. It was no defence that there was no intent to cause an obstruction, nor that the road was only blocked for five minutes. *DPP v Jones* [1999] 2 AC 240 moderates this strict approach. This consisted of a peaceful, non-obstructive assembly of 21 people, including Margaret Jones, on the verge of the A344 road at Stonehenge. Lord Chancellor Irvine said, at p. 257, that:

> the public highway is a public place which the public may enjoy for any reasonable purpose, provided the activity in question does not amount to a public or private nuisance and does not obstruct the highway by unreasonably impeding the primary right of the public to pass and repass: within these qualifications there is a public right of peaceful assembly on the highway.

The Lord Chancellor thought this was the case irrespective of the right guaranteed under Article 11 of the ECHR, as the Human Rights Act was not yet in force at the date of this case.

Margaret and her friends would have a stronger argument that they have the right to protest now that the Act is in force, as they are only causing minor inconvenience to motorists.

Lord Irvine referred to public nuisance, which is a more serious charge than obstruction of the highway. The House of Lords stated in *R v Rimmington, R v Goldstein* [2006] 1 AC 459, that this offence should now be rarely used, when there was a statutory equivalent available, which might give the defendant the benefit of statutory defences. So the prosecution should use obstruction of the highway, to which, as we have seen, Margaret may have a defence.

The Public Order Act 1986 gives the police powers to control a public assembly, which is defined in s. 16 as 'an assembly of 20 or more persons in a public place which is wholly or partly open to the air'. The minimum number was reduced to two by **s. 57 of the Anti-Social Behaviour Act 2003**, so Margaret's gathering would meet the definition. Also, under **s. 16**, a 'public place' includes a highway. By **s. 14** a senior police officer may impose conditions on a public assembly such as the place it is held, its maximum duration or the maximum number of persons. Ignoring police directions is a criminal offence. It is important to note that the police may only impose conditions if they reasonably believe the assembly may result in serious public disorder, serious disruption to the life of the community, intimidation to others or serious damage to property. The 'attack' on the aircraft could be damage or intimidation, so this probably gives the police power to act under this section. However, the **1986 Act** gives the police no power to ban or forbid a public assembly of this kind. This can only be done if the protest is moving and therefore becomes a 'procession' or if it is a 'trespassory assembly' under the **Criminal Justice and Public Order Act 1994**. A trespassory assembly has to cause serious disruption to the life of the community or damage to some sort of historical monument. Neither seems to be the case here.

The actions of Janet and Steve in entering the air base and damaging an airplane could be aggravated trespass under **ss. 68 and 69 of the Criminal Justice and Public Order Act 1994**. They have trespassed on land. Even entering the aircraft hanger is included, because although the offence originally only covered land in the open air, this was changed by the **Anti-Social Behaviour Act 2003** to include all land. They have obstructed or disrupted 'lawful activity': the activities of the military. These issues were discussed, by the House of Lords, in *R v Jones* **[2006] 2 WLR 772**. Jones (the same Jones as in *DPP v Jones* above) and others had entered RAF Fairford and carried out or planned to carry out various acts of damage to military property. They argued that they could not have committed aggravated trespass, because the military were not engaged in 'lawful activity'. The war against Iraq was the crime of aggression and the military were preparing for it. Their Lordships accepted that, ever since the Nuremberg Military Tribunal at the end of the Second World War, 'aggressive war' was a recognised crime in international law. However, it had never been made a crime in the domestic law of the UK, as only an Act of Parliament could do this. Anyway, this crime could only be committed by the leaders of a state, not by low-ranking service personnel. The decision to go to war and to conduct foreign policy was part of the prerogative power of the Crown, with which the courts would not interfere. The defendants were also guilty of criminal damage under **s. 1(1) of the Criminal Damage Act 1971**. This offence is not committed if the defendants have a 'lawful excuse', so they tried to argue the same defence as with aggravated trespass. They claimed that they were using reasonable force to prevent the crime of aggressive war from being committed. This too was rejected by the House of Lords for the same reasons. So it does not seem likely that Janet and Steve have any defence to the charges of aggravated trespass and criminal damage.

Janet destroyed the 'Stars and Stripes', but it is not a crime to destroy a flag, even the flag of the United Kingdom. In *Percy v DPP (2002) 166 JP 93*, Ms Percy performed a similar action at RAF Feltwell, by writing 'Stop Star Wars' across the US flag and standing on the flag. Five US service personnel gave evidence that this caused them distress, so Percy was charged under **s. 5 of the Public Order Act 1986**. The offence is that she used insulting words and behaviour likely to cause harassment, alarm or distress. On appeal, the court held that her right to freedom of expression, under **Article 10 of the European Convention**, outweighed any distress she might have caused. Janet could use a similar argument.

The police could use the ancient common law power to control a breach of the peace, to justify their dispersal of the demonstration. In another case involving Ms Percy, *Percy v DPP [1995] 1 WLR 1382*, breach of the peace had to involve violence or a threat of violence. This could include provoking others to violence, or as the court put it where violence from some third party was a natural consequence of her action. In that case Percy had repeatedly trespassed on a military base, but she had not committed a breach of the peace as highly trained military personnel were unlikely to respond to an unarmed trespasser with violence. So applying this case, it does not look like Janet has committed a breach of the peace.

According to older cases such as *Moss v McLachlan [1985] IRLR 76*, if a police officer honestly and reasonably considers that there is a real risk of a breach of the peace in close proximity both in place and time, then the officer may take reasonable measures to prevent the breach of the peace. This permitted a police road block in *Moss*. In *R (Laporte) v Chief Constable of Gloucestershire Constabulary [2007] 2 AC 105*, the police prevented three coachloads of demonstrators from joining an anti-Iraq war demonstration outside RAF Fairford in Gloucestershire. They were stopped at some distance from RAF Fairford and then conducted non-stop back to London. The House of Lords did not think that the police could reasonably apprehend that a breach of the peace was imminent. The protesters were nowhere near the protest site and there were plenty of police at Fairford to deal with any breach of the peace. This can be contrasted with the later Court of Appeal case, *Austin v Metropolitan Police Commissioner [2008] 1 All ER 564*, where there was a large May Day demonstration in London. The police confined around 3,000 people in Oxford Circus for seven hours, without toilet facilities or food and drink. Not all the persons detained were protestors. It was held that a breach of the peace was imminent and that these were extreme and exceptional circumstances as violence had occurred at previous May Day demonstrations. On appeal to the House of Lords, **[2009] 3 All ER 455**, it was argued that the police action infringed **Article 5**, the right to liberty. It was held that other rights had to be considered, such as the right to life of those threatened by mob violence. The police decision took into account the interests of the whole community, was taken in good faith and was proportionate and therefore not unlawful.

So, in conclusion, the police are probably justified in moving Janet and Steve away. They have committed the crimes of aggravated trespass and criminal damage and breach of the peace does include violence against property, not just people: *R v Howell* [1982] QB 416. Janet and Steve are inside the perimeter fence and can be easily separated from Margaret and the other protesters, which was not the case in *Austin v Metropolitan Police Commissioner* [2008] 1 All ER 564. Following *R (Laporte) v Chief Constable of Gloucestershire Constabulary* [2007] 2 AC 105, Margaret and the other demonstrators should be allowed to continue their peaceful protest. The European Court of Human Rights would agree that as long as a protest is peaceful the law should not forbid it: *Steel v UK* (1999) 28 HHRR 603.

Question 3

Article 11 of the European Convention on Human Rights refers to the right to freedom of peaceful assembly, subject to the imposition of lawful restraints on the exercise of that right. Consider whether citizens of the UK enjoy the right to peacefully assemble or whether the lawful restraints mean that such right exists only so far as the police in the exercise of their discretion allow it.

Discuss.

Commentary

For a number of reasons, this looks to be a fairly intimidating essay question! For a start it seems to cover what to many students would seem to be two quite separate topics, the European Convention on Human Rights and public order law. However, since the Human Rights Act 1998 came into force, on 2 October 2000, such questions will be seen as increasingly relevant. Whether the existing law measures up to human rights standards could be asked of several areas of constitutional law. Fortunately, there is plenty of material with which to answer this question. A critical account of the existing public order law would just about get by. Ask yourself the question, how much freedom to protest have we really got when all the various offences and police control powers are taken into account? There are also some cases, involving the UK, which the European Court of Human Rights has already decided. The issue of police discretion seems tricky, but has been dealt with in cases as old and as well-known as *Beatty v Gillbanks* (1882) 9 QBD 308. Structure and argument are everything in an essay like this. Do not just write down every case that you can remember and list all the offences in the Public Order Act 1986, but select the cases and offences that you want to discuss. Only use those that advance your argument, i.e., do they reveal a respect for peaceful protest or are they unnecessarily restrictive?

Freedom to Protest and Police Powers

Answer plan

- **Article 11 of the European Convention of Human Rights** declares that everyone has the right to freedom of peaceful assembly
- Protest must be peaceful
- Processions may be prohibited if there is a threat of violence
- Violence or the threat of violence is an essential constituent of breach of the peace
- Restrictions on the right to protest must be clearly prescribed by law
- Peaceful protest may allow obstruction of the highway
- The State has a duty to protect peaceful protest.

Suggested answer

Some have suggested that English law unduly hinders peaceful protest. Take, for example, the views of Lord Bingham in *R (Laporte) v Chief Constable of Gloucestershire Constabulary* [2007] 2 AC 105 at 126–7: 'The approach of the English common law to freedom of expression and assembly was hesitant and negative, permitting that which was not prohibited. Lord Hewart CJ reflected the then current orthodoxy when he observed in *Duncan v Jones* [1936] 1 KB 218 at 222 that "English law does not recognise any special right of public meeting for political or other purposes".'

The **1998 Act**, giving effect to **Articles 10 and 11 of the Convention**, represented what Sedley LJ in *Redmond-Bate v DPP* [2000] HRLR 249 at 256 aptly called a 'constitutional shift'. **Article 11.1 of the European Convention on Human Rights** states that: 'Everyone has the right to freedom of peaceful assembly . . . '. **Article 11.2** allows this right to be restricted, but the restrictions must be 'prescribed by law' and must meet one at least of the legitimate aims listed there such as, 'national security', 'public safety', 'the prevention of disorder or crime' or 'the protection of the rights and freedoms of others'. The restriction on the right to protest must also be justified as 'necessary in a democratic society'. In other words it must be genuinely designed to protect, for example, 'public safety', but must go no further than is necessary to achieve that purpose. This is known as 'proportionality'. **Article 10.1** states that 'Everyone has the right to freedom of expression. . . ' and there are similar restrictions on this right in **Article 10.2**. This essay aims to explore whether Sedley LJ is right, and whether English law does now guarantee a right of peaceful protest in accordance with the **European Convention**.

It is clear that any protest must be peaceful, as the European Commission held in *Christians against Racism and Fascism v United Kingdom* (1980) 21 DR 138 at 148: 'Disruption incidental to the holding of the assembly will not render it "unpeaceful", whereas a meeting planned with the object of causing disturbances will not be protected by Article 11.' Therefore there seems to be nothing objectionable to the offences in the Public Order Act 1986, for an essential element of riot, violent disorder and affray is that violence or threats of violence are used, so, by definition, they are not 'peaceful' actions. Even the 'threatening, abusive or insulting words or behaviour' in s. 4 must carry with them a threat of violence or at least provoke violence. Section 5, which merely requires the 'threatening, abusive or insulting words' etc. to be likely to cause 'harassment, alarm or distress' seems more suspect, as violence is not a constituent of the offence. In Chorherr v Austria (1993) 17 EHRR 358, however, the European Court of Human Rights held that a protest that caused annoyance or agitation was not protected by Article 11. Hence, s. 5 of the Public Order Act 1986 might well be acceptable.

Some have argued that it is an undue interference with public protest to prohibit processions, under what is now s. 13 of the Public Order Act 1986. This has, however, been considered acceptable under the European Convention, if there is a likelihood of violence in the area: *Christians against Racism and Fascism v United Kingdom* (above) and *Rai v United Kingdom* (1995) 82 ADR 134. Turning aside from the statutory provisions of the Public Order Act 1986, the ancient common law power to control a breach of the peace has often caused concern amongst civil libertarians. According to Lord Denning in *R v Chief Constable of Devon and Cornwall ex parte CEGB* [1982] QB 458, at 471: 'There was a breach of the peace whenever a person who was lawfully carrying out his work was unlawfully and physically prevented by another from doing it.' Other cases have preferred a tighter definition, which involve threats of harm or violence. This was expressed in *R v Howell (Erroll)* [1982] 2 QB 416 as 'an act done or threatened to be done which actually harms a person, or in his presence his property, or is likely to cause such harm or which puts someone in fear of such harm being done'. This was further explained in *Percy v DPP* [1995] 3 All ER 124, that to be conduct that was a breach of the peace, it had to involve violence, a threat of violence or carry a real risk that it would provoke violence in others.

The use of breach of the peace has been questioned three times in the European Court of Human Rights. Each time the Court has been satisfied that the restriction that breach of the peace makes upon the right to protest is 'prescribed by law'. In other words it is sufficiently well-defined for someone to be able to understand what it is they are forbidden to do. The Court has, however, preferred the definition in *Howell* and *Percy*, which stresses the need for violence to make the conduct unlawful, for 'peaceful assembly' is a right. On the facts though, the court has disapproved of the use of breach of the peace in some circumstances. In *Steel v United Kingdom* (1999) 28 EHRR 603, Ms Steel walked in front of a grouse shoot and Ms Lush stood in front of a JCB digger in order to hinder the building of the M11. This was an acceptable restriction upon their rights to protest as Ms

Steel might have been accidentally shot and Ms Lush might have provoked violence, so their protests were not peaceful. Ms Needham, Mr Polden and Mr Cole were conducting an entirely peaceful protest, outside a sale of 'fighter helicopters', when they were arrested. This was unacceptable under Article 11, Article 10, which guarantees freedom of expression and Article 5.1, which guarantees that no one will be deprived of their liberty unless they break the law. The three had not broken English law as they had not threatened or provoked any violence and so there was no breach of the peace. The use of anti-terrorism legislation powers of stop and search were also found to interfere with the right to protest in *Gillan & Quinton v UK* [2010] 50 EHRR 45.

In *McLeod v United Kingdom* (1999) 27 EHRR 493, the police had been present when Mr McLeod entered and removed items from his ex-wife's house, because they claimed that they feared a breach of the peace. The Court held that this was unjustified, as there was in fact little or no risk of disorder or crime occurring, as Mrs McLeod was not there at the time. This was a breach of Article 8, Mrs McLeod's right to respect for her home.

Finally, in *Hashman and Harrup v United Kingdom* (2000) 30 EHRR 241, hunt saboteurs were bound over to keep the peace. The words used by the English magistrates were to be of 'good behaviour'. The European Court of Human Rights found this to be unacceptable, because it did not tell the protesters what it was they were forbidden to do. It was particularly difficult for them to know, because they had not been convicted of or charged with any offence. Restrictions on the right to protest must be 'prescribed by law' and this lacked any clear definition.

The English courts have been moving tentatively towards accepting a right of peaceful protest on the public highway. Completely peaceful assemblies, protests and demonstrations have often fallen foul of s. 137 of the Highway Act 1980, because it is a criminal offence to obstruct the highway. Cases such as *Arrowsmith v Jenkins* [1963] 2 QB 562, have held that the only lawful use of the highway is for passage and repassage, so a public meeting in the street was an obstruction. Other cases, such as *Hirst v Chief Constable of West Yorkshire* (1987) 85 Cr App R 143, have taken a slightly more lenient line, that very minor protests, which cause no real obstruction, can be tolerated. Some judges have been willing to go further and find that a right of peaceful assembly on the highway might exist. The Lord Chancellor, Lord Irvine and Lord Hutton, gave tentative support for such an idea in *DPP v Jones* [1999] 2 All ER 257 and felt that, if necessary, the common law should develop in order to conform to Article 11. The House also accepted that the peaceful protest, of 21 people on the grass verge of the A344 at Stonehenge, was not only not an obstruction of the highway, but also not a trespassory assembly under the Criminal Justice and Public Order Act 1994. The English courts seem to be gradually getting into line with the rulings of the European Commission, in *Rassemblement Jurassien et unite*

Jurassiene v Switzerland (1979) 17 DR 93 and the European Court of Human Rights, in *Platform Arzte fur das Leben* (1988) 13 EHRR 204, where it was held that there is a *right* to hold meetings in public places. However, a permanent protest encampment on Parliament Square Gardens was not a proportionate use of the right to protest. It interfered with the rights of others to use the gardens and might lead to public health and crime problems: *Mayor of London v Hall* [2010] EWCA Civ 817.

The *Platform* case also made clear that the State does not merely have a duty to permit peaceful protest, in certain circumstances there may be a duty to protect peaceful protesters from those who would oppose them with violence. Even the English courts have occasionally endorsed this approach and asserted that the authorities should not merely take the easy way out and prevent those with an unpopular message from speaking, for fear of the possible reaction. In *Beatty v Gillbanks* (1882) 9 QBD 308, it was held that the Salvation Army should not be forbidden from marching through Weston-super-Mare, just because they might be opposed by the Skeleton Army. In a modern version of this case, the police were not permitted to stop women preaching from the steps of Wakefield Cathedral just because some of their audience were hostile: *Redmond-Bate v DPP* [2000] HRLR 249.

It might be apparent from the contrasting cases given above, that the police have many difficult decisions to make. Do they permit free speech or step in to prevent a possible outbreak of public disorder? The English courts have usually been most unwilling to interfere with police discretion. In *R v Chief Constable of Devon and Cornwall ex parte CEGB* [1982] QB 458, even though the Court of Appeal seemed confident that criminal offences were occurring, they were unwilling to instruct the police to act. Similarly, in *Re E (a child)* [2009] 1 All ER 467 the police were not obliged to stop a Protestant protest that was menacing Roman Catholic schoolchildren. *Article 11 of the European Convention on Human Rights* explicitly allows for the balancing of conflicting interests and, indeed, the few decisions of the European Court of Human Rights in this area do not seem any more willing to 'overrule' the decisions of the police than the English courts. Perhaps all the English courts need to do is to try and be a bit more consistent and not forget the basic principle that peaceful protest should be permitted.

Question 4

Jennifer has been arrested for allegedly committing an armed robbery. While being taken to the police station, she escapes from police custody and is pursued. She flees into Brian's house where she has a room. Brian refuses to let the police enter his house, but the police overcome his slight resistance and enter anyway. Jennifer is seized by the police in Brian's living room. The police search Jennifer and the living room but do not find anything.

Brian is asked by the police whether they can search Jennifer's rented room and he consents, even though Jennifer objects. While searching her room, the police find documents that seem to indicate her involvement in a financial fraud. The police ask Jennifer about these documents and she explains that her solicitor, Peter, deals with her business affairs and that they will have to ask him about the documents.

The police go to Peter's office with Jennifer and gain entry by claiming that they are delivering office equipment. Peter insists that they need a search warrant, but the police say that they do not as they have just arrested Jennifer. The police search the office and remove all the files relating to Jennifer's business affairs.

Jennifer, Brian and Peter seek your advice on the legality of the police conduct.
Advise Jennifer, Brian and Peter.

Commentary

Earlier in the chapter we have seen that it is accepted that people are allowed to protest and express their views. This has subtly changed from a liberty to a right since the **Human Rights Act 1998** and protest should now be allowed as long as it is not violent. There are, however, other liberties or freedoms that English law has long upheld. One is the idea that people should be secure in their own homes and that the authorities should not interfere with them there. This was expressed as long ago as the early seventeenth century in *Semayne's Case* **(1604) 77 Eng Rep 194**, at 195:

> That the house of everyone is to him as his castle and fortress, as well as for his defence against injury and violence, as for his repose . . .

If a police office or government official wants to gain entry to someone's home or other property, there must be some clear legal authority to permit this. This was the point of the famous case of **Entick v Carrington (1765) 19 St Tr 1030**: no official could enter and search the home of Entick, unless the official could clearly point to an Act of Parliament or case that authorised this. Similarly, the law would clearly identify the correct procedure for an official to gain entry as seen in *Semayne's Case* **(1604) 77 Eng Rep 194, at 195**: 'But before he breaks it, he ought to signify the cause of his coming, and to make request to open doors.'

This approach can only be reinforced by the rights guaranteed by the **European Convention on Human Rights. Article 8** provides a 'right to respect for his private and family life, his home and his correspondence' and **Article 1 of the First Protocol** concerns the protection of property. As far as personal liberty is concerned, **Article 5** states that 'Everyone has the right to liberty and security of person.'

So when we look at the problem question above, we must be sure that the police actually have the legal power to do what they have done and that they have followed the correct procedures. This can be ascertained by knowledge of the major statute on police powers, the **Police and**

Criminal Evidence Act 1984. This gives the police the power to arrest and search and lays down sometimes quite complicated procedures. There is also a considerable case law on what these powers actually mean in practice. These cases make an answer both much more interesting to write and to read and some have entertaining and interesting facts. Pick your favourite examples, as there is usually more than one case on every point. A convoluted problem like this is best approached line by line and you should try to identify each legal point and be prepared to comment upon it. Is this legal? Which power are the police likely to be using here? Are our facts similar to any reported case? Then gradually you should be able to construct your answer step by step and come to a conclusion.

Answer plan

- Arrest upon reasonable suspicion
- Informing the suspect of their arrest
- **Section 17 PACE 1984** entry and search
- Consent to search of premises
- **Section 32 PACE 1984** search of premises where a person is arrested
- **Section 18 PACE 1984** search of premises occupied and controlled by the person arrested
- **Section 19 PACE 1984** lawful entry and seizure of evidence of an offence
- Search warrants.

Suggested answer

We must first consider whether Jennifer has been lawfully arrested and then go on to consider the various powers that the police have to enter private premises and to search those premises. Most of those powers of entry and search depend upon whether a person has been arrested, so the first question to ask is whether Jennifer has been lawfully arrested.

No warrant has been issued for the arrest of Jennifer, so we must consider the powers that the police possess to arrest without warrant. Under **s. 24 of the Police and Criminal Evidence Act 1984** a police constable may arrest anyone who is guilty of an offence or anyone whom he has reasonable grounds to suspect of being guilty of an offence. Previously, these arrest powers only applied to 'arrestable offences', but they were extended by the **Serious Organised Crime and Police Act 2005** to include all offences. 'Suspicion' was defined by Lord Devlin in *Shaaban Bin Hussien v Chong Fook Kam* [1970] AC 942, at 948 as 'a state of conjecture or surmise where proof is lacking . . . I suspect but I cannot prove'. It would seem that the police have reasonable grounds for suspecting Jennifer, for she has escaped from police custody, which is a crime, and allegedly committed armed robbery, for which they could re-arrest her.

Blackstone defined arrest as 'the apprehending or restraining of one's person in order to be forthcoming to answer an alleged or suspected crime' (Blackstone's *Commentaries* p. 289). The old case of *Genner v Sparks* (1705) 6 Mod Rep 173, which also involved the recapture of a fugitive, requires that their must be some touching or seizure of the person. This seems to have occurred. The police must also tell the person that they are under arrest and the reasons for the arrest: s. 28 Police and Criminal Evidence Act 1984 and *Christie v Leachinsky* [1947] AC 573. The explanation must be in simple, non-technical language that the arrested person can understand, as explained in *Taylor v Thames Valley Chief Constable* [2004] 3 All ER 503, where a 10-year-old boy was arrested. It appears that Jennifer has been told nothing, but it appears from the case law that she can be told later. This might be because it was impracticable to tell her at the time, say if she was resisting arrest or trying to escape again: *DPP v Hawkins* [1988] 3 All ER 673. Even if there was no particular reason to delay, if she is told the reasons, for example when she is taken to the police station, then the failure to inform her when first arrested will not make the subsequent police actions unlawful: *Lewis v Chief Constable of South Wales* [1991] 1 All ER 206.

As seen from the Blackstone quotation above, the original purpose of arrest was to secure the suspect so that they could be taken before a court. Nowadays the police often arrest so that they can investigate the offence and question the suspect at the police station. This is perfectly acceptable, according to the House of Lords in *Holgate-Mohammed v Duke* [1984] AC 437.

A more contentious issue is that the police appear to have forced entry to Brian's house, without a warrant and without his permission. Section 17(1)(d) of the Police and Criminal Evidence Act 1984 allows a constable to enter and search for the purpose 'of recapturing a person who is unlawfully at large and whom he is pursuing'. This was possibly allowed by *Genner v Sparks* (1705) 6 Mod Rep 173 mentioned above, but the 1984 Act makes clear that the police can enter Brian's house as long as it is a genuine and continuous pursuit. In *D'Souza v DPP* [1992] 4 All ER 545 a woman was absent without leave from a psychiatric hospital and had returned home. The police could not force entry, but had to obtain a warrant, as they had not pursued her from the hospital. The police here seem to be in pursuit of Jennifer and it does not matter that it is not her house: *Kynaston v DPP* (1987) 84 Cr App R 200. According to s. 117 of the Police and Criminal Evidence Act 1984 the police may use 'reasonable force, if necessary' when exercising their powers under the Act; so pushing their way past Brian, if that is what they did, is not unlawful.

Once they have gained entry the police commence to search the house. Under s. 17(4) of the Police and Criminal Evidence Act 1984 the police may only search 'to the extent that is reasonably required for the purpose for which the power of entry is exercised'. In other words they can search for Jennifer, but for nothing else under this section. They have, however, already found her, so does Brian's consent make their further searching lawful? This is not dealt with in the sections of the Police and Criminal Evidence Act 1984, because it has been clear, at least since the great case of Entick v Carrington (1765) 19 St Tr 1030, at 1066, that if the owner or occupier consents to another entering, it cannot be unlawful:

> . . . every invasion of private property, be it ever so minute, is a trespass. No man can set foot upon my ground without my licence, but he is liable to an action though the damage be nothing.

Under the Codes of Practice that accompany the Police and Criminal Evidence Act 1984, the police should obtain Brian's consent in writing. Again, according to the Codes, Brian is unable to consent to the search of a room that is occupied by Jennifer, not him. The fact that the provisions of the Codes have been infringed does not necessarily render the search unlawful. Under s. 67(11) of the Act breach of the Codes of Practice is just something that 'shall be taken into account' in any subsequent proceedings.

Even if there are doubts about the validity of the consent of Brian, the police have other powers to search under the Police and Criminal Evidence Act 1984. Section 32 allows a constable to search the arrested person, but it also allows the police to use s. 32(2)(b) and 'to enter and search any premises in which he was when arrested or immediately before he was arrested for evidence relating to the offence for which he was arrested'. There is some doubt about whether the police can use this power to arrest a person and then, later, return and search the site of arrest (McLorie v Oxford [1982] QB 1290), but here the search is contemporaneous. It would seem reasonable for the police to assume that there could be further evidence of an armed robbery at the suspect's home. The permitted search is not unlimited, because s. 32(3) of the Act only allows 'search to the extent that is reasonably required for the purpose of discovering. . . any such evidence'.

In addition the police have powers to search the home of a person that they have arrested, under s. 18 of the Police and Criminal Evidence Act 1984. They can either search when they arrest the person or return later. Entry and search is permitted if the constable 'has reasonable grounds for suspecting that there is on the premises evidence' of that offence or a connected or similar offence. The police cannot use the section to go on a general 'fishing expedition' to search and see whether they can find evidence of an offence, any offence, as illustrated in Jeffrey v Black [1978] QB 490. The defendant was arrested for the theft of a sandwich from a public house, but the police searched his house and found illegal drugs. This was an unlawful search as there were no reasonable grounds for the police to suspect that there would be evidence of further sandwich theft at his home. It would seem reasonable, however, to suspect that there could be further evidence of Jennifer's armed robbery at her home. There is a further trap for the unwary police officer in s. 18. They can only 'search premises occupied or controlled' by the arrested person and Khan v Commissioner of Police of the

Metropolis [2008] EWCA Civ 723 stresses that this is actual occupation or control by the arrested person. It is not enough for the police to reasonably suspect that the person lives there, they must actually do so. Fortunately, for the police, Jennifer does.

The police find documents that they suspect indicate involvement in a financial fraud, while they are searching for something else, evidence of an armed robbery. It is legal to seize evidence of a crime, when the police are lawfully on the premises, according to Lord Denning in *Ghani v Jones* [1970] 1 QB 693. This is confirmed by **s. 19 of the Police and Criminal Evidence Act 1984**, the 'General power of seizure'. When a constable is lawfully on any premises, he may seize anything that he has reasonable grounds for believing is evidence of any offence. It does not have to be evidence of the offence that he is investigating. If the police suspicions are reasonable, they may take Jennifer's documents.

The search of the solicitor's office is illegal. The police should have obtained a search warrant under **s. 8 of the Police and Criminal Evidence Act 1984**. As indicated by the recent case of *Redknapp v Commissioner of the City of London Police* [2009] 1 All ER 229, the police must follow the correct procedure to apply for the warrant, including practical details such as including the correct address. Jennifer's business records would be held in confidence by the solicitor, so they would be regarded as 'special procedure material' under **s. 14** of the Act. The police should apply to a circuit judge, who could issue a Production Order to the solicitor, if the judge agreed that it was likely to be evidence of substantial value to the investigation. A search warrant would only be issued as a last resort, if it seemed that Peter was not likely to comply. Gaining entry to Peter's office by a subterfuge is not necessarily unlawful, because in *R v Longman* [1988] 1 WLR 619 the police pretended to be delivering flowers from Interflora in order to gain entry. In that case, however, the police did actually have a warrant, which they produced upon entry.

Surprisingly, it is not unlawful to search a solicitor's office, but the police are not permitted to search for legally privileged material. This is defined in **s. 10 of the Police and Criminal Evidence Act 1984** as legal advice to a client or material connected with legal proceedings. Jennifer's business documents do not seem to be legally privileged and are not protected from search (*R v Crown Court at Northampton ex parte DPP* (1991) 93 Cr App R 376), but the police do need a warrant, which they have not got.

So, in conclusion, Jennifer has little to complain about, as the police had the legal power to search under **ss. 18 and 32** at the least. Her arrest was probably lawful, though the procedure followed leaves a little bit to be desired. The search of Peter's office was unlawful, as the police needed a search warrant or Peter's permission, which they did not obtain. Peter could make an official complaint about the police or sue them for trespass, as suggested in *Entick v Carrington* (1765) 19 St Tr 1030.

Further reading

Barnett, H. *Constitutional and Administrative Law*, 8th edn (Routledge, 2011), chs. 20 and 21.

Bradley, A. and Ewing, K. *Constitutional and Administrative Law*, 15th edn (Longman, 2010), chs. 24 and 21.

Bailey, S. and Taylor, N. *Bailey, Harris and Jones: Civil Liberties, Cases, Materials and Commentary*, 6th edn (Oxford University Press, 2009) chs. 5 and 4.

10

Freedom of Expression

Introduction

Freedom of speech is one of the most important civil liberties in a democratic society. It enables citizens to say or write what they like. This could include criticism of the government or other powerful institutions and discussion of alternative policies. Without free and open debate it is difficult to see how a democratic system could work.

In English law, freedom of speech is traditionally a civil liberty and not a right so we need to study the various laws that restrict free speech. One can say or write whatever one likes unless there is a law against it. Unfortunately there are a lot of laws that may need to be considered. The main areas would be obscenity, official secrets, breach of confidence and contempt of court. Other relevant laws might be incitement to racial hatred, sedition, incitement to disaffection, incitement to racial and religious hatred and civil and criminal defamation. Different public law courses will have different emphases and may concentrate on only some areas. Read the syllabus and listen to what your lecturers and tutors are telling you! If this does not work, a study of past examination papers should usually give you a clear idea of the areas that are required study.

Different lecturers will often have very different ideas of what should be studied. A traditional concern was the freedom of expression of writers and artists. This was reflected in the 'reform' of the law in the **Obscene Publications Act 1959**. A more modern way of looking at this area might be to assume that the battle for artistic freedom was won back in the 1960s and 1970s and that the worry now might be whether there is sufficient control over 'extreme pornographic images' as defined in the **Criminal Justice and Immigration Act 2008**. A topical concern here might be paedophilia and as well as the above laws there might be a consideration of the **Protection of Children Act 1978**.

Yet again there has been recent concern over the government's control over official information. Here one would look at not just the **Official Secrets Acts** but also the **Public Record Acts**, breach of confidence and the Spycatcher trials. The convention of ministerial responsibility can also play a role in controlling the flow of information. See **Chapter 3**, Prime Minister and Cabinet and the *Scott Report of the Inquiry into the*

Export of Defence Equipment and Dual-use Goods to Iraq and Related Prosecutions. When John Major became Prime Minister he announced that he was in favour of open government and a White Paper of this name was issued in 1993 (Cm 2290). This scheme relied on voluntary disclosure, but the Labour government, elected in 1997, promised a legally binding Freedom of Information Act, which was enacted in 2000.

The Human Rights Act 1998 came into force in 2000, meaning that the courts of Britain had to take account of the European Convention on Human Rights, when establishing the meaning of case law and interpreting Acts of Parliament. Article 10 guarantees a right to freedom of expression. Even before 2000, English courts had been considering Article 10, in their attempts to make sense of conflicting case law in the various areas of law that affect freedom of expression. Examples would include *Derbyshire v The Times* [1993] AC 534, which concerned libel and *A-G v Observer, The Times (Spycatcher)* [1990] AC 109, which involved the equitable doctrine of breach of confidence. The general tendency has been to conclude that English case law usually conforms to the demands of Article 10. There has also been a slight change, in favour of liberalising the law to uphold freedom of expression, but the Human Rights Act has not yet produced major changes in favour of freedom of expression. For example, *The Times* tried to claim that it would be in the public interest, for them to be able to discuss the conduct of politicians and be protected from libel actions. The House of Lords rejected this in *Reynolds v Times Newspapers* [2001] 2 AC 127, but did say that responsible journalism should be protected from libel actions. On the other hand, the courts have developed breach of confidence to protect the private life of celebrities in *Campbell v Mirror Group Newspapers* [2004] 2 AC 457 and *Douglas v Hello!* [2002] 1 FCR 289, among other cases.

The common law offences of blasphemy and blasphemous libel had been criticised for only protecting Christianity and no other religion or for being an unnecessary restraint upon freedom of expression when people follow a variety of religions or no religion at all. Blasphemy was abolished by the Criminal Justice and Immigration Act 2008 and replaced by an offence of incitement to religious hatred in the Racial and Religious Hatred Act 2006.

It is unlikely, nowadays, that any constitutional and administrative law course would attempt to cover all of the possible aspects of freedom of expression. So our suggested answers only try to cover the main and, we hope, most likely areas.

Question 1

Humbert, who lives in Alphaville, is interested in computing and child pornography. He obtains from his computer images of young children engaged in sexual activity. These he prints out and exchanges with his friends. He also exchanges DVD recordings dealing with similar subject matter. He is arrested by the police and prosecuted.

In his defence, he wishes to argue that his sexual desires are incurable and that looking at such pictures is beneficial in that it satisfies those desires. He also wishes to argue that some of the computer images are of artistic merit. Eminent psychiatrists and art experts are willing to give evidence on his behalf.

Two days before his trial, the local newspaper, *The Alphaville Record* publishes an article under the headline, 'Hanging is Too Good for Humbert' and reveals that he has previously been convicted for sexual offences. The editor defends publication as in the public interest.

Advise Humbert and the editor of *The Alphaville Record*.

Commentary

This is a fairly typical problem designed to raise most of the main issues on obscenity law. The cases are interesting in themselves and fairly easy to remember. All that is needed is to apply them to the facts. In common with many questions on obscenity the student would also be expected to know about other laws that cover roughly the same area. There are quite a number of them and it is hard to predict which ones would come up in a particular question. So it is best to have a general idea of most of these laws. The examples here are the **Protection of Children Act 1978**, the **Video Recordings Act 2010** and conspiracy to corrupt public morals.

Another common tactic is to expect students to be aware of fairly obscure changes in the law, here those made in the **Criminal Justice and Public Order Act 1994** will need to be mentioned.

It is hard to make a problem question about obscenity long enough, so it is not unusual to include another area of law in the question. Here it is contempt of court. Again it would be hard to devise a full problem question on contempt. There are only so many points that could be raised.

Answer plan

- Obscenity is a tendency to deprave and corrupt
- Those who are likely to read, hear or see the 'obscene' article
- Expert evidence on artistic merit is allowed
- Extreme pornographic images
- Offence to possess indecent electronic data
- Freedom of expression can be restricted for the protection of morals
- Contempt is a substantial risk that the course of justice will be impeded or prejudiced
- A discussion in good faith of public affairs is not contempt.

Suggested answer

The first offence that springs to mind is that Humbert might have contravened the **Obscene Publications Act 1959. Section 1** makes it an offence to publish an obscene article.

Publishing includes any form of distribution. It is not necessary to show that Humbert did this for gain, for distributing or circulating is enough according to the Act. Even if this was not the case, an 'exchange' might well be held to be for gain. Whether obscene material stored on a computer was an 'article' was open to doubt until the Criminal Justice and Public Order Act 1994 (s. 168 and sch. 9, para. 3) made it clear that the transmission of electronically stored data was covered by the 1959 Act.

The test for obscenity is set out in s. 1 of the Obscene Publications Act 1959. It is that the article is obscene 'if its effect . . . is, if taken as a whole, such as to tend to deprave and corrupt persons who are likely, having regard to all relevant circumstances, to read, hear or see' it. This test has eluded precise definition. *R v Secker and Warburg* [1954] 2 All ER 683 stated that the material being merely shocking and disgusting was not enough. The famous, though unreported, case concerning the book, *Lady Chatterley's Lover* in 1960 suggested that it meant 'to make morally bad, to pervert, debase or corrupt morally'. The old case, *R v Hicklin* (1868) LR 3 QB 360 mentioned 'exciting impure or libidinous thoughts'. It is not necessary to show that anyone was actually depraved or corrupted, merely that the material has that tendency.

The statutory definition above also demands that the likely audience is taken into account. If it is children, obscenity is more likely to be proved: *DPP v A & BC Chewing Gum* [1968] 1 QB 519 and *R v Anderson* [1972] 1 QB 304. Here though, although the material concerned children, they are most unlikely to be the 'target' audience. This is likely to be adults. Humbert cannot argue that they are likely already to be paedophiles and so incapable of further corruption. The argument that the 'audience' for pornography is already corrupt has not succeeded: *R v Anderson* [1972] 1 QB 304; *DPP v Whyte* [1972] AC 849.

The vague definition of obscenity may not be a problem. The jury will decide. Expert evidence is not permitted to help them on this issue unless the type of obscene material is outside the normal experience of adults. Expert evidence was allowed upon the effects of cocaine in *R v Skirving* [1985] QB 819 and the effects of horrific pictures upon children in *DPP v A & BC Chewing Gum* (ibid). There seems no justification for this type of expert evidence in this case, as the 'target audience' for the material are adults.

Section 4 of the 1959 Act does, however, permit expert evidence upon 'artistic merit' (*R v Anderson*; *Lady Chatterley* (above)). If the material can be shown to be for the 'public good' it is not obscene. The jury decide first whether material is obscene and then, if it is, whether considerations of public good outweigh this and if publication is desirable. More general arguments and evidence that pornographic material has therapeutic effects has never been permitted: *DPP v Jordan* [1977] AC 699 and *A-G's Reference (No. 3 of 1977)* [1978] 3 All ER 1166.

On balance it seems that Humbert's computer images and DVDs will be judged to be obscene. If this is not so, there are other offences that could be considered.

Humbert's pictures are unlikely to be regarded as 'extreme pornographic images' under s. 63 of the Criminal Justice and Immigration Act 2008 as we are not told that they involve violence, corpses or animals. Mere possession of an 'indecent' photograph is an offence under the Protection of Children Act 1978. The prosecution must prove that Humbert had 'knowledge' of what he possesses, but on the facts here that does not seem too difficult: *Atkins v DPP* [2000] 2 All ER 425. Section 84, Criminal Justice and Public Order Act 1994 makes very clear that 'photographs' include both the electronic data and the print-out. Even if he had deleted the images from his computer, if he had the necessary skill to recover them, he would still be guilty: *R v Porter* [2006] 1 WLR 2633. There is no defence of the public good for this offence nor for the common law offence of 'conspiracy to corrupt public morals': *Shaw v DPP* [1962] AC 220. Paedophile 'rings' have been dealt with under this offence. Lastly it is highly unlikely that Humbert's DVDs have been given a classification under the Video Recordings Act 2010 by the British Board of Film Classification. This is particularly so, since the Board was urged to have 'special regard' to DVDs dealing with 'human sexual activity' in s. 90 of the Criminal Justice and Public Order Act 1994. It is a criminal offence merely to supply such a video, punishable by imprisonment. The Video Recordings Act 1984 had to be re-enacted in 2010, because the original Act had never complied with European Community law, but even if Humbert's offence was committed before 2010, he will have no defence: *R v Budimir* [2010] 2 Cr App R 29.

The Human Rights Act 1998 may not help him very much. Under s. 2, a British court must 'take into account' decisions of the European Court of Human Rights. This Court has consistently allowed contracting States a 'margin of appreciation' in the area of obscenity law, because they cannot find an agreed European standard of morals in the domestic law of these States. So the Court has refused to say that obscenity laws infringed the Article 10 right to freedom of expression in both *Handysides v UK* (1976) 1 EHRR 737 and *Muller v Switzerland* (1991) 13 EHRR 212.

The Alphaville Record is almost certainly guilty of contempt of court. Under s. 2(2) of the Contempt of Court Act 1981 there needs to be a 'substantial risk that the course of justice will be seriously impeded or prejudiced'. The publication of previous convictions has long been held to be contempt: *R v Odhams Press* [1957] 1 QB 73. The proceedings are clearly 'active' because Humbert has been arrested (s. 2(3)).

There is a defence under s. 5 that the risk of prejudice is purely incidental to 'a discussion in good faith of public affairs'. A passing mention in a newspaper article about a forthcoming trial might benefit from this section: *A-G v English* [1983] 1 AC 116. Here, though, the main purpose of the article seems to be to discuss Humbert, his trial and his previous convictions. It is a clear contempt. The Contempt of Court Act 1981 was enacted to bring English law into line with the European Convention on Human Rights, following Britain's defeat in *Sunday

Times v United Kingdom (1979) 2 EHRR 245. *R v Sherwood ex parte The Telegraph Group* [2001] I WLR 1983, confirms that contempt laws are necessary to guarantee a fair trial under Article 6.

Indeed, it could be argued that the editor obviously knows about the trial and is deliberately trying to interfere with the administration of justice. This intentional contempt is not covered by the Act (s. 6), but remains as a common law offence: *A-G v Hislop* [1991] 2 WLR 219. It would be treated most seriously by the courts if, as would be likely here, the Attorney-General brought a prosecution against the editor.

In conclusion both Humbert and the editor face conviction. In a strange way the contempt might help Humbert. If convicted, he might be able to appeal successfully on the grounds that the contempt meant that he did not receive a fair trial: *R v Taylor* (1993) 98 Cr App R 361.

Question 2

Jane is a civil servant working for the Ministry of Defence. Because of the nature of her work she signed the Official Secrets Act on commencing her employment. During the course of her work Jane comes across a document indicating that a British company is selling artillery shells to the government of Fantasia. She knows that this is contrary to British law and contrary to the stated policy of Her Majesty's government. Jane asks a more senior civil servant what she should do. He tells her that the Secretary of State for Defence knows all about it but the matter is to be kept secret.

Jane is still concerned that the law is being broken so she hands over a copy of the document to a journalist who works for the *Sentinel* newspaper. That journalist discovers that there is a DA-notice relating to arms sales to Fantasia. He and his editor decide to publish the document anyway.

The government learns about the proposed publication and wants to stop it. It also wishes to punish the parties responsible.

Advise the government.

Commentary

The problem with this sort of question is that at first glance it might seem unclear which area of constitutional law is relevant. The inspiration for the question is the 'Arms to Iraq' scandal, but it is not about the main concerns there of ministerial accountability and public interest immunity. Reading the rubric carefully, what you are actually asked to do with the facts given, is often helpful. Here it tells you that we are looking at the laws protecting government information.

Freedom of Expression

The **Official Secrets Act** should immediately spring to mind, but so should breach of confidence, even though it is now some years since the Spycatcher trials. As will be seen from the suggested answer there are a few other bits and pieces of law that come in handy for questions like this.

Although this is a problem question, this sort of area is more often examined by means of an essay. The same material could be 'recycled' to answer an essay. With an essay, though, you would be expected to be critical rather than analytical as with a problem.

Answer plan

- Communicating to an enemy information that is prejudicial to the safety and interests of the State
- Disclosure of defence information that is damaging to British defence
- Disclosure of information relating to international relations that is damaging to British international relations
- Knowing receipt of such information
- The document belongs to the government
- Damages can be recovered for breach of contract
- Breach of confidence can be restrained to protect national security.

Suggested answer

The most obvious avenues for the government to explore are the **Official Secrets Acts 1911 and 1989**, but there are other possibilities. A civil action, perhaps for breach of confidence, might be possible and as Jane remains a civil servant, she is subject to Civil Service discipline.

Jane has signed the **Official Secrets Act**. This is a common procedure, but has no legal effect. All it does is warn her that she is in the sort of job that may be subject to the Act. Despite the reforms of 1989, **s. 1 of the Official Secrets Act 1911** remains in force. Breach of this is a serious offence and can be committed by communicating to an enemy information that may be 'prejudicial to the safety and interests of the State'. Jane might well argue that she has not communicated to an enemy and that her actions are not 'prejudicial to the safety and interests of the State'. *Chandler v DPP* **[1964] AC 763** indicates that only the government can decide what is in the interests of the State. In *R v Ponting* **[1985] Crim LR 318** Clive Ponting, another civil servant, tried to argue that he was helping the State by revealing to an MP information that ministers were hiding from Parliament. This is the 'whistle-blower' argument: he had a duty to expose wrongdoing. In *Ponting* the court ruled that this argument was unacceptable, for, as in *Chandler*, only the government of the day could rule on what was 'in the interests of the State'. Despite the ruling the jury acquitted Ponting. For this reason, it is unlikely that the government would use **s. 1** against Jane or the journalist, who would also be liable.

The old **s. 2 of the 1911 Act** was replaced by the **Official Secrets Act 1989**. The Act is meant to focus only on those areas where the Crown is genuinely concerned with the revelation of official information. **Section 1** warns Crown servants, such as Jane, that she must not reveal information acquired during her work if it relates to the security or intelligence services. Her revelation would not seem to affect security or intelligence, but it might affect defence. Under **s. 2** it is an offence to disclose 'defence' information. 'Defence', as defined in **s. 2(4)(b)**, includes 'weapons' but only those used by the Armed Forces of the Crown. Foreign Armed Forces are not included. Maybe it is possible that foreign weapon sales come under **subsection (d)**, the more general 'defence policy'. Not only this but the prosecution must prove that disclosure of information is 'damaging' to British defence. It is difficult to see how this could be so. Damage to British interests abroad is also mentioned in **s. 2** and might be easier to prove on our facts. There is also a 'did not know' defence in **s. 2(3)** of the Act, which was considered in *R v Keogh* [2007] 1 WLR 1500 together with a similar defence in **s. 3(4)**. Read literally, the subsections seem to reverse the burden of proof and require Jane to prove that she did not know that it was defence information and did not know that it was damaging to reveal it. The Court of Appeal held that this was incompatible with the presumption of innocence in **Article 6 of the European Convention on Human Rights**. It would be up to the prosecution to prove that Jane knew that it was defence information and that it would be damaging to reveal it. Another government possibility is **s. 3** of the Act, which protects information relating to 'international relations' in a similar way. Conceivably arms sales to a foreign country might well be connected to foreign policy matters. Again the prosecution would have to prove that Jane knew that the information was damaging to international relations.

Chandler v DPP (above) suggests that the courts would accept the government's view upon what was 'defence', 'international relations' or 'the interests of the United Kingdom abroad'. It was hoped that the courts would take a more liberal line under the **1989 Act** and allow defendants, such as Jane, to put forward their own evidence on what was damaging to the country's defence or international relations. In *R v Shayler* [2003] 1 AC 247, however, the defendant claimed that he had tried to reveal the wrongdoings of the security services and that this was in the public and national interest. He also argued that the **Official Secrets Act 1989** was incompatible with **Article 10 of the European Convention of Human Rights**, because it infringed his right to freedom of expression. The House of Lords did not agree. They followed decisions of the European Court of Human Rights, where the needs of 'national security' were deemed to outweigh freedom of expression: *Engel v Netherlands (No. 1)* (1976) 1 EHRR 647 and *Klass v Germany* (1978) 2 EHRR 214.

Shayler's 'whistle-blower' argument also fell on stony ground. *R v Ponting* [1985] Crim LR 318 had stated that a civil servant, concerned about wrongdoing, should report their worries to their superiors, not the press. The House of Lords suggested that Shayler should have told his Secretary of State. A minister may authorise the disclosure of 'secrets' under s. 7 of the 1989 Act. It seems, on these precedents, that Jane's best hope would be to use *R v Keogh* [2007] 1 WLR 1500 and argue a defence that she did not know that the information that she revealed would be damaging, but instead hoped that her revelation of wrongdoing would be for the benefit of the country.

The journalist too, commits an offence if he knowingly receives the information and knowingly passes it on (s. 5). This the *Sentinel* newspaper seems determined to do. It is necessary, however, for the information to contravene the foregoing provisions of the Act for this to be an offence. As we have seen, it is by no means clear that it is 'defence' or 'international relations' information. The journalist also has a 'not damaging' defence.

Under s. 8 it is a specific offence for a Crown servant like Jane to retain the actual document 'contrary to her official duty'. Again, though, for the offence to be committed it has to relate to 'defence' or 'international relations'.

The government has other measures that it could utilise against Jane. The 'Defence Advisory notice' is just a non-statutory warning issued by a committee of members of the media, civil servants and the military, known as the Defence, Press and Broadcasting Advisory Committee. It advises the media not to publish information relating to certain military and intelligence matters. It is not an offence to ignore the notice, but it acts as a warning that publication might infringe the law. Civil injunctions can be sought to prevent breach of the Official Secrets Act, as occurred in the Zircon Affair of 1986–7. As such an injunction would probably be issued ex parte, the government might be successful in obtaining it. The court would await the full trial before looking into the finer legal points.

There is possibly a very simple way to recover the document. The document and copies of it are personal property that belong to the government. It could simply sue in tort for its return. In *Secretary of State for Defence v Guardian Newspapers* [1984] Ch 156. Sarah Tisdall, a civil servant, had handed a document about cruise missiles to *The Guardian* newspaper. Section 10 of the Contempt of Court Act 1981 allows a journalist to protect his sources, but not if it is an issue of national security. This might well be such an issue and the document's return would be ordered. Although it is in the discretion of the court, journalists are usually ordered to reveal their sources: *Ashworth Security Hospital v Mirror Group Newspaper Ltd* [2004] 4 All ER 1. The European Court of Human Rights might be more inclined to protect a journalist, in a commercial case, but probably not if there were national security implications: *Financial Times v UK* (2010) 50 EHRR 46.

Jane, as a civil servant, would be subject to dismissal for breach of contract. If the newspaper paid her, the fee could be recovered as damages according to *A-G v Blake* [2001] 1 AC 268.

The most flexible remedy that the government has, is to seek an injunction for breach of confidence. It is clear that Jane has an obligation of confidence as a civil servant. The government would need to show that it was in the public interest to prevent disclosure: *A-G v The Observer, The Times (Spycatcher)* [1990] 1 AC 109. Damage to the security services was the reason for non-disclosure in that case. Here, though, Jane, wishes to reveal breaches of the law. It is permissible to reveal criminal wrongdoing, even if it is a breach of confidence: *Cork v McVicar* (1984) Times, 31 October. The court did not extend this approach to the revelation of government wrongdoing in *Attorney-General v The Observer, The Times* [1990] AC 109 and advised a civil servant, such as Jane, to report their worries to their superiors and not the press.

It is possible though, that the entry into force of the Human Rights Act 1998 might help Jane. Decisions of the European Court of Human Rights have emphasised the importance of freedom of expression. Although the Court found the law on breach of confidence acceptable in *Observer v UK* (1991) 14 EHRR 153, they thought that the 'Spycatcher' injunction should have been lifted earlier, as the material was already in the public domain. Now, under s. 12 of the Human Rights Act 1998, the courts of the UK must have special regard to freedom of expression. In *Attorney-General v The Times* [2001] 1 WLR 885 the newspaper was about to publish extracts from a book by Tomlinson, a former MI6 officer. The court allowed this as the material had already been published elsewhere. It was up to the government to prove that there was a need to restrict freedom of expression 'in the interests of national security'. The newspaper did not have to prove that the material was already in the public domain, the government had to prove that it was not.

Jane's problem is that her material is not already in the public domain. I would suggest that the court is more likely to follow the approach in *Shayler* (above) and issue an injunction to protect national security. The *Sentinel* would also be injuncted and all other newspapers that could reasonably be expected to know about the injunction would also be bound as happened when *Punch* magazine published some of the *Shayler* material in *Attorney-General v Punch Ltd* [2003] 1 All ER 289. So, in conclusion, Jane risks conviction under the Official Secrets Act 1989, damages for breach of contract and an injunction forbidding her disclosures. The Human Rights Act 1998 does not seem to have allayed the courts' fears about endangering national security.

Question 3

In a democracy, people should have information about the workings of government. Without it, they cannot call their representatives to account and make informed use of their rights as citizens and electors.

(Cm 7285 White Paper on reform of the Official Secrets Act 1911)

> Consider whether a Freedom of Information Act would give people more information about the workings of government.

Commentary

The 1997 Labour government promised a Freedom of Information Act in their election manifesto. This was the culmination of a long-running campaign to introduce such legislation, which already existed in other countries. The question itself is perfectly straightforward; would a Freedom of Information Act be a good thing?

The **Freedom of Information Act 2000** finally became law after making very slow progress through Parliament. It was not until late in 2005 that it finally came fully into force. Campaigners for freedom of information want more rights of access to information than any government, of any political persuasion, is likely to concede. The Act has been much criticised, particularly because of the large number of exemptions to the right of information contained within it and, also, because of the considerable powers that the government has retained to decide what those exemptions should be. Therein lies valuable material for your essay! The suggested answer below is slightly more ambitious, in that it attempts to set a Freedom of Information Act in the context of the various powers that the government has to control the flow of information. Here you could show your knowledge of legislation such as the **Official Secrets Acts**, which you might have revised or studied anyway. Another possibility would be to try and compare the British Act with similar legislation in other countries. That would, however, require a reasonably detailed knowledge of that foreign legislation.

Answer plan

- The **Public Records Acts** allow the release of some government documents
- The **Official Secrets Act 1911** prevents the release of information for a purpose prejudicial to the safety and interests of the State
- The **Official Secrets Act 1989** protects information relating to security and intelligence, defence, international relations and criminal investigations
- Breach of confidence protects government information
- A voluntary Code of Practice promoted the release of government information
- The **Freedom of Information Act 2000** requires public authorities to publish information
- The public may request information from a public authority
- But there are many exemptions
- Government ministers have a strong role in exempting information
- Appeal to the Information Commissioner.

Suggested answer

The Home Office's 1999 consultation paper on freedom of information starts by stating that:

> Freedom of information is an essential component of the government's programme to modernise British politics. This programme of constitutional reform aims to involve people more closely in the decisions which affect their lives.

While this may be true, the government did not plan to repeal the laws that successive governments had used to control the release of government information.

The Official Secrets Act 1911 can always be used in a serious case, for s. 1 remains and makes it a serious offence to obtain or communicate any document or information 'for a purpose prejudicial to the safety or interests of the State'. *R v Ponting* [1985] Crim LR 318 held, in the case of a whistle-blowing civil servant, who wanted to reveal documents about a controversial military act to an MP, that only the government could decide what was in 'the safety or interests of the State'. The Official Secrets Act 1989 was a reform, but the crucial areas of information, that a government would wish to keep secret, are still protected by criminal sanction. These are security and intelligence, defence, international relations and criminal investigations. The Defence Advisory Notice, which warns journalists not to investigate certain areas, for fear of prosecution, also still exists, as does the practice of 'signing' the Official Secrets Act, which serves a similar warning function for individuals.

Failing this, a government could always use the civil remedy of breach of confidence to restrain, by injunction, government employees, ex-employees and those they pass the information to, such as newspapers and publishers, from betraying confidences. The most spectacular example of this was the protracted litigation against the ex-security agent Peter Wright's book *Spycatcher* in the late 1980s and early 1990s, culminating in the House of Lords' decision *A-G v Guardian (No. 2)* [1990] 1 AC 109, where the injunctions were only lifted because the information was, by now, so well known that to continue them would be pointless. Governments have not tired of pursuing such actions for in *A-G v Blake* [2001] 1 AC 268, an ex-member of the Secret Intelligence Service had been sued for breaching his contractual obligation, not to reveal what he had learnt from his employment. The House of Lords decided that Blake would have to account (i.e. restore) the profits made from the book, that he published about his career.

Legal proceedings against Blake actually began in 1991, under the Conservative government of John Major. At the same time the PM was proclaiming his belief in 'open government'. This started with the release of hitherto secret information, such as the names and composition of the various cabinet committees, the guidelines for ministerial behaviour 'Questions of Procedure for Ministers' (now known as the Ministerial Code) and some details about M15 and M16. Later on a Code of Practice was introduced that, for instance, required government to routinely release far more information than previously. The law on government information remained the Public Records Act 1958 with its famed '30 year rule'. Under this scheme, government records were released after 30 years, so documents from 1973 would be released on 1 January 2004. Some records were retained for longer or never released, the decision being made by the Lord Chancellor. The system has been further reformed by the Constitutional Reform and Governance Act 2010, with the standard release period being reduced to 20 years. In the year 2000, a Freedom of Information Act was enacted to replace the voluntary Code of Practice. The Public Records system was also changed by the Public Records Act 2005. In principle all public records, even if they are not 20 years old, are accessible to the public under the Freedom of Information Act 2000. Requests for information are now enforceable in court and there are some improvements in access to information, but there are many exemptions from the obligation to release information.

The government wanted to promote a 'change of culture within the public sector' and encouraged all 'public authorities' to voluntarily publish far more information. Public authority is broadly defined, to mean any body or office exercising a public function and includes those providing services of that nature to the public authority. There is a list of over 400 public authorities in the Freedom of Information Act and all must draw up a publication scheme. This includes things like schools admission criteria and how priorities on hospital waiting lists are determined, which are matters of concern to the general public, not just to those interested in politics.

Otherwise any person can request information from a public authority. The public authority has a duty to confirm or deny whether they hold the information or not. If they do they must provide it, although a small fee may be charged. The applicant may even express a preference about whether they want the information to be provided as a copy of a document, a digest or summary or whether they just want to inspect it. There are a number of grounds upon which the public authority can refuse to supply the information, such as that it is already available, about to be published, would be too expensive or the request is 'vexatious', e.g. the applicant has made repeated requests for the same information.

The main criticism of the Act is that there are a large number of exempted categories of information where there is no duty to disclose. Apart from this obvious criticism, the different exemptions are differently defined, which may cause confusion amongst the public. There are categories of information that are absolutely exempt from disclosure such as that relating to security organisations, court records, personal data, information obtained in confidence, and information whose disclosure is forbidden by statute, European Community obligation or would be in contempt of court. There is a longer list of information categories where it has to be decided whether the public interest requires disclosure or withholding of the information. Defence, international relations, the economy, public investigations, law enforcement, the formulation of government policy, the award of honours, and communications with the Queen are just some of the 'public interest' exempt category.

Another problem is the strong government role in these exemptions, when the government is the very organisation that may be trying to conceal information. Government ministers certificate whether information has been supplied by a security or intelligence agency and whether it is a threat to national security. Communications between government ministers, cabinet communications and advice from civil servants on policy formulation are all exempted information. What is more, a government minister can also give an opinion that information should be withheld because it could prejudice the convention of collective responsibility, inhibit the free and frank provision of advice or prejudice public affairs. The courts of Scotland have held, in *Scottish Ministers v Scottish Information Commission* [2007] SC 330 that this does not allow ministers to say that all documents containing advice to ministers should be withheld. The Information Commissioner was entitled to examine individual documents to assess whether they could safely be released. The Information Tribunal can and does order the revelation of minutes of Cabinet meetings. *Cabinet Office v Information Commissioner* EA/2008/0024 and EA/2008/0029 ordered the release of minutes relating to the decision to invade Iraq, which contained the controversial advice from the Attorney-General on the legality of military action. Most controversially, under s. 53 of the Freedom of Information Act 2000, a Secretary of State can add to the list of exempt information, merely by using delegated legislation. Parliament have to agree to this delegated legislation, as the Act requires the affirmative resolution procedure and Parliament did agree in the case of the 'Iraq minutes'.

Fortunately, the Freedom of Information Act comes complete with a fairly robust enforcement system. First, the public authority needs to provide an internal complaint procedure. Then the applicant can apply to the 'Information Commissioner', an independent official created by the Act. Either the applicant or the public authority has an appeal to an Information Tribunal, with further appeals on a point of law to the High Court and then upwards to the Court of Appeal and House of Lords, if necessary. The courts ordered the disclosure of MPs' expenses in *Corporate Officer of the House of Commons v Information Commissioner* [2009] 3 All ER 403, which provoked a huge public scandal and the retirement of many MPs. Even on the issue of the Attorney-General's legal advice, mentioned earlier, although the courts accepted that such advice is normally confidential, they insisted on having the final say on its release: *HM Treasury v Information Commissioner* [2010] 2 All ER 55. The Information Commissioner also has pretty impressive enforcement powers and she will be able to investigate, obtain search warrants and order the release of information. The penalty for defying her or lying to her could be proceedings in the High Court for contempt of court.

When compared to freedom of information legislation in other countries, such as the US Freedom of Information Act 1966, or the Australian or Swedish equivalents, the same problem of exemptions occurs. The British Act, in comparison, does seem to have rather a lot of exemptions and they are rather widely drawn.

The government also seems to have undue power to widen the scope of these exemptions. A strong Information Commissioner would help to counteract this and it is to be hoped, in the post-**Human Rights Act 1998** era, that courts dealing with the inevitable appeals will interpret the Act in a way that promotes freedom of information. There are some small signs that that they are trying to do so.

Figure 10.1 The Freedom of Information Act 2000

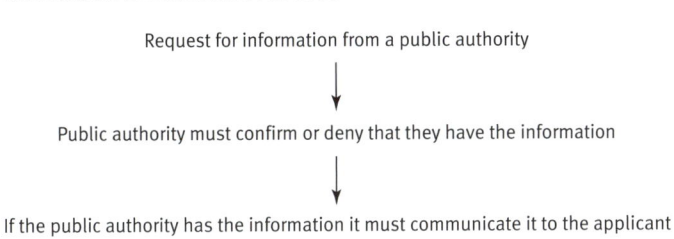

Request for information from a public authority

↓

Public authority must confirm or deny that they have the information

↓

If the public authority has the information it must communicate it to the applicant

UNLESS the information falls into an exempt category
There are 2 exempt categories

ABSOLUTE EXEMPTION if the information is:	PUBLIC INTEREST EXEMPTION
Reasonably accessible by other means	The public interest in not disclosing outweighs the public interest in disclosing.
Relating to bodies dealing with security matters	This is information:
Court records	Intended for future publication
Covered by Parliamentary Privilege	Safeguarding national security
Prejudicial to the effective conduct of public affairs e.g. the convention of collective responsibility	Prejudicial to defence
	Prejudicial to international relations
A communication with the Sovereign or the heir to the throne	Prejudicial to relations between the different governments of the UK
Personal data	Prejudicial to the economy
Prohibited from disclosure by another enactment	Concerning criminal investigations
	Prejudicial to the prevention or detection of crime
	Prejudicial to the audit of public authority accounts
	Relating to the formulation of government policy
	Likely to endanger health and safety
	Relating to the environment (separate statutory scheme of disclosure)
	Protected by legal professional privilege
	Constituting a trade secret or prejudicial to commercial interests

Appeal to the Information Commissioner

↓

Appeal to First-tier Tribunal (Information Rights)

Question 4

Is there a right of privacy in English law?
Discuss.

Commentary

It is very hard to define exactly what privacy is and how a legal right to privacy should be defined. Many sorts of activities could be covered by a right to privacy and there could be many possible infringements of that right by the State, the media, powerful business interests or, maybe, other people. Historically, English law does not have a specific right of privacy, but the tort of trespass and the equitable doctrine of breach of confidence both give some protection to specific aspects of privacy. In contrast, the **European Convention on Human Rights** clearly does grant a right to a 'private life' in **Article 8.1**:

> Everyone has the right to respect for his private and family life, his home and his correspondence.

The **European Convention** is now enforceable in UK courts under the **Human Rights Act 1998**. The European Court of Human Rights has made many decisions on what can be covered by **Article 8**, and, under **s. 2 of the Human Rights Act 1998**, UK courts are required to take such decisions into account. A change of sex was held to be a matter concerned with a person's private life in *Goodwin v UK* (2002) 35 EHRR 44, it was not acceptable to criminalise homosexuality in *Dudgeon v UK* (1981) 4 EHRR 523, telephone tapping was a breach of human rights in *Halford v UK* (1997) 24 EHRR 523, and the placing of a bugging device in a private house was unacceptable in *Khan v UK* (2001) 31 EHRR 1016.

The major concern has, however, been media intrusions into the private lives of famous and not so famous people. The UK courts have been able to adapt the old law of breach of confidence to meet some of those concerns, reinforced by the **European Convention on Human Rights (ECHR)**. There is a steady stream of new cases, usually involving celebrities, and so they even make the mainstream news, not just the pages of legal journals. That makes this an interesting subject to write about.

A comprehensive survey of the law is not possible in such a relatively short essay, so the key to a good answer is a good structure and some clear arguments, backed up by some good examples from the case law.

Answer plan

- Trespass does not include a right of privacy
- Breach of confidence
- Breach of confidence depends upon a confidential relationship
- The public interest must also be considered
- There is no confidence in iniquity

Freedom of Expression | **171**

- **Article 8 ECHR**—right of respect for private life
- **Article 10 ECHR**—freedom of expression
- The private life of public figures may be protected
- Private life may be revealed if it is a legitimate subject of public debate
- Personal information is now protected without the need for a confidential relationship
- Should there be a more extensive right of privacy?

Suggested answer

Historically, no right of privacy has been recognised in English law, unlike the situation in other European countries such as France or Germany, where the protection of privacy is a recognised part of the law. In England, privacy did not become accepted as a recognised tort nor has there been legislation on the subject, despite the recommendations of the Younger Committee on Privacy in 1972 (Cmnd 5012) and the Calcutt committee in 1990 (Cm 1102).

Although unauthorised entry to someone's house has long been recognised as a trespass in famous cases like *Entick v Carrington* (1765) 19 St Tr 1030, the courts felt unable to extend trespass to cover other intrusions into a person's home or private life. In *Malone v Metropolitan Police Commissioner* [1979] Ch 344, Megarry VC was unable to grant a remedy to Malone, whose telephone had been tapped by the Metropolitan Police, but thought that the matter needed legislation. Similarly, there was nothing unlawful about taking aerial photographs of a person's house, without their permission, in *Bernstein v Skyviews Ltd* [1978] 1 QB 479. It is not possible to trespass by flying over someone's land. Even as late as 2004, the courts declined to recognise a right of privacy when visitors to a prisoner sued after being strip searched: *Wainwright v Home Office* [2004] 2 AC 406.

Yet the courts were not completely without the means to deal with some of the grosser intrusions into a person's private life. In *Kaye v Robertson* [1991] FSR 62, a well-known actor was lying injured in a hospital bed after an accident, when journalists photographed him and published the pictures without his permission. The courts stopped this, on the slightly dubious grounds that this was a malicious falsehood. A better legal doctrine to use would have been the old equitable doctrine of breach of confidence.

The Court of Chancery decided in *Prince Albert v Strange* (1849) 1 Mac & G 25 that Strange could not publish etchings that Prince Albert had made of members of his immediate family. Prince Albert had not given permission for any publication and Strange had obtained copies from an employee of the printer, who had been entrusted with the printing. To publish them would be a breach of confidence. Many years later, this precedent was followed in the notorious case of *Argyll v Argyll* [1967] Ch 302, where the Duke and Duchess of Argyll were divorcing and the Duke sold a story, with intimate details of their married life, to the *People* newspaper. Publication could be restrained, because this was information from a confidential relationship, marriage.

The concept of the confidential relationship was developed in *Attorney-General v Guardian Newspapers (No. 2)* [1990] 1 AC 109, where Peter Wright, a retired intelligence services officer, published a book, *Spycatcher*, revealing what he had allegedly done during his working life. The government tried to stop publication of the book and newspaper reports of what it contained, by suing for breach of confidence. Lord Keith, at 255, held that:

> The law has long recognised that an obligation of confidence can arise out of particular relationships. Examples are the relationships of doctor and patient, priest and penitent, solicitor and client, banker and customer. The obligation may be an express or implied term in a contract, but it may also exist independently of any contract on the basis of an independent equitable principle of confidence.

Third parties, outside the relationship of confidence, could also be restrained from revealing the confidential information. The public interest also had to be taken into account. Here it was not in the public interest for government secrets to be revealed, particularly as it might encourage other intelligence officers to follow Wright's example. By the time this case came to court, however, the book had been widely distributed and Wright's allegations were well known. There was little point in continuing injunctions against the newspapers, forbidding them to reveal what Wright claimed. The injunction remained against Wright.

It could be in the public interest to reveal confidential information, which was an argument unsuccessfully raised by Wright, but accepted in other cases. It was held that there was 'no confidence in iniquity' in *Woodward v Hutchins* [1971] 1 WLR 760, where the *Daily Mirror* published details of the private life of the singer, Tom Jones, revealed by a former employee. Jones had courted publicity in the past, so he could not complain about unwelcome publicity now. It would be in the public interest to reveal a crime, as in *Cork v McVicar* (1984) Times, 31 October, where McVicar taped private conversations with Cork, a retired police officer, which seemed to provide evidence of police corruption. The *Daily Express* was free to publish. Similarly it was acceptable for the police to publish the photograph of a suspect in *Hellewell v Chief Constable of Derbyshire* [1995] 1 WLR 804.

The confidential relationship that is being protected is not always well defined. In *Prince of Wales v Jim Regan* (1981) Times, 7 May, telephone conversations between the Prince of Wales and his fiancée, Lady Diana Spencer, were intercepted, but publication was forbidden. Presumably, engagement was the relationship, but in *Francome v Mirror Group Newspapers Ltd* [1984] 2 All ER 408, the court disapproved of a journalist tapping a famous jockey's telephone when there was no relationship.

It seemed that some judges, at least, were willing to extend the protection given by breach of confidence, and this process was accelerated by the European Commission on Human Rights in *Spencer v United Kingdom* (1998) 25 EHRR CD 105. Earl Spencer complained about newspaper reports relating to his marriage. He lost, but the Commission did say that there was a remedy in UK law for breach of Article 8, the right to respect for private life and that was breach of confidence. So since the coming into force of the Human Rights Act 1998 there has been an increase in court actions attempting to protect confidential information and a person's privacy, as Lord Woolf CJ remarked in *A v B plc and Another* [2003] QB 195. There a married professional footballer was having sexual relationships with two other women, who had sold their stories to a national newspaper. He wanted to stop publication, but failed on the grounds that the court set great store in protecting the confidentiality of marriage and other permanent relationships, but far less value in protecting the confidentiality of this sort of liaison. The court had to consider not just the right to a private life, which was protected by Article 8, but also the newspaper's right to freedom of expression, which was guaranteed by Article 10, as A was a public figure. This balancing of interests was familiar from the equitable origins of breach of confidence, as Lord Woolf CJ explained at p. 202.

> The court is able to achieve this by absorbing the rights which articles 8 and 10 protect into the long-established action for breach of confidence.

In *Douglas v Hello! Ltd* [2001] QB 967, Michael Douglas and Catherine Zeta Jones had sold exclusive rights to their wedding photographs to *Hello!* magazine and wanted to stop a rival magazine publishing surreptitious photographs taken by a wedding guest. They failed, because they had not imposed an obligation of confidentiality on all the people at the wedding. Naomi Campbell gained a partial victory in *Campbell v Mirror Group Newspapers* [2004] 2 AC 457, where a newspaper had revealed that she was receiving treatment for drug addiction. This was acceptable, but publishing photographs of her leaving the place of treatment was not. Lord Nicholls had some important things to say about the development of the right of privacy. Although s. 6 of the Human Rights Act says only that 'public authorities' can be sued for breaching human rights, this type of action can be brought between individuals and between individuals and a non-governmental body such as a newspaper. He also wanted to abandon the use of the term 'duty of confidence' and the insistence that only 'confidential' information could be protected. He preferred to refer to it as 'private' information and stated at p. 465: 'The essence of the tort is better encapsulated now as misuse of private information.'

Article 10 can be outweighed by more important and fundamental rights. In *Venables v News Group Newspapers* [2001] Fam 430, the court ordered all the media never to reveal the new identities or whereabouts of the child murderers,

Venables and Thompson, who were about to be released from prison. Freedom of expression and the public interest in uncovering crime were outweighed by the possible threat to the lives and safety of the two young men, protected by *Article 2*, the right to life, and *Article 3*, freedom from inhuman and degrading treatment.

The 'public interest' is not at all the same thing as the public being interested in something, as the court held in *HRH Prince of Wales v Associated Newspapers Ltd* [2008] Ch 57. An employee of Prince Charles gave the Prince's diaries to a newspaper, which was a breach of the employee's contract. Although there was some public interest in the diaries, the Prince was a public figure and the diaries criticised the leaders of China, which might be seen as a matter of political debate; the extreme confidentiality of a person's private diaries outweighed this.

The law continues to evolve. According to the European Court of Human Rights, it is not permissible to publish photographs of the private life of a public figure unless it contributes to political debate. In *Von Hannover v Germany (2005) 40 EHRR 1*, Princess Caroline of Monaco successfully complained that German newspapers should not publish photographs of her with her husband and children, when engaged in their private life. The State has an obligation to protect the private life of individuals from other individuals. Sometimes it is permissible to look at the private life of public figures if it relates to a political debate, but that was not the situation here.

This case has been reflected and further developed in decisions in the UK courts. In *Murray v Express Group Newspapers* [2008] HRLR 33, the Court of Appeal suggested that taking a photograph, without permission, of the young child of J. K. Rowling on an Edinburgh street was a breach of the child's 'reasonable expectation of privacy'. Similarly, in *Mosley v News Group Newspapers* [2008] EWHC 1777, the *News of the World* was condemned for publishing a story, photographs and a video of the head of motor racing's Formula 1 engaged in an orgy with five prostitutes. He was a public figure, but his sexual preferences were private and did not relate to his work. The right of privacy does not now depend upon any confidential relationship existing. It might be enough to show that the information was of a strictly personal nature, relating, say, to sexual relationships, health, financial or family matters: *Author of a Blog v Times Newspapers* [2009] EMLR 22.

So there does now seem to be a right of privacy, but the granting of this right is highly discretionary and depends upon many factors. We can see that the law has changed. Revelations about the private sexual lives of the famous were allowed in *Woodward v Hutchins* [1971] 1 WLR 760 and *A v B plc and Another* [2003] QB 195, but not in *Mosley v News Group Newspapers* [2008] EWHC 1777. *Mosley* has proved unpopular with those who run newspapers, who claim that it will prevent the legitimate investigation of the private lives of public figures. The media claim that they need to do this in order to show whether these people are fit to hold public office. The cynical might say that the newspapers are just worried about their profits, but there may be something in the argument that free expression requires that newspapers should be able to investigate the rich and powerful, without being intimidated by the threat of costly court actions. The right of privacy is still very limited and only seems to have been developed to deal with the excesses of the tabloid press. There are signs that the right of privacy might also extend into State intrusions into the lives of less affluent people, such as the retention of photographs of protesters by the police in *R (Wood) v Metropolitan Police Commissioner [2009] 4 All ER 951,* but as yet this case seems to be an isolated example.

Further reading

Bradley, A. and Ewing, K. *Constitutional and Administrative Law*, 15th edn (Longman, 2010), ch. 23 and ch. 13F.

Barnett, H. *Constitutional and Administrative Law*, 8th edn (Routledge, 2011) ch.19.

Stone, R. *Textbook on Civil Liberties and Human Rights*, 8th edn (Oxford University Press, 2010) chs. 8–11.

11

Administrative Law: Judicial Review

Introduction

This chapter covers one of the most important growth areas of the law. Some courses have found it impossible to include it within the general constitutional law course and have hived it off into a separate administrative law or public law course. These questions are designed to cover all the aspects likely to be included in a general, rather than a specialised course.

This subject lends itself particularly well to problem questions, and is for that reason popular with examiners seeking to give a more legal slant to what might otherwise be an excessively political subject. Students will need to demonstrate their legal skills in identifying and applying the appropriate case law.

The diagram opposite provides a template for answering problem questions on judicial review. It is most unlikely that any one question will raise all the issues identified, or all the grounds of review. Questions 2, 3 and 4 of this chapter are typical in raising a limited number of issues. But examination questions, unlike seminar questions, do not come with a convenient heading identifying the topic, such as 'questions on natural justice'. So, if you are not sure which issues are being raised, working through the questions on the diagram will help. It will also ensure that you do not miss out on the extra marks that may be available for, e.g. discussing the applicant's locus standi, or identifying the appropriate remedy.

Question 1

The twentieth century saw both the decline of administrative law to virtual extinction, and its revival and development to unprecedented heights.

Discuss. Why has the development of administrative law been so erratic?

Administrative Law: Judicial Review | **177**

Commentary

The basis of the answer to this question will be a description of the way administrative law, particularly judicial review, has developed in the last century, illustrated with the appropriate cases. What will make the answer a good one will be the discussion of the reasons for its erratic progress. There are no cut and dried answers on this; the student's answer will be judged on the way the arguments are presented and the evidence marshalled in support.

Figure 11.1 Tackling problems on judicial review

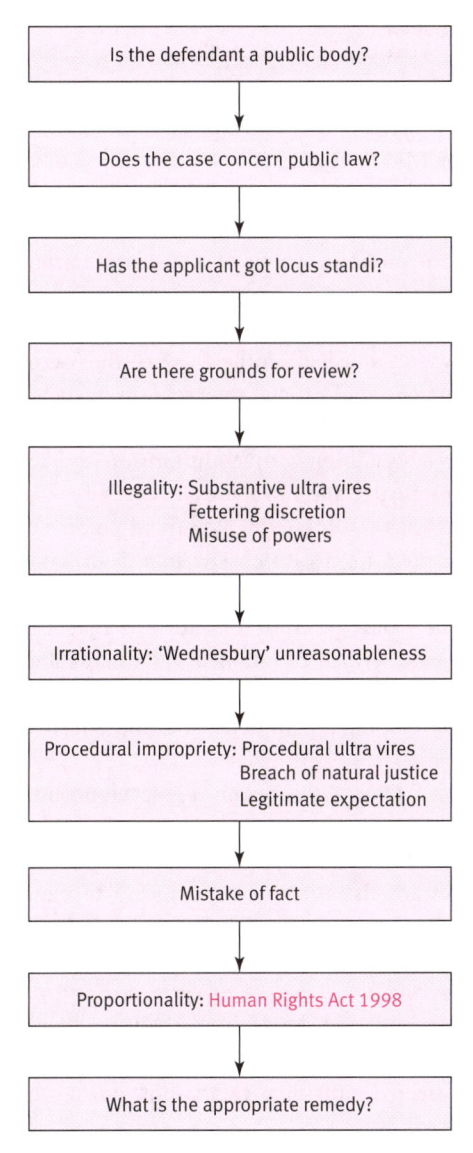

```
┌─────────────────────────────────────────┐
│      Is the defendant a public body?    │
└─────────────────────────────────────────┘
                    ↓
┌─────────────────────────────────────────┐
│       Does the case concern public law? │
└─────────────────────────────────────────┘
                    ↓
┌─────────────────────────────────────────┐
│      Has the applicant got locus standi?│
└─────────────────────────────────────────┘
                    ↓
┌─────────────────────────────────────────┐
│         Are there grounds for review?   │
└─────────────────────────────────────────┘
                    ↓
┌─────────────────────────────────────────┐
│      Illegality: Substantive ultra vires│
│                  Fettering discretion   │
│                  Misuse of powers       │
└─────────────────────────────────────────┘
                    ↓
┌─────────────────────────────────────────┐
│  Irrationality: 'Wednesbury' unreasonableness │
└─────────────────────────────────────────┘
                    ↓
┌─────────────────────────────────────────┐
│ Procedural impropriety: Procedural ultra vires │
│                         Breach of natural justice │
│                         Legitimate expectation │
└─────────────────────────────────────────┘
                    ↓
┌─────────────────────────────────────────┐
│              Mistake of fact            │
└─────────────────────────────────────────┘
                    ↓
┌─────────────────────────────────────────┐
│   Proportionality: Human Rights Act 1998│
└─────────────────────────────────────────┘
                    ↓
┌─────────────────────────────────────────┐
│       What is the appropriate remedy?   │
└─────────────────────────────────────────┘
```

Answer plan

- Historical prerogative and other remedies
- Initial development of ultra vires and natural justice
- Decline in review during and after the Second World War
- Alternatives proposed
- Revival from 1960s.

Suggested answer

The history of English administrative law can be traced back through many centuries. The prerogative writs of certiorari, prohibition and mandamus were originally developed in the Middle Ages, but first came to prominence with the growth of a more effective administrative system under the Tudors. The seventeenth century sees the first precedents concerning the rules of natural justice (*Baggs Case* (1615) 11 Co Rep 93b) and the doctrine of ultra vires (*Hetley v Boyer* (1614) Cro Jac 336).

It was during the nineteenth century that something approaching a system of administrative law was established, in the wake of the Victorian reforms of central and local government, and official intervention in such areas as health, factory conditions and sanitation. The courts were able to use the old prerogative remedies against the new administrative authorities, and to develop and refine the concepts of natural justice and ultra vires, in cases like *Cooper v Wandsworth Board of Works* (1863) 14 CB (NS) 180. Maitland pointed out in 1888 that half the reported cases in the Queen's Bench Division dealt with aspects of administrative law. New remedies also became available; in *Dyson v Attorney-General* [1911] 1 KB 410, the Court of Appeal confirmed that a declaration could be granted to a person who wished to establish the unlawfulness of administrative action. By the beginning of the twentieth century, it seemed that English law was well on the way to developing a comprehensive and effective system of administrative law.

But during the next 50 years, this promising development was halted; in some respects the law went into reverse. One of the main factors was a conceptual problem about judicial and administrative decisions. Until the nineteenth century reforms, much local administration was conducted through the justices of the peace, and it was natural to describe their power as judicial and their decisions as judicial, whether they were convicting a thief or allocating poor relief. The availability of the prerogative remedies of certiorari and prohibition were also described as being dependent on the decision challenged being judicial. This presented no problems as long as the courts were willing to define decisions as judicial whenever they affected individual rights. But, during the 1920s and 1930s, the courts started to distinguish between judicial and administrative decisions more strictly, confining the definition of judicial decisions to those where Parliament had imposed some kind of judicialised procedure. As a consequence, the rules of natural justice were no longer applied to decisions affecting individual rights where these were classified as administrative: see *R v Metropolitan Police Commissioner ex parte Parker* [1953] 1 WLR 1150.

Over the same period, the courts showed some antipathy to the very idea of administrative law, perhaps under the influence of Dicey, who was critical of the French idea of a special body of rules governing the conduct of the administration, assuming that it would give them too much protection. The term '*droit administratif*' was used almost as a term of abuse! Perhaps, as a further effect of this, academic lawyers paid little heed to the subject, and it was not taught except as a minor part of constitutional law.

What was perhaps most unfortunate in these developments was that the courts abdicated their responsibility for protecting the rights of the individual at the very time when the government's activities put those rights most at risk. A notorious example is the case of *Liversidge v Anderson* [1942] AC 206, where the Secretary of State had the power to detain persons without trial if he had reasonable cause to believe them to be of hostile origin or associations, a power justifiable enough in wartime. But the House of Lords, with the honourable exception of Lord Atkin, held that the reasonableness of the Secretary of State's belief was not reviewable, turning an objective power into a wholly subjective one. A similarly unfortunate ruling was made in *Duncan v Cammel Laird* [1942] AC 624, when the House of Lords held that the Crown had an absolute and unreviewable privilege to withhold documents in litigation, if ministers felt it was in the public interest to do so.

The courts' attitude was not surprising in wartime, but even after the war, the courts remained very reluctant to interfere in the work of the administration in any way. In *Franklin v Minister of Town and Country Planning* [1948] AC 87, the House of Lords refused to apply the rule against bias to an administrative decision taken by a minister, even where Parliament had imposed a quasi-judicial process. In *Smith v East Elloe RDC* [1956] AC 736, the House of Lords accepted as effective a clause excluding judicial review, even where bad faith was alleged. Perhaps the most likely explanation for this lies in the effect of the doctrine of precedent. It will always be difficult to convince a court that the recent precedents should be disregarded and an ancient ruling preferred. A rare example of such a decision was *R v Northumberland Compensation Appeal Tribunal ex parte Shaw* [1952] 1 KB 338, where the Court of Appeal revived the doctrine of error of law on the face of the record after a century of disuse, as a means of controlling the increasing numbers of statutory tribunals.

Overall, anyone surveying the condition of administrative law in the early 1960s would have found a depressing sight. Natural justice was restricted, discretionary power not subject to judicial control, and remedies constrained by ancient rules and obscurities. As a consequence, few applicants considered the risks of litigation to be worthwhile, causing the law to fall yet further into decline. It was generally assumed that the law could not offer a means of controlling the administration, and attention turned to other methods, such as the reform of tribunals and inquiries after the Franks Committee report in 1957, and the introduction of an Ombudsman. Some even advocated the importation of the French system of *droit administratif*, and the establishment of an English *Conseil d'Etat*.

But, to the surprise of many, the English courts showed themselves to be capable of reviving this moribund area of law. In *Ridge v Baldwin* [1964] AC 40, the House of Lords attacked the dichotomy of judicial and administrative decisions, restoring the rule that decisions affecting the rights of subjects were subject to natural justice, even if Parliament was silent on the need for a hearing. This was followed by a stream of cases, extending the right to a fair hearing even into areas that had always been characterised as administrative. Other precedents were reversed. In *Conway v Rimmer* [1968] AC 910, the House of Lords removed the Crown's power to withhold documents in litigation, replacing it with the power of the court to grant public interest immunity. In *Anisminic v Foreign Compensation Commission* [1969] 2 AC 147, the House of Lords found a way of defeating the express exclusion clause that had been held effective in *Smith v East Elloe RDC* (above), and in so doing extended the courts' powers to review errors of law. In *Padfield v Minister of Agriculture* [1968] AC 997, the House of Lords rejected the idea of the unfettered and unreviewable administrative discretion.

Why did the courts change the law so radically and so unexpectedly?

One important factor was certainly a change in judicial personnel, with judges used to Diceyan orthodoxy being replaced by others with a less restricted outlook. One of the most influential was Lord Reid, who came to the House of Lords from Scotland, where administrative law had never fallen to such a low ebb. Lord Denning also played a significant part, as he did in so many branches of the law. Some credit is also due to academic lawyers, such as S. A. de Smith and Sir William Wade, whose publications and research into administrative law established it as an important academic subject. It is possible that the courts may have felt that, if the law was not reformed, they would lose out to other methods of redress, such as the Parliamentary Commissioner for Administration, who was introduced in 1967. Such statutory reforms also demonstrated that governments were willing to contemplate improved methods of redress, and the courts would not be risking political controversy if they joined in.

Once the process of revival began, there was no shortage of litigants seeking redress for what would once have been inescapable injustices. Within a few years, a new body of precedents had been built up, and cases decided between 1910 and 1960 are almost always viewed with suspicion. To consolidate this new law, procedural reforms were introduced on the advice of the Law Commission: see **s. 31 of the Supreme Court Act 1981.**

Administrative Law: Judicial Review | **181**

The overall effect has been a huge expansion in the role of judicial review, which now shares with criminal justice the highest profile and the most media attention. In October 2000, its importance was recognised by the formal establishment of the Administrative Court as a specialised section of the Queen's Bench Division. Few other branches of the law can show such dramatic changes. It is to be hoped that the courts will maintain their role of protecting individual rights against abuse at the hands of the administration, as they have during the last 50 years.

Question 2

Under the (imaginary) Radiation Protection Act 1993, any person wishing to use radioactive materials must obtain a licence from the Radiation Protection Agency (RPA). On receipt of an application, the RPA must consult any organisation that it considers to be representative of those affected, and must publish notice of the application in the national and local press, and in any other way it considers desirable. The RPA must allow three months for the submission of comments and objections, which should include the name and address of the sender. After considering all representations submitted to it, and giving the applicant a hearing, the RPA may grant or refuse a licence.

The Sulphurous Chemical plc applied for a licence to use radioactive materials in its factory in Coketown. The RPA published notice of the application in three national and two local newspapers, and put up a small notice in the Coketown public library. The RPA wrote to the Coketown Borough Council and the Cokeshire County Council asking for comments. It received a reply only from the Coketown Borough Council. The RPA made no attempt to consult the National Union of Chemical Workers, which represented the majority of Sulphurous Chemical's employees.

The RPA received many objections, including several from an unknown and unidentified group calling itself the Green Anti-Nuclear Faction; the RPA threw these away. A petition signed by 25,000 inhabitants of Coketown was presented the day after the three month submission period had expired, but the RPA refused to accept it.

After completing its consideration and giving Sulphurous Chemical a hearing, the RPA granted the licence.

Consider the validity of the licence.

Commentary

This question is concerned with judicial review, primarily though not exclusively with procedural ultra vires. The student will need to identify and explain the general principle involved, the distinction between mandatory and directory procedural requirements. It is then simplest for the student to work through the problem point by point. Although some issues raised in this type of question may bear a sufficient resemblance to decided cases to be straightforward, others will require the student to argue by analogy. Where issues are debatable, the student will be assessed on the quality of the argument, whichever conclusion is reached. Refer back to the diagram on p. 177 for advice.

Answer plan

- Distinguish mandatory and directory conditions
- Notice of application
- Consulting representative organisations
- Challenge by judicial review
- Locus standi.

Suggested answer

The validity of this licence can be challenged by judicial review, because, as laid down in *O'Reilly v Mackman* [1983] 2 AC 237, it concerns the activities of a public body in matters relating to public law. The grounds of challenge mostly concern procedural defects in the way the RPA dealt with the application.

In dealing with procedural defects, the courts have to balance the need to ensure that statutory procedural safeguards are carefully observed against the risk that trivial procedural defects are used as a pretext by objectors seeking to halt or delay an unpopular scheme. To do this the courts have generally drawn a distinction between mandatory and directory procedural requirements. A mandatory requirement is one that is regarded as so essential that failure to observe it justifies treating the decision reached as invalid. A directory requirement is one whose non-observance will not invalidate the decision. In *London & Clydeside Estates v Aberdeen District Council* [1980] 1 WLR 182, Lord Hailsham LC suggested that these two categories should not be regarded as the only two alternatives, but as the extremes of a range of possibilities. An example of a more subtle approach can be found in *Coney v Choyce* [1975] 1 WLR 422, where various detailed publication requirements were only partially complied with. The court held that it was mandatory that there be substantial compliance with the requirement of publication, but that the exact details were merely directory.

It is possible for statute to specify the precise consequences of failure to comply with procedural requirements, but in practice this rarely occurs. It is therefore left to the courts to decide retrospectively whether the failure has invalidated the decision. This area of the law is criticised as uncertain, but some guidance may be obtained from decided cases.

The RPA is required by the Act to publish notice of the application 'in the national and local press'. They published it in three national and two local newspapers. In *Bradbury v Enfield London Borough Council* [1967] 1 WLR 1311, the court held that giving notice was to be construed as a mandatory requirement as it was essential for the protection of the rights of the individual citizen. But in that case there was a complete failure to give notice. In *Coney v Choyce* substantial compliance was held to be sufficient. It could be argued here that there has been substantial compliance. The size of the petition is evidence that there was widespread awareness of the application. In *Coney v Choyce* it was considered material that all those affected had become aware of the proposal in spite of the defects in the publication. The RPA is given a discretion to publicise the application 'in any other way it considers desirable'. It could be argued that one small notice in the library is hardly sufficient. But any challenge would have to be on the ground of 'Wednesbury' unreasonableness: see *Associated Provincial Picture Houses v Wednesbury Corporation* [1948] 1 KB 223. It is unlikely that the courts would consider this to be beyond the limits of a reasonable exercise of discretion.

The RPA is required to consult 'organisations that it considers to be representative of those affected'. Consultation is generally held to be a mandatory requirement, as it is a means of protecting the interests of those affected: see *R v Secretary of State for the Environment ex parte Association of Metropolitan Authorities* [1986] 1 WLR 1. The consultation of the Coketown Borough Council seems to have been satisfactory. But in *Agricultural Training Board v Aylesbury Mushrooms Ltd* [1972] 1 WLR 190, sending a letter that went astray, and failing to make further enquiries was held not to amount to adequate consultation. If the RPA has made no attempt to follow up its letter to the Cokeshire County Council and check that it indeed has no comment to make, it will be considered to have broken a mandatory requirement. As this is a licence application to use radioactive materials, in fairness the RPA should disclose the scientific information, on which their decision is based, to the groups consulted: *R v Health Secretary ex parte US Tobacco International Inc* [1992] QB 353 and *R (Eisai) v National Institute for Health and Clinical Excellence* [2008] EWCA Civ 438.

The RPA's failure to consult the National Union of Chemical Workers could be challenged as an unreasonable use of discretion, as in *Secretary of State for Education v Metropolitan Borough of Tameside* [1977] AC 1014; no reasonable authority could have failed to consider the Union representative of those affected.

The RPA is required to consider 'all representations submitted to it', but it throws away the objections from the Green Anti-Nuclear Faction. The only possible justification for this is the provision in the Act that objections should include the name and address of the sender. This requirement could be classed as mandatory if it is essential for the conduct of the administration. In *Chapman v Earl* [1968] 1 WLR 1315, the failure of a tenant to indicate the proposed rent in an application to a rent tribunal was held to be a breach of a mandatory requirement. However, requirements imposed merely for the convenience of the administration are likely to be classified as directory only. In *Jackson Developments v Hall* [1951] 2 KB 488, the requirement that the tenant supply the landlord's name to a rent tribunal was held to be directory. In this problem, the objectors' failure to identify themselves hardly seems of sufficient importance to be treated as breach of a mandatory requirement. Their objections should therefore have been considered.

The petition is rejected because it is submitted one day late. Time limits will be held to be mandatory where they are essential in establishing legal rights and obligations. In *Howard v Secretary of State for the Environment* [1975] QB 235, the statutory time limit of 42 days for appealing against an enforcement notice was held to be mandatory, because it determined the legal powers of the local authority. But if no such compelling reasons exist, time limits will be treated as directory. In *James v Minister of Housing and Local Government* [1966] 1 WLR 135, a local authority was held to be entitled to make a planning decision after three months, though regulations imposed a limit of two months. In this problem, as the RPA will be spending some time considering the application, there seems no reason to treat the time limit for receipt of representations as mandatory.

An application for judicial review to challenge the validity of the licence under s. 31 of the Supreme Court Act 1981 and Part 54 of the Civil Procedure Rules could be made by any person with locus standi, that is, with a sufficient interest in the matter. Cokeshire County Council and the National Union of Chemical Workers would clearly have a sufficient interest, as would members of the Green Anti-Nuclear Faction, if willing to identify themselves. In *R v Secretary of State for the Environment ex parte Greenpeace* [1994] 4 All ER 352, Greenpeace was held to have locus standi, as a pressure group with local members, to challenge the licensing of the THORP nuclear plant. It could further be argued that any of the inhabitants of Coketown who had signed the petition would have locus standi. In *R v Inland Revenue Commissioners ex parte National Federation of Self-Employed & Small Businesses* [1982] AC 617, Lord Diplock referred to the desirability of 'a single public-minded taxpayer' being able to challenge the validity of unlawful administrative action.

The most appropriate remedies in this case would be a quashing order to quash the licence, or a declaration that it was invalid. It would, however, be open to Sulphurous Chemical plc to make a further application for a licence.

Question 3

Under the (imaginary) Social Services Act 2000, all residential homes for the elderly must be licensed by the local authority. Unsatisfactory homes will be refused a licence and closed down, but there is a right to appeal against the refusal of a licence to an Appeal Tribunal.

Mrs Danvers applied to the Cokeshire County Council for a licence for the Manderley Home. The application was referred to the Social Services Committee, which instructed Rebecca, one of its employees, to investigate the suitability of the Home. Rebecca visited the Home, posing as someone looking for accommodation for an elderly relative. After completing her researches, Rebecca produced a report recommending that a licence be refused, because the kitchens and bathrooms were not cleaned properly and few of the staff had the appropriate professional qualifications.

The Committee considered the report and then invited Mrs Danvers to a meeting to discuss her application. She came to the meeting accompanied by her husband, a solicitor, but he was asked to wait outside. At the meeting, she was handed a copy of Rebecca's report and asked to comment on it. She asked for an adjournment so she could consult her husband, but the Committee refused. She denied the allegations in the report and invited the members of the Committee to visit the Home and talk to the residents. The Committee declined to do so and, after deliberating in private, refused the licence.

Mrs Danvers appealed to the Tribunal, which gave her a hearing, but refused to hear evidence from the staff of the Home or allow her to cross-examine Rebecca, who gave evidence in person. The Tribunal confirmed the original decision. Mrs Danvers has now discovered that the wife of the Chair of the Committee is a member of the board of a charity that campaigns for better care for the elderly.

Advise Mrs Danvers.

Commentary

This problem raises a number of issues relating to judicial review, principally concerning natural justice. Such a problem may appear at first sight rather long and daunting, but if you have a reasonable understanding of the issues it is actually quite straightforward. It is best tackled as advised earlier by working systematically through the facts of the problem, picking up each issue as it arises, explaining the law on that point, citing the relevant authority and then applying the law to the problem. You may, if you wish, introduce your answer by a few general remarks on the topic, though this answer does not. What you should not do is to attempt to answer this, or any other problem, by writing an essay. It is the ability of the student to select from the material they have learnt just those points that are relevant that marks out the competent student.

Answer plan

- Challenge by judicial review
- Has she a right to a fair hearing
- Notice of charges
- Legal representation
- Article 6: the right to a fair hearing
- Evidence
- Real possibility of bias.

Suggested answer

As Mrs Danvers has exhausted the statutory procedure, she will have to use judicial review if she wishes to challenge the refusal of a licence. Both the Council Committee and Tribunal are clearly public bodies and her grounds of challenge derive from public law, making judicial review the appropriate procedure to use. She must apply to the Administrative Court *ex parte* for permission to make an application for judicial review promptly and in any event within three months of the Tribunal's decision. As the person directly affected by the decision she has locus standi.

It appears that Mrs Danvers will have grounds for arguing that there has been a breach of the rules of natural justice, but she must first establish that she was entitled to a fair hearing. In *Ridge v Baldwin* [1964] AC 40 it was held that natural justice applied whenever a decision affected the rights of the individual, and it was made clear in *Re HK* [1967] 2 QB 617 that this applied even if the decision was of an administrative nature. By imposing a requirement that a licence must be obtained for an activity that could previously have been carried on without restriction, the law is affecting individual rights and so a fair hearing must be given. This was applied in *R v Gaming Board ex parte Benaim* [1970] 2 QB 417 to the grant of gaming licences and is clearly applicable here.

At what stage in the procedure is Mrs Danvers entitled to be heard? There is no general right to be heard during preliminary investigative or preparatory processes. In *Pearlberg v Varty* [1972] 1 WLR 534, it was held that there was no right to a hearing by the Inland Revenue as they prepared a taxpayer's assessment; he would be heard at the proper time before the relevant tribunal. It is therefore acceptable for Cokeshire County Council to conduct a covert investigation. Nor is there an objection to the matter being referred to a committee, as the Local Government Act 1972 specifically authorises this form of delegation. But, before any decision is made about the licence, Mrs Danvers must be given an opportunity to state her case. For this it is necessary that she be informed of the matters that are causing concern, otherwise she cannot offer an effective defence. In *Fairmount Investments v Secretary of State for the Environment* [1976] 1 WLR 1255, a compulsory purchase decision was held to be invalid because the inspector had based his decision on defects in the building that he had noticed but had not mentioned to the parties. Here Mrs Danvers is not shown Rebecca's report in advance or even informed of its contents. The Committee could argue that she was shown the report at the hearing, but this did not allow her any time to prepare a defence. In *R v Thames Magistrates' Court ex parte Polemis* [1974] 1 WLR 1371, it was held that it was a breach of the rules of natural justice to serve a summons on a defendant in the morning and try him that afternoon as he had no chance to prepare a defence. It therefore appears that there has been a breach of the rules of natural justice.

Mrs Danvers was refused permission to be accompanied by or to consult her husband, who was presumably also her legal adviser. It appears, from *R v Maze Prison Visitors ex parte Hone* [1988] AC 379, that there was no absolute right to legal or other representation. Article 6 of the European Convention of Human Rights reinforces the right to a fair hearing. A teacher who stood to lose his job had the right to legal representation in *R (G) v Governors of X School* [2010] 2 All ER 555, as did a doctor in a similar position in *Kulkarni v Milton Keynes Hospital* [2009] EWCA Civ 789. Mrs Danvers also stands to lose her livelihood, so must have a strong case to be permitted a legal representative. The Committee is obliged to hear all relevant evidence: see *R v Hull Prison Visitors ex parte St Germain (No. 2)* [1979] 1 WLR 1401. It could be argued that they should have visited the Home and spoken to the residents, but in cases such as *Osgood v Nelson* (1872) LR HL 636, it has been held to be acceptable for a subordinate to collect evidence for submission to those who decide, as was done here.

The breach of natural justice committed by the Committee will render its decision invalid, and it can be argued that as a matter of logic no subsequent procedures can cure that initial invalidity. If the outcome of the first hearing is likely to influence the decision in the appeal, which seems likely here, then there is still a breach of natural justice: *R (G) v Governors of X School* [2010] 2 All ER 555.

The Tribunal refused to hear evidence from the staff of the Home. This seems to be a clear breach of the obligation to hear all relevant evidence discussed above, as the qualifications of the staff seem to be one of the principal issues of concern. In older cases, natural justice did not always include the right to cross-examination e.g. *Bushell v Secretary of State for the Environment* [1981] AC 75. Nowadays, as Mrs Danvers' livelihood is at stake, Article 6 would require it: *R (G) v Governors of X School* [2010] 2 All ER 555.

The final substantive issue is the allegation that one member of the Tribunal was biased. It is clear that the presence of one biased person is enough to invalidate a decision. A breach of natural justice could involve several forms of bias, which are conveniently subdivided into 'actual bias' and 'apparent bias' according to the House of Lords in *R v Abdroikov* [2008] 1 All ER 315. Actual bias leads to automatic disqualification and includes: a financial interest in the decision, as in *Dimes v Grand Junction Canal Co* (1852) 3 HLC 759; the decision makers have already decided the matter before the hearing, as in *Eszias v North Glamorgan NHS Trust* [2007] 4 All ER 940; or direct association with a party to the case, as in *Ex parte Pinochet* [1999] 1 All ER 577. The last two seem the more likely on the facts here, but neither seems strong enough to invalidate the decision of the Tribunal. For other, more indirect, forms of 'apparent bias', the courts have formulated various tests, such as looking for a 'real likelihood' or 'reasonable suspicion' of bias. In *Porter v Magill* [2002] 1 All ER 465, the House of Lords formulated a general test for bias as follows:

> whether the fair-minded and informed observer, having considered the facts, would conclude that there was a real possibility that the Tribunal was biased.

This was confirmed as the correct approach in the more recent House of Lords case of *Helow v Secretary of State for the Home Department* [2009] 2 All ER 1071.

Can it be argued that there is such a real possibility here? It is doubtful; the Tribunal's very existence is in order to improve the care of the elderly and there is nothing in the background of the Chair of the Tribunal to indicate any connection with or prejudice against Mrs Danvers.

If Mrs Danvers is successful in establishing grounds for judicial review, as seems likely, the most appropriate remedy would be a quashing order to quash the decisions of the Committee and Tribunal, though a declaration would also be a possibility. She could in addition ask for a mandatory order to compel them to reconsider her application. The award of remedies is at the discretion of the court, but there seems no reason why the court should decline to give redress. However, the court's decision will not necessarily mean that Mrs Danvers will obtain the licence she seeks. That decision will be made by the Committee and Tribunal and will be based, as it should be, on the suitability of the Home she runs.

Question 4

As a result of local elections, the Radical Party has taken control of the Coketown District Council. It has implemented the following changes and wishes to know whether there could be any legal challenge to them. It also wishes to know who could make such a challenge and by what legal process.

(a) To revoke, with immediate effect, the licences given to Able (A), Baker (B) and Charlie (C) to sell ice creams from their vans in council owned parks.

(b) To refuse to give any more discretionary grants for the insulation of homes.

(c) To save money by closing the three old people's homes that it runs and instead paying privately-run old people's homes to house these old people.

(d) To increase the pay of its lowest paid workers to 20% more than the statutory minimum wage.

(e) To licence no more taxis in Coketown, because 300 taxis is too many. (In fact there are only 250 taxis in Coketown.)

Administrative Law: Judicial Review

Commentary

This question raises a variety of issues relating to judicial review and must be tackled by identifying the material relevant to each part of the problem. It will be appropriate to introduce the answer by dealing with those issues that are clearly common to all parts of the question. But there is no need to write an essay on judicial review before tackling the problems and little credit will be given for doing so. The good student will look separately at each part of the problem, identify one or two relevant grounds and support them with references to cases. Putting in far-fetched suggestions, such as challenging a perfectly sensible decision on the grounds of irrationality, is likely to make the examiner think you do not really understand the law. Note also that the question specifically asks about locus standi and process, and it will be appropriate as part of this to suggest which remedy or remedies should be sought.

Answer plan

- Public body, public law, judicial review
- Breach of natural justice
- Proportionality
- Fettering discretion
- Legitimate expectation
- Misuse of discretion
- Unreasonableness
- Giving reasons
- Mistake of fact.

Suggested answer

Because the Council is a public body, its decisions can be challenged by way of judicial review. Any person who has a sufficient interest will be able to bring a case on the grounds characterised by Lord Diplock as illegality, irrationality and procedural impropriety. Such a person must apply to the Administrative Court for permission to make an application for judicial review within the three-month time limit. If permission is granted, the case will proceed to a full hearing.

(a) No information is given about the grounds on which the Council has acted, but it is clear from the facts given that the way the decision was made is open to challenge. A, B and C, as licence holders, have rights and under the general principle laid down in *Ridge v Baldwin* [1964] AC 40, decisions affecting the rights of individuals must be made in accordance with the rules of natural justice. Indeed it was specifically held in *R v Wear Valley DC ex parte Binks* [1985] 2 All ER 699 that contractual as well as statutory licences were protected. It therefore appears that if the revocation of the licences was not preceded by an opportunity for A, B and C to state their cases, it can be challenged. It has been held, however, that in situations of extreme urgency a decision can be made before any hearing is given. In *R v Secretary of State for Transport ex parte Pegasus* [1989] 2 All ER 481, it was held that an air charter company's licence could be revoked with immediate effect because of fears over public safety. If the Council's decision in this problem was provoked by, for example, fears that the ice cream posed a threat to public health, there would be no breach of natural justice, provided a proper hearing was given at a later stage. Nowadays, the court might also consider the issue of proportionality, when a person's livelihood is at stake. 'Proportionality' has been defined by Bradley and Ewing's *Constitutional and Administrative Law*, 14th edn (2007) at p. 737:

> In outline, if action to achieve a lawful objective is taken in a situation where it will restrict a fundamental right, the effect on the right must not be disproportionate to the public purpose sought to be achieved.

So Coketown DC would have to prove that there really was a public health problem and that there was no other way of dealing with it, short of shutting down the businesses of A, B and C. In an early case, *R v Barnsley MBC ex parte Hook* [1976] 1 WLR 1052, Lord Denning MR quashed the council's decision to revoke the licence of a market trader, who had urinated in the street. The punishment was out of all proportion to the crime. A, B and C clearly have locus standi as the persons directly affected by the decision and are likely to seek either a quashing order to quash the Council's decision or a declaration that it is invalid.

(b) The Council appears to have a discretion to make these grants. It is entitled to adopt general policies to guide it in allocating such grants, but that does not permit it to adopt a rule and refuse to depart from it. In *R v London County Council ex parte Corrie* [1918] 1 KB 68, the Council was held to have acted ultra vires in adopting a rule against the sale of pamphlets in parks and refusing even to consider making an exception to it. In *A-G ex rel Tilley v Wandsworth LBC* [1981] 1 WLR 854, the court declared invalid a council's decision never to use a statutory power to rehouse homeless families with children.

There is, however, nothing unlawful in the adoption of a policy, provided that consideration is given to each individual case. In *British Oxygen v Board of Trade* [1971] AC 610, a decision to refuse the applicant an investment grant, in accordance with a stated policy, was held to be valid, because consideration had been given to the individual application. The easiest way to demonstrate that individual cases are considered is to offer applicants an opportunity to state their case either orally or in writing. The Council would therefore be well advised to adopt a procedure that shows its willingness to consider applications;

it can then lawfully reject any applications that it does not feel justify a departure from its policy.

If the Council does not do so, its decision could be challenged by anyone who has applied for a grant and been rejected. Such an applicant could ask for a declaration that the Council was acting unlawfully or a mandatory order to compel them to consider the application again. It will remain within the Council's discretion, however, whether any particular grant is made or not.

(c) This situation seems to resemble *R v North Devon Health Authority ex parte Coughlan* [2001] QB 213. In 1993, North Devon moved Coughlan and other geriatric patients into a new home and assured them that this could be their home for life. However, in 1998, North Devon decided to close the home and move the residents into local authority care. The court held that North Devon could not go back on its promise to the residents as they now had a 'legitimate expectation' that they could stay and it would be an abuse of power to break the promise. This case seems to do justice, but as a precedent it has caused problems for public authorities, who often need to change their policies, particularly if the financial situation changes. *R (Bibi) v Newham Borough Council* [2002] 1 WLR 237 is a comparable case, where Newham had told some refugees that it would place them in permanent, secure accommodation within 18 months. The Council had thought that they were legally obliged to do this, but when a House of Lords decision held that this was not so, Newham continued just to provide temporary accommodation. The refugees claimed that they had been promised permanent accommodation and the court agreed that the Council had created a legitimate expectation. The court did not, however, order the Council to provide permanent accommodation, because that would be a court assuming the power of the executive. Instead, the problem would be referred back to the Council for it to determine how best to keep their promise of permanent, secure accommodation. In contrast, our facts do not reveal that Coketown DC have made any specific promises to any of the residents of the old people's homes. This would seem to be an important element of legitimate expectation, as it was held in *R (Niazi) v Secretary of State for the Home Department* [2008] EWCA Civ 755 that there either has to be a distinct promise to a specific person or group that an existing policy would be maintained, or that the policy affected a specific person or group and it was reasonable for that person or group to expect that policy to continue. Coketown have made no promises that the old people's homes would remain open, so if there was a challenge to the closure by one or more of the residents, it is likely that it would fail.

(d) The Council will have a discretion over the rates of pay it adopts and this discretion must be exercised on the basis of relevant considerations and to achieve proper purposes. In examining this problem, it is clear that the Council must take into account its fiduciary duty to its rate and tax payers, as laid down in *Roberts v Hopwood* [1925] AC 578, and *Bromley LBC v Greater London*

Council [1982] 1 AC 768. In *Roberts v Hopwood* excessively generous wages were found to breach that principle. The radical Poplar Borough Council had ignored such relevant considerations as the cost of living and the rates of pay agreed by collective bargaining with the trade unions. If it could be shown here that the Council had made an arbitrary decision to increase the wages, its decision might be open to challenge. If, on the other hand, the increase was part of a negotiated wage settlement, or a response to an acute shortage of workers, no objection could be made.

This decision could be challenged by a council tax payer by way of judicial review. The courts have generally accepted the locus standi of those who pay local taxes to challenge councils' activities: see *Barrs v Bethell* [1982] Ch 294. The most appropriate remedy would be a declaration.

(e) This final decision could be challenged on three grounds. Firstly, it is based on facts that are clearly incorrect, so it could be suggested that the decision is unreasonable or irrational, within the strict test laid down by Lord Greene in *Associated Provincial Picture Houses v Wednesbury Corporation* [1948] 1 KB 223, at 229: 'something so absurd that no sensible person could ever dream that it lay within the powers of the authority'.

Secondly, there is a breach of natural justice. Although there is no general duty in administrative law to give reasons for a decision, fairness would probably require that the Council gave some kind of explanation for their decision to the local taxi drivers: *R v Home Secretary, ex parte Doody* [1994] 1 AC 531. The taxi drivers should be given an opportunity to respond and make their own representations, before a final decision is taken: *Re Liverpool Taxi Fleet Operators' Association* [1972] 2 QB 299.

Thirdly, although judicial review is not an appeal against a finding of fact and usually only involves legal mistakes made by public bodies, a new head of challenge has recently emerged, that of mistake of fact. A decision cannot be based on facts that can be shown to be incorrect, are material to the decision and cause unfairness. It is the Council that is mistaken about the number of taxis and there is no error or misleading on the part of the taxi drivers themselves. These principles were laid down by the House of Lords in *R v Criminal Injuries Compensation Board ex parte A* [1999] 2 AC 330, where the Board did not see a vital doctor's report. Mistake of fact was further developed in *E v Secretary of State for the Home Department* [2004] QB 1044, where a Tribunal did not consider relevant new evidence and was upheld in the recent *R (March) v Secretary of State for Health* [2010] EWHC 765, where the government minister was mistaken as to the true facts of the case.

The taxi drivers have a good case. The Council decision could be held unlawful by a declaration. Then Coketown would have to take their decision again, based on the correct number of taxis and giving the taxi drivers the opportunity to make representations.

Administrative Law: Judicial Review | 193

Question 5

What are the main procedural difficulties facing someone who wishes to make an application for judicial review? Should any of the rules in this area be reformed?

Commentary

This is a straightforward question, requiring the student to examine just the procedural aspects of judicial review, not the substantive law. There is scope for differences of emphasis about what is included; the selection made here covers the principal issues, but other issues could properly be included. What will make for a good answer is the assessment of the law and discussion of whether reform is needed. This answer concludes with a defence of the present law, but it would be just as acceptable to conclude with criticism and calls for changes.

Answer plan

- The public/private divide
- Applying for permission to sue
- Time limit
- Locus standi.

Suggested answer

From the earliest times, when the courts developed the prerogative writs, there have been special procedures for obtaining judicial review, which have differed from those used in ordinary civil proceedings. Generally such procedures have made it more difficult to seek judicial review, because they have been imposed to protect public authorities. Whether the retention of special procedures can be justified has been widely debated. Some changes to the rules have been made, but other aspects remain problematic.

An applicant who is thinking of seeking judicial review must first of all be sure that judicial review is the appropriate procedure to use. The defendant must be a public body, not a private body. But because the conceptual difference between public and private is not a traditional part of English law, this rule may be difficult to apply, and litigants have failed through using the wrong procedure. The courts have little difficulty in identifying as private those bodies whose legal authority derives only from contract, such as trade unions and sporting bodies: see *R v Disciplinary Committee of the Jockey Club ex parte Aga Khan* [1993] 1 WLR

909. But where bodies of uncertain status perform a public function, the courts tend to classify them as public, in order to subject them to judicial review, as in *R v Panel on Takeovers and Mergers ex parte Datafin* [1987] QB 815. The Panel had been established by the London Stock Market to regulate company takeovers and mergers. It was not created by Act of Parliament. The view of the court was that the Panel was performing a vital public function and, if it did not exist, a statutory body would have had to have been created to take its place. Other non-statutory bodies, such as the Advertising Standards Authority, LAUTRO and university visitors, have also been confirmed as public bodies and therefore subject to judicial review. If this was not so, it would be difficult to subject the decisions of these bodies to legal control.

In the early days of the, then new, judicial review procedure the courts were strict in insisting, that if the case involved a public law matter, the judicial review procedure must be used: *O'Reilly v Mackman* [1983] 2 AC 237. The claimant could not use ordinary High Court procedure to challenge the decision of a public body. However, since the reform of High Court procedure in 1998, the courts are much more relaxed about this, because even if a case is begun by writ in the High Court, it can be transferred to the judicial review procedure: *Clark v University of Lincolnshire and Humberside* [2000] 1 WLR 1988.

Having decided to use judicial review, applicants are faced with one of the main procedural hurdles. They cannot commence proceedings as of right, but must apply for permission (formerly leave). The defendant public authority will be informed, and then a judge in chambers will consider the papers and decide whether to grant permission. If the judge is minded to refuse, the request will be considered in open court, and the applicant can appeal against a refusal to the Court of Appeal. Why is permission needed? The justification offered is that attempts are made to seek judicial review in cases that are plainly hopeless, sometimes as a publicity stunt or as a last desperate throw of the dice. There would be a great waste of resources if public authorities had to defend all such cases at a full hearing. Instead, these cases are filtered out at the permission stage, and this also saves the applicant unnecessary expense. The counter-argument is that it is wrong in principle that litigation should need the permission of the court. In no other branch of the law is permission needed. An action against a public authority in tort or contract can be commenced as of right. Frivolous or vexatious claims are deterred sufficiently by the risk of liability for costs. Although every applicant with an arguable case should be granted permission, there is a danger that someone with a good case may be unable even to start proceedings. There have been cases where an applicant, having initially been refused permission, went on to win the case on its merits.

When the Law Commission examined this issue in 1994 it recommended that the permission stage should be retained as the only means of preventing a flood of hopeless cases. Many writers have criticised this finding, but public authorities are happy with it. Provided that judges are generous in their initial assessment of cases, the current law can be defended.

The next problem for the applicant is the time limit. Application must be made promptly and in any event within three months of the decision being challenged. This is a much shorter time limit than applies in normal civil proceedings, but it is justified by the need for the legal position of public authorities to be firmly settled at the earliest opportunity. Short time limits are normal in administrative law. Under Article 230 of the EU Treaty, the limit for challenging the actions of European Union institutions is only two months, a period adopted from French administrative law. The courts do have the power to extend the period for a good reason; in *R v Stratford on Avon DC ex parte Jackson* [1985] 1 WLR 1319, the applicant justified his delay by showing that he was waiting for a decision from the Legal Aid Board. But the court will not allow a belated application if this would cause administrative difficulties. In *R v Dairy Produce Quota Tribunal ex parte Caswell* [1990] 2 AC 738, the court refused to allow a challenge after two years to the way milk quotas had been allocated to farmers, as there would have been enormous problems in trying to undo previous allocations. It seems reasonable to expect applicants to be prompt and no change to this rule seems necessary.

The final issue that may cause problems for applicants is locus standi. When the Application for Judicial Review was introduced, locus standi was deliberately described in words without a previous legal meaning, as a 'sufficient interest' in the matter. The meaning of this expression was discussed by the House of Lords in *R v Inland Revenue Commissioners ex parte National Federation of Self-Employed and Small Businesses* [1982] AC 617. The applicants wished to challenge the validity of an agreement between the IRC and Fleet Street casual workers about past and future payments of tax. Although the challenge failed on the facts, the House of Lords felt that only 'busybodies, cranks and other mischief makers' should be regarded as not having locus standi to seek judicial review of the actions of public authorities. Pressure groups and even 'a single public-spirited taxpayer' should be allowed to bring such cases, in order to ensure that the rule of law applies.

The effect of this decision was a general liberalisation of the rules of locus standi. The 'single public-spirited taxpayer' has brought actions for judicial review. In *R v HM Treasury ex parte Smedley* [1985] 1 QB 657, a taxpayer challenged, albeit unsuccessfully, the UK's payment of certain sums to the European Community. The locus standi of pressure groups has been generally accepted, though in *R v Secretary of State for the Environment ex parte Rose Theatre Trust* [1990] 1 QB 504, the judge refused to allow a pressure group formed specifically for the purpose of saving the Rose Theatre to challenge the government's decision. Other cases have been more generous. Most striking was the decision in *R v Foreign Secretary ex parte World Development Movement* [1995] 1 WLR 386.

The applicants were a respected voluntary organisation whose interest in challenging the use of UK aid to fund the Pergau Dam in Malaysia was purely moral. But, as the court said, if WDM did not have locus standi, no one would be able to challenge the decision, except people living in a remote area of Malaysia whose opportunity to take legal action in the English High Court is limited. It seems therefore that locus standi will not cause a problem to genuine applicants and no change to the law on this point is needed.

In conclusion, it can be argued that, although there are practical problems in bringing any type of legal action, the special rules relating to judicial review do not act as too great a hindrance to litigants. The need to obtain permission is the most contentious issue but even this can be defended. It would be a great problem for those seeking judicial review if frivolous or vexatious cases filled the courts and caused delay to genuine applicants.

Question 6

The (imaginary) Protection of Airfields Act 2005 empowers the Secretary of State to make regulations, in the form of a statutory instrument, 'in order to protect and maintain the security of airfields used by the Royal Air Force'. The Act provides that, before drafting such regulations the Secretary of State 'shall consult organisations and groups appearing to him to be representative of those who may be affected by the regulations'. It is further provided that before the regulations become law the draft statutory instrument must be approved by the House of Commons under the affirmative resolution procedure.

In 2008 the Secretary of State for Defence made SI 1688, the RAF Crookwaters Protection Regulations, under which it is an offence, punishable with a maximum fine of £200, for anyone to go within one mile of the perimeter fence of RAF Crookwaters. The Secretary of State only consults the RAF and the regulations are not laid before the House of Commons.

Alan is a farmer, whose fields border on RAF Crookwaters. He has been threatened with prosecution if he enters any of his fields that are within a mile of the airfield. He has never heard of these regulations and nor has the National Farmers Union as the regulations have not yet been published.

Advise Alan.

Commentary

Delegated legislation can seem a somewhat dry topic and most law students probably think that Acts of Parliament are more important. In fact, most modern law making is done by way of delegated legislation and there can be 10,000 or more new pages of it every year. Governments prefer

Administrative Law: Judicial Review   197

to make delegated legislation, because it is less time-consuming than passing a new Act of Parliament and new laws can be passed almost instantaneously. Similarly, some delegated legislation is very technical and detailed and would just clog up parliamentary time with draft laws that few of the MPs understand anyway. Most modern Acts only lay out the general principles with the details to be filled in later by means of statutory instrument. Critics see this as undemocratic, in that Parliament should make the law, not ministers and civil servants. Some suspect that governments could be tempted to hide controversial new laws in delegated legislation, which does not attract as much publicity as an Act of Parliament. Therefore the courts might be persuaded to judicially review delegated legislation, particularly if the court considers the legislation fundamentally unfair: see *R (C) v Secretary of State for Justice* **[2009] QB 657** in the Suggested Answer as an example.

Problem questions on delegated legislation will usually focus on the main grounds that the courts have used to overturn ultra vires legislation. Knowledge of just a few cases should enable you to answer most questions of this type.

Agricultural, Horticultural and Forestry Training Board v Aylesbury Mushrooms **[1972] 1 WLR 190** shows that lack of consultation can mean that the delegated legislation is void and of no effect. It is as though that legislation never existed.

Council of Civil Service Unions v Minister for the Civil Service **[1985] AC 374** is always a good case on judicial review, generally, as it sets out the main grounds in a clear way, but it also shows that a failure to consult can make legislation void.

No taxation without legislation raises a major constitutional theme, linking back to the **Bill of Rights 1689** and is nicely illustrated by *Attorney-General v Wiltshire United Dairies Ltd* **(1921) 37 TLR 884**.

Human Rights are an important new element in this area, particularly since the **Human Rights Act 1998**. An Act of Parliament is still valid, even if it is incompatible with the human rights protected by the Act, but delegated legislation can be held void by the courts if it is contrary to human rights.

Lastly, the defence that a statutory instrument has not been published always makes a nice little point in problems of this kind, as illustrated by *Simmonds v Newell* **[1953] 1 WLR 826**.

Answer plan

- Judicial review of a statutory instrument
- A matter of public law
- Procedural impropriety—lack of consultation
- Procedural impropriety—lack of parliamentary approval
- Illegality—criminal penalty must be authorised by the Act
- Illegality—regulations must be within the purpose of the Act
- Irrationality
- Breach of human rights
- Failure to publish the regulations may provide a defence
- Collateral challenge.

Suggested answer

It seems that Alan's livelihood is threatened by the RAF Crookwaters Protection Regulations, yet he faces prosecution for allegedly infringing them. It is not possible for him to challenge the fairness and legality of the Protection of Airfields Act 2005. Due to the doctrine of the supremacy of Parliament, it is not possible for the courts to even begin to question the legal authority of an Act of Parliament: *Pickin v BRB* [1974] AC 765.

There is nothing, however, to stop Alan seeking to challenge the legal validity of the statutory instrument. This could be done by seeking a judicial review. The Secretary of State for Defence is a government minister and he has made delegated legislation, so the Secretary of State is clearly a public body exercising a public law power. So, according to *R v City Panel on Takeovers and Mergers ex parte Datafin Ltd* [1987] QB 817, the matter is susceptible to judicial review. All types of delegated legislation can be judicially reviewed under the three main grounds of illegality, irrationality and procedural impropriety: *Council of Civil Service Unions v Minister for the Civil Service* [1985] AC 374.

For Alan to succeed in a judicial review on the grounds of procedural impropriety, he would need to show that the Secretary of State for Defence has failed to follow the correct procedure when making the RAF Crookwaters Protection Regulations. The correct procedure is laid down in the parent Act, the Protection of Airfields Act 2005, and requires that before making the regulations, the Secretary of State consults those who may be affected by the regulations. Such consultation requirements are common in Acts of Parliament that allow ministers to make delegated legislation and, despite the wording, 'appearing to him', that seems to allow the Secretary of State to consult whoever he chooses, the courts have held that a minister does not have complete discretion on this matter. There was a similar statutory consultation requirement in *Agricultural, Horticultural and Forestry Training Board v Aylesbury Mushrooms* [1972] 1 WLR 190 and the court held that, although the minister had a discretion on whom to consult, he must exercise that discretion reasonably and in good faith. In the *Aylesbury Mushrooms Case*, just sending a letter and sending a copy of the draft regulation, which did not arrive, was not proper consultation. Similarly, allowing insufficient time for the consulted body to study the proposals before replying, does not amount to genuine consultation: *R v Secretary of State for Social Services ex parte Association of Metropolitan Authorities* [1986] 1 WLR 1. Here, the Secretary of State for Defence has not consulted at all, except for the RAF, who would presumably agree to the Regulations anyway. There may be an expectation of consultation, particularly as Alan is so personally affected by the Regulations. The courts have certainly held that, where there has been a previous practice of consultation, it should continue and not to consult is a breach of natural justice: *Council of Civil Service Unions v Minister for the Civil Service* [1985] AC 374.

If the court agrees that there is a procedural impropriety, then the Regulations are ultra vires and of no legal effect.

It also seems, from the facts, that the affirmative resolution by the House of Commons has not taken place. This, too, is a statutory requirement, but there is little case law on the matter. Older cases, such as *Bailey v Williamson* (1873) LR 8 QB 118, suggest that this might only be a directory requirement and not mandatory, but where an affirmative resolution is required it would seem logical to argue that the resolution must be granted by Parliament or the Regulations will be null and void and of no effect: *R v Department of Health and Social Security, ex parte Camden LBC* (1986) Times, 5 March.

Illegality, as grounds of judicial review, means that the court will closely inspect the wording of the delegated legislation and the parent Act and decide whether the delegated legislation goes beyond what is permitted under the Act. If the delegated legislation allows the authorities to charge a fee or levy a fine, this must be clearly permitted under the parent Act. In *Attorney-General v Wiltshire United Dairies Ltd* (1921) 37 TLR 884, the Food Controller charged a duty of 2d per gallon on milk imported from another county. This was not legal as the Defence Regulations did not authorise charging citizens money. Similarly the tax authorities could not charge extra taxes that were not statutorily authorised: *Commissioners of Custom and Excise v Cure and Deeley* [1962] 1 QB 340. So the Secretary of State for Defence will have to show that the Protection of Airfields Act 2005 does allow fines to be imposed for breach of a statutory instrument.

The court will also try to interpret the Protection of Airfields Act 2005, to see whether it allows the restriction of the citizen's freedom of movement. In *R (Spath Holme Ltd) v Secretary of State for the Environment* [2001] 2 AC 349, the House of Lords held that the court must look for the overall purpose of the Act. A statute called the Protection of Airfields Act would suggest that it would allow the government to take reasonable measures to protect the security of an airfield.

However, is a complete ban on anyone approaching within a mile of the airfield reasonable? Judicial review is also permitted on the grounds that a measure is irrational. This was defined by Lord Diplock in *Council of Civil Service Unions v Minister for the Civil Service* [1985] AC 374 at 410 as 'a decision so outrageous in its defiance of logic or of accepted moral standards that no sensible person who had applied his mind to the question to be decided could have arrived at it'. It is fairly unusual for the courts to overturn delegated legislation on the grounds that it is irrational, because the decision on how to exercise the statutory power generally turns on political and economic considerations, which are better evaluated by the minister and Parliament than the courts: *R (Javed) v Home Secretary* [2001] 3 WLR 323. It is much more likely, however, that the court will hold the delegated legislation to be irrational if it infringes human rights. In the *Javed* case the Home Secretary had the power to make statutory instruments designating safe countries, to which asylum-seekers could be returned. The Court of Appeal disagreed with the Home Secretary's assessment that Pakistan was a safe country to which to return women and Ahmadis (a religious minority) and overturned the Order. This was despite the fact that Parliament had actually approved the Order, as required, by affirmative resolution. So Alan's case seems stronger as there has been no parliamentary approval on our facts, so the court would not fear that they were obstructing the wishes of the democratically elected Parliament. In *R (C) v Secretary of State for Justice* [2009] QB 657, the Court of Appeal overturned a statutory instrument that allowed for the physical restraint of children held in privately run secure training centres, partly on the grounds that *Articles 3 and 8 of the European Convention on Human Rights* had been infringed. *Article 3* prohibits inhuman and degrading treatment and *Article 8* protects a person's private life. But have any of Alan's human rights actually been infringed? His farm is also likely to be his home and restricting access to it would be a breach of *Article 8*, respect for his home, and *Article 1 of the First Protocol*, the right to peaceful enjoyment of his possessions. The Secretary of State would have to show that there really was a security reason for stopping him from using his farm.

So it seems that Alan would have a good case for a successful judicial review of the RAF Crookwaters Protection Regulations on a number of grounds, but he might not want to take this course of action. Judicial review cases are heard in the High Court in London, and this would make it expensive and maybe inconvenient for Alan. He could, instead, just wait to be prosecuted in his local magistrates' court and then there are two defences that he could use.

A huge volume of delegated legislation is enacted each year and there are sometimes delays in publishing it, particularly if the statutory instrument is lengthy. Therefore there is a defence in *s. 3(2) of the Statutory Instruments Act 1946* to a prosecution for breach of a statutory instrument if it has not been published. This would give Alan a defence to a prosecution as we are told that the RAF Crookwaters Protection Regulations have not been published: *Simmonds v Newell* [1953] 1 WLR 826. This defence will not, however, be available if the government has taken reasonable steps to bring the contents of the statutory instrument to the attention of the public or to the persons affected by it, as seen in *R v Sheer Metalcraft* [1954] 1 QB 586. As neither Alan, who is directly affected by them, nor the National Farmers Union, who represent other farmers, have heard of these new regulations it would seem that the government has not taken reasonable steps to publicise the Regulations. So the non-publication defence is still available to Alan.

There is another defence that Alan could use if he is taken to court, which is sometimes known as a collateral challenge. He, or more likely, his lawyers, would argue that if the Regulations are ultra vires, then they are void and of no effect and therefore he cannot be prosecuted under them. This was permitted in *DPP v Hutchinson* [1990] 2 AC 783, where some 'Greenham Common' women succeeded in their defence to a prosecution for breaking a by-law not to enter RAF

Greenham Common, by showing that the parent Act stated that the Secretary of State could not make a by-law 'to take away or prejudice any rights of common'. This was what is known as substantive ultra vires, which we classified as illegality and irrationality and it was thought, at first, that collateral challenge did not allow a defence based on procedural ultra vires, which we classified as procedural impropriety. The House of Lords ruled in *Boddington v British Transport Police* [1998] 2 All ER 203 that the magistrates' court had jurisdiction to rule on both substantive and procedural ultra vires.

So in conclusion this is probably Alan's best option: carry on using his fields, wait to be prosecuted and then argue that the RAF Crookwaters Protection Regulations are ultra vires.

Further reading

Barnett, H. *Constitutional and Administrative Law*, 8th edn (Routledge, 2011), chs. 24, 25 and 26.

Bradley, A. and Ewing, K. *Constitutional and Administrative Law*, 15th edn (Longman, 2010), chs. 30 and 31.

Leyland, P. and Anthony, G. *Textbook on Administrative Law* 6th edn (Oxford University Press, 2009), chs. 10–16 and 19.

Turpin, C. and Tomkins, A. *British Government and the Constitution*, 6th edn (Cambridge, 2007), ch 10.

DELEGATED LEGISLATION

Bradley, A. and Ewing, K. *Constitutional and Administrative Law*, 15th edn (Longman, 2010), ch. 28.

Craig, P. *Administrative Law*, 6th edn (Sweet and Maxwell, 2008), ch. 22.

12

Public Authority Proceedings

Introduction

The topics dealt with in this chapter are more likely to be included in an administrative law course than in a general constitutional law course, with the exception of public interest immunity, which is of such constitutional interest that it may be included where the other aspects are not. Students will need to be guided by their own examiners and syllabus.

Examples of both essay and problem questions are included. Good answers will require the student to show skills of legal analysis and application. A student who has studied or is studying tort or contract need not be afraid to bring that extra knowledge into the answer. The law may be divided into discrete subjects for the purpose of teaching and examining, but in reality it is an undivided whole.

Question 1

The Home Office decided, as part of its policy of reducing the prison population, to establish hostels where long-term prisoners could spend the last year of their sentences, being gradually rehabilitated into the outside world. One of these hostels was established in Coketown. It was a converted house in a residential area, occupied by eight prisoners, who went out to work during the day, but were otherwise supervised by a warden and his staff.

Consider the liability of the Home Office in the following situations.

(a) White, Black and Gray, who live in the same street as the hostel, consider that it has reduced the amenity and value of their homes. They consider that the hostel should have been established somewhere else.

(b) Brown, who lives next door to the hostel, thinks that the choice of site for the hostel was made because he is a prominent campaigner against Home Office policies: he suspects that there is evidence of this hidden in Home Office files.

(c) The Home Office decided that prisoners convicted of violent crimes could if considered suitable, be sent to the hostel. Reg had been sentenced to 15 years for attempted murder and, because he had behaved impeccably throughout his time in prison, was due for release next year. He was sent to the hostel, obtained a job, and apparently settled in well. But last week, on the way home from work, he went to the pub, got drunk, and punched Green, the landlord. The previous week, Reg had threatened Green.

Commentary

This question raises various issues relating to the liability of public authorities. It is important for students to deal both with the general rules applicable to all public authorities and with the special rules governing the liability of the Crown. The student will not be expected to examine issues of tortious liability in as great depth as would be appropriate in a tort examination, but should concentrate on those aspects peculiar to public authorities. The question also touches on public interest immunity.

Answer plan

- Nuisance, subject to statutory authority
- Breach of **Article 8 ECHR**
- Misfeasance in public office
- Public interest immunity
- Liability in negligence for policy and operation
- Breach of **Article 2 ECHR**.

Suggested answer

(a) White, Black and Gray will have to prove that the hostel constitutes an actionable nuisance if they wish to obtain redress. Under **s. 2 of the Crown Proceedings Act 1947** the Crown is subject to the same liabilities as any other person in respect of torts committed by its servants or agents, and torts arising from its ownership, occupation or control of property. But there are circumstances in which a body may be able to plead that it has statutory authority. If a statute specifically authorises some activity that will inevitably result in the commission of a nuisance, no action will lie. In *Allen v Gulf Oil Refinery Ltd* **[1981] AC 1001**, the defendants obtained a private Act of Parliament authorising them to construct a refinery on a particular site, from which some nuisance would inevitably result. They were held to be immune from action, unless they negligently operated the refinery in such a way as to increase the nuisance beyond what was inevitable.

But this defence does not operate where the authorisation is general and the nuisance not inevitable. In *Metropolitan Asylum District v Hill* (1881) 6 App Cas 193, the plaintiff had statutory authority to build hospitals, and chose to build one in a place where it would cause a nuisance. As it would have been possible to exercise the statutory power without causing a nuisance, no defence of statutory authority existed.

In this problem, it appears that the choice of site was in the hands of the Home Office. It can be argued that the hostel could have been established anywhere, including places where it would not have constituted a nuisance.

In contrast, Thames Water escaped liability for nuisance, when their sewers overflowed and flooded the property of Marcic: *Marcic v Thames Water Utilities Ltd* [2004] 2 AC 42. The sewers were properly maintained, but the volume of sewerage had increased since the sewers were built. The House of Lords held that there was no liability for nuisance, particularly as there was a detailed statutory scheme for making complaints, which Marcic had not used. There is no statutory scheme under which White, Black and Gray can complain but, as in *Marcic v Thames*, the court would probably say that the wider interests of the population, in having criminals rehabilitated, outweighed the interests of White, Black and Gray. Marcic also claimed that Thames Water had infringed his right of respect for his home under *Article 8 of the European Convention of Human Rights*. The House of Lords rejected his claim and applied *Hatton v UK* (2003) 37 EHRR 28, a decision of the European Court of Human Rights concerning aircraft noise at Heathrow Airport. In these types of claim the interests of the householder had to be weighed against the wider interests of society. It could not be said that the statutory scheme for regulating sewage failed to keep a balance between the interests of Marcic and the interests of everyone else in having their sewers emptied. Following *Marcic v Thames*, it seems less likely that the interference, which the hostel causes to surrounding property, is sufficient to amount to nuisance. If it did, White, Black and Gray will be able to sue for damages. They will not, however, be able to obtain an injunction against the Crown to order the closure of the hostel. By *s. 21 of the Crown Proceedings Act 1947*, no injunction may be awarded against the Crown, though a declaration may be awarded instead.

(b) Brown is alleging that the choice of site for the hostel was made maliciously. This would constitute grounds for judicial review, the decision being made for an improper purpose or even in bad faith. Such proceedings would be an appropriate way of getting the decision quashed but would not lead to the award of any compensation to Brown unless he can demonstrate the existence of some established form of liability.

To make a decision that subsequently proves to be unlawful does not in itself give rise to any liability. In *Dunlop v Woollahra Municipal Council* [1982] AC 158, the Privy Council refused to impose any liability on a local authority whose decision, based on a misunderstanding of their legal powers, was later held to be ultra vires.

Brown may be able to recover damages for the tort of misfeasance in a public office, which is designed to provide redress for the victims of malicious abuses of public power. The House of Lords held in *Three Rivers DC v Bank of England* [2000] 3 All ER 1 that there are two different forms of this tort. First, there is targeted malice by a public officer, where he uses his statutory power, specifically to injure a person for an improper or ulterior motive. Secondly, where a public officer acts, knowing that he has no power to do the act and knowing that what he does will probably injure the claimant. In the second form of this tort there is still liability if the public officer is reckless as to whether he has the power and whether he injures the claimant. Brown's claim is based on the first form of this tort, intentional or targeted malice. If the tort involves outrageous, arbitrary or unconstitutional behaviour it is possible to award exemplary damages: *Abdillaahi Muuse v Secretary of State for the Home Department* [2010] EWCA Civ 453. According to *Watkins v Home Secretary* [2006] 2 All ER 353, for both types of the tort, Brown would have to prove that the opening of the hostel had caused him material damage, in the sense of financial loss or physical or mental injury.

Brown would have to prove that the decision was in fact made with the deliberate intention of causing him injury and had caused him financial loss, perhaps the decline in value of his house, in order to recover damages. His difficulty will be to obtain proof.

Any attempt by Brown to obtain the documents that he thinks will reveal misfeasance may be met by a claim for public interest immunity from the Home Office. Such a claim may be based on the contents of the particular document, or on the assertion that that class of document needs, in the public interest, to be kept secret. As was made clear in *R v Chief Constable of the West Midlands Police ex parte Wiley* [1994] 3 All ER 420, if the Home Office does not think that the public interest would be harmed by revealing these documents, there is no obligation on it to claim public interest immunity.

The case of *Conway v Rimmer* [1968] AC 910 established that the decision on disclosure or otherwise rests with the court, not the government. The court has to balance two aspects of the public interest; on the one hand, the public interest in secrecy and confidentiality, and, on the other hand, the public interest in the fair administration of justice. Where necessary, the court may inspect the documents to help it decide whether disclosure should be ordered.

The Home Office may have two possible grounds for arguing that these documents should be kept secret. One is that the security of the hostel, its inmates and neighbours might be compromised if the documents were revealed. This does not appear to be very plausible, though security would generally be taken as a reasonable ground to use as a basis for secrecy. The other ground might be the confidentiality of Civil Service advice to ministers. It has been asserted in various cases that the candour of public officials, and hence their usefulness to ministers might be impaired if they knew their words might be revealed in later litigation. But the courts have shown themselves very unsympathetic to such claims, refusing to believe that officials, whose advice will in any case be preserved on file, will be frightened by the remote possibility of later litigation into failing to do their job properly. In *Williams v Home Office* [1981] 1 All ER 1151, this argument concerning candour was rejected and documents relating to penal policy revealed. In that case, inspection of the documents revealed them to be essential to the plaintiff's case, so that the court had no difficulty in holding that the public interest in the fair administration of justice prevailed.

In this problem, it may well be that the court will find it necessary to inspect the documents to discover whether they are necessary to Brown's case, because, if unnecessary, they need not be disclosed. In *Burmah Oil Co. v Bank of England* [1980] AC 1090, where sensitive papers were concerned, the court inspected them before deciding that their evidential value to the plaintiff was so limited as not to outweigh the genuine claim to confidentiality put forward by the Attorney-General. Brown is therefore in the hands of the court, which must perform the difficult task of balancing the two aspects of the public interest.

(c) The Home Office's liability to Green would have to be based on the claim that it has been in some way negligent. The basic principles governing the liability of public authorities in negligence have been laid down by the House of Lords in the cases of *X v Bedfordshire CC* [1995] 2 AC 633 and *Jain v Trent Strategic Health Authority* [2009] 1 All ER 957. When a state authority acts under statutory powers, designed for the benefit or protection of a particular class of persons, a duty of care is not owed to others, who might be adversely affected by those actions. According to *Barrett v Enfield LBC* [2001] 2 AC 550, the court should not be drawn into deciding between different policy choices, because that is the task of ministers and councillors. Applying these principles to Green's case, it is difficult to see how he could succeed, as the prison authorities have to protect all of society, not just Green. The choice of appropriate penal policies is one that the Home Office has to make and, in the absence of some extreme irrationality, the courts will not intervene in such a decision: *Connor v Surrey County Council* [2010] EWCA Civ 286. Green might attempt to assert that the Home Office was negligent in choosing Reg for admission to the hostel. Such negligence would have to be established on ordinary tort principles, and this might prove difficult. It is not clear whether the court would find it fair, just and reasonable to impose a duty of care. In *Hill v Chief Constable of West Yorkshire* [1989] AC 53, the court held that the police owed no duty of care to members of the public in respect of the investigation and prevention of crime. Even if Green had warned the Home Office about the previous threat from Reg, it seems unlikely that there would be any liability for negligence, according to *Van Colle v Chief Constable of Hertfordshire Police, Smith v Chief Constable of Sussex Police* [2008] 3 All ER 977. Smith had warned the police that his former partner, Jeffrey, had threatened to kill him and Jeffrey eventually succeeded in seriously injuring him. The House of Lords declined to hold that the police had any duty of care to protect victims and witnesses of crime. To impose such a duty would be contrary to public policy, as it would make the police fearful of legal action and cause them to perform their duties in a defensive manner, which would be detrimental to the whole of society. Although there was no cause of action in negligence, the House endorsed the principle, laid down by the European Court of Human Rights, in *Osman v UK* (1998) 29 EHRR 245. The police could be liable for a breach of the right to life under Article 2 of the European Convention of Human Rights, if they knew, or ought to have known at the time, of the existence of a real and immediate risk to the life of the claimant and then failed to take reasonable steps to prevent it. Reg's threat does not seem to be serious or persistent and there is no evidence that Green reported it to the Home Office. In *Van Colle*, only Lord Bingham was willing to extend the *Osman* principle to cover not just threats to life, but threats of serious injury, so Green would not seem to have a human rights case either.

Green will have a much stronger case if he can show that the warden and staff were under instruction to keep the inmates under supervision and had failed to do so. In *Home Office v Dorset Yacht Co* [1970] AC 1004, the Home Office were held to be vicariously liable for the negligence of prison officers, who had failed to keep a party of borstal boys under supervision as they had been instructed to. But if, as seems to be the case here, the whole reason for the inmates' stay in the hostel is that they are not under constant supervision, no negligence on the part of the warden and staff can be shown. It would therefore appear that Green may be unable to establish any liability on the part of the Home Office, in which case he will be left only with the right to sue the probably impecunious Reg.

Question 2

How far is it true to say that the Crown, when involved in litigation, is in the same position as any other litigant before the English courts? Are any further reforms to proceedings involving the Crown necessary?

Commentary

This question covers a fairly wide range of issues relating to Crown proceedings and the student will need to be careful to pick up issues that may not all have been covered under that heading. Clearly, the **Crown Proceedings Act** will form the core of the answer, but there are still areas where common law rules remain applicable. There are further areas where other changes to the law have had an incidental effect upon the Crown, such as Crown service, which has been affected by the development of statutory rights for workers. The **Human Rights Act 1998**, which binds the Crown, is also beginning to extend the liability of the Crown.

Answer plan

- 'The king can do no wrong'
- Normal tort liability
- Liability to Armed Forces
- European Convention on Human Rights
- Crown service
- Contractual liability
- Procedural immunities.

Suggested answer

Until 1947, the Crown enjoyed substantial immunities from liability in English law, and benefited from various procedural advantages in litigation. These derived from historical developments. The impossibility of subjecting the king to the jurisdiction of his own courts produced the paradoxical saying that 'the king could do no wrong'; because there was no remedy for those wrongs, they did not legally exist. But an immunity that originally attached to the person of the Monarch also applied if he exercised his powers through his servants and ministers. Though the individual servant might be personally liable, the Crown remained immune. When, through the development of parliamentary government, the exercise of the Crown's power was controlled by a government, the immunity remained intact. It was therefore impossible to sue the Crown in tort, and possible to sue in contract and restitution only with the permission of the Crown, if the Attorney-General granted his fiat to a petition of right.

It was, however, possible, in appropriate cases, for the victim of a tort to sue the individual Crown servant responsible. Dicey indeed regarded this as a powerful demonstration of the rule of law, as it forced the individual to accept responsibility for his or her own actions, rather than being able to hide behind some official immunity. But as a means of ensuring adequate compensation for the victim it was seriously defective, until the Crown developed the practice of standing behind its servants and paying any damages awarded against them. Even this did not help in those circumstances where tortious liability attached to the Crown itself, perhaps as employer or landowner, and not to any individual Crown servant. The cases of *Adams v Naylor* [1946] AC 543 and *Royster v Cavey* [1947] KB 204 showed that the courts were no longer willing to co-operate in evading the effects of Crown immunity by making findings of liability against nominated defendants who were not personally liable. Statutory reform, which had been under discussion for some years, was finally introduced.

The Crown Proceedings Act 1947, s. 2 subjects the Crown to the same liabilities in tort as a person of full age and capacity in the following respects. Most importantly, it is vicariously liable for torts committed by its servants or agents; by s. 6, Crown servants are defined as those directly or indirectly appointed by the Crown and paid out of the Consolidated Fund or other Treasury-controlled moneys. To avoid any suggestion of Crown interference in the judicial system, no such liability exists in respect of those acting in a judicial capacity. The only significant limitation on this form of liability, s. 2(1), gives the Crown the right to plead any defence that the servant could have pleaded. This includes not only the ordinary tort defences but defences like Act of State, which had developed to limit the liability of Crown servants. But as the case of *Nissan v Attorney-General* [1970] AC 179 showed, this defence is very limited in scope and, in recent cases involving UK military activity abroad, the Crown has chosen not to plead Act of State as a defence: *R (Al Skeini) v Secretary of State for Defence* [2007] 3 WLR 33 and *Bici v Ministry of Defence* [2004] EWHC 786 (QB).

The other forms of tortious liability imposed by s. 2 are employers' liability to employees and liability arising from the ownership or occupation of property.

The Crown is also subjected to liability for breach of statutory duty, but this is subject to two limitations. First, the statutory duty must also be binding on persons other than the Crown. The Crown Proceedings Act is concerned only to extend the ordinary forms of tort liability to the Crown, not to create new forms of liability to which only the Crown could be subject. Secondly, by a common law rule expressly preserved by s. 40(2)(f), the Crown is not bound by statutes unless the statute so provides, expressly or by necessary implication. This rule has been the subject of stringent criticism, as making it far too easy for the Crown to evade liabilities and obligations to which it should be subject, but was confirmed by the House of Lords in *Lord Advocate v Dumbarton Council* [1990] 2 AC 580. Most modern Acts of Parliament now expressly state that they apply to the Crown, as seen in s. 22(5) of the Human Rights Act 1998.

There remain some specific limitations on the liability of the Crown in tort. Under s. 40(2) the Act only applies to liabilities arising in the UK. No action could therefore be brought, for example, in respect of a nuisance committed by the British Army in Berlin; *Trawnik v Lennox* [1985] 1 WLR 532. This seems an undesirable rule as the doctrine of state immunity may well prevent any action being brought in the foreign state either. A major problem arose as a result of **s. 10**, which exempted the Crown from liability for injuries caused to one member of the Armed Forces by the negligence of another, if the injury was classed as pensionable. After sustained criticism of this rule, the **Crown Proceedings (Armed Forces) Act 1987** repealed **s. 10**. The repeal, however, did not have retrospective effect. In *Matthews v Ministry of Defence* [2003] 1 All ER 689, it was argued that the continuing exemption for pre-1987 injuries was a breach of the right to a fair trial under **Article 6 of the European Convention on Human Rights**. But the House of Lords held that this was a substantive bar to action, not a procedural one, so **Article 6** did not apply. In the **1987 Act**, the Crown reserved the right to revive its immunity in case of war or emergency, but in recent conflicts it has not done so. It has in any case been held in *Mulcahy v Ministry of Defence* [1996] 2 All ER 758 that in battle conditions no soldier owes a duty of care to his fellow soldiers, nor does the Crown, as employer, owe any duty of care to military personnel in active combat. This so-called 'combat immunity' does not extend to policing and peacekeeping operations. So in *Bici v Ministry of Defence* [2004] EWHC 789 (QB), the Ministry of Defence was vicariously liable for soldiers, who negligently shot Albanian civilians during an operation in Kosovo.

There may also be liability under the **Human Rights Act 1998**, because, under **Article 1, the European Convention on Human Rights** applies whenever a Member State has 'jurisdiction'. It has been held, in a number of cases, that this includes foreign territory when it is under the 'effective control' of the Member State. So **Article 2**, the right to life, applied when an Iraqi civilian was killed while held in custody on a British base in Iraq: *R (Al Skeini) v Secretary of State for Defence* [2007] 3 WLR 33. So far, the Strasbourg court has confirmed that the Convention only applies to British controlled bases, hospitals, detention centres etc., but not to the rest of Iraq: *Al Saadoon & Mufdhi v UK* (2009) 49 EHRR SE11. There is no reason why other Articles of the Convention could not apply as well as seen with **Article 5**, the right to liberty, in *R (Al-Jedda) v Secretary of State for Defence* [2008] 2 WLR 1 and **Article 3**, inhuman and degrading treatment, in *Al Saadoon*. The soldiers themselves are not protected by the **Human Rights Act 1998** when they are on active service outside UK territory. Private Smith was only protected by **Article 2**, because he died of heat stroke on a British base: *R (Smith) v Secretary of State for Defence* [2010] 3 WLR 223.

The final issue in relation to tort liability is the provision in **s. 40(1)** which excludes the possibility of any action in tort against the Monarch in his or her personal capacity. Although this could be criticised, it is perhaps an appropriate way of preserving the Monarch's dignity. It is in any case difficult to imagine any circumstances in which the Monarch would have the opportunity to commit torts in person—perhaps a bite from a royal corgi? In any such case compensation would no doubt be paid ex gratia.

Turning to liability in contract, the Crown Proceedings Act 1947, s. 1 simply states that actions that could formerly have been brought by petition of right can now be brought as of right. Actions in contract against the Crown are now therefore straightforward, with the exception of actions against the Monarch in person that would have to use the old petition of right procedure.

The only area of contractual liability that has given rise to any substantial amount of litigation is the law of Crown service. At common law, Crown servants, both civil and military, were employed at the pleasure of the Crown and could therefore be dismissed at any moment, regardless of any terms in the contract; see *Dunn v R* [1896] 1 QB 116. This rule remains in the case of military personnel, whose engagement is not contractual at all; see *Mitchell v R* (1890), noted at [1896] 1 QB 121. But for civil servants, the law has been transformed by the extension to them of most of the statutory provisions governing employment. Civil servants are now entitled to redundancy payments, to compensation for unfair dismissal and to protection from racial and sexual discrimination. Although their common law rights remain limited, these are in general insignificant compared with statutory rights. Some categories of Crown servants continue to be governed by special rules, such as prison officers who are subject to strict disciplinary codes. The Crown's treatment of its employees has given rise to some disputes, such as the *GCHQ case* [1985] AC 374, but on the whole its behaviour compares satisfactorily with that of most large employers. Under the Constitutional Reform and Governance Act 2010, the Civil Service Commission, which controls the appointment of civil servants, has been put on a statutory basis and the Minister for the Civil Service, who is always the Prime Minister, has been given statutory powers of management. This will further increase the legal accountability of civil servants' employers.

There have been suggestions in some cases that the Crown may be entitled to certain immunities in contract, but the Crown does not seem to assert these. Most sweeping was the suggestion in *Rederiaktiebolaget Amphitrite v R* [1921] 3 KB 500 that the Crown cannot by contract fetter its future freedom of action in matters affecting the welfare of the State. Taken literally, this would entitle the Crown to break any contract it has entered into, but it is doubtful that such a wide proposition can be supported. Indeed, it can be argued that in the case itself there was no actual contract, so the remarks were merely obiter. The Crown has in any case sufficiently wide statutory powers, especially in emergencies, to make such a common law doctrine unnecessary.

Another limitation on the contractual power of the Crown was suggested by the case of *Churchward v R* (1865) LR 1 QB 173, where a contract was awarded to Churchward on condition that moneys were voted by Parliament. When Parliament voted against the payment, the contract necessarily fell. It was argued that this made all government contracts dependent on money being voted by Parliament, but this was refuted by the Australian case of *Attorney-General of New*

South Wales v Bardolph (1934) 52 CLR 455, where the State was held liable even in the absence of a specific vote of money, provided that the contract was a proper one and was covered by a general vote of funds. It remains possible, under the doctrine of parliamentary supremacy, for Parliament to forbid payments under a contract, and that would be legally effective. It is not, however, the practice of the Crown to bankrupt its contractors by refusing to pay its debts.

The **Crown Proceedings Act** preserves certain procedural immunities. By **s. 25(1)** awards of damages against the Crown cannot be enforced by the usual machinery of execution or attachment but this is no real problem. The Crown will always be able to pay damages awarded against it and, on the rare occasions when it does not wish to do so, as in *Burmah Oil v Lord Advocate* [1965] AC 75, it will procure the passage of legislation to reverse the decision. More serious is the provision in **s. 21(1)** that the courts cannot grant an injunction, specific performance or an order for the delivery up of land against the Crown. It was long thought that this would prevent the award of an injunction against a Crown servant acting in his or her official capacity. But in *M v Home Office* [1994] 1 AC 377 the House of Lords, acting under the influence of European Community law, held that the Act did not preclude the grant of an injunction against a particular Crown servant, even a government minister. So although the Crown is not subject to this coercive remedy, its servants who carry out its tasks are so subject. This case demonstrates the willingness of the courts to restrict the immunities and privileges of the Crown, which is further illustrated by the historic decision in *Conway v Rimmer* [1968] AC 910, which removed the Crown's absolute right to withhold evidence.

Such immunities as do survive do not seem to cause too many problems for litigants, particularly as the Crown does not seek to rely on the more extreme privileges suggested in the cases. But there needs to be continuing vigilance to ensure that the rule of law is observed and the Crown subjected to the proper degree of liability.

Question 3

To what extent has English law developed special rules to govern the liability in negligence of public authorities? Do you consider the law on this subject to be satisfactory?

Commentary

This question raises an issue that has given rise to a good deal of litigation and a lot of debate among academic lawyers. There are many different opinions as to what the law should be. As usual, it does not matter so much what opinion you express as how well you express it. Some students may be studying or have studied tort, and so would be able to give a more sophisticated discussion of the tort issues involved than is given here. It is important to remember that, though the law is divided into separate topics for teaching purposes, it is not divided in reality.

Answer plan

- One law of tort for all
- Relevance of public law principles
- Imposing a duty of care
- Finding negligence
- Liability for breach of human rights
- Liability for omissions.

Suggested answer

Because English law did not traditionally distinguish between public and private law, the ordinary principles of tort liability were developed to apply to public and private bodies alike. In *Mersey Docks and Harbour Board Trustees v Gibbs* **(1866) LR 1 HL 93**, it was held that public bodies enjoyed no inherent immunity from liability in negligence. The only exception related to the Crown, which was immune from tortious liability until the **Crown Proceedings Act 1947**. The Act expressly made the Crown liable 'as if it were a private person' so confirming the general principle that there is just one law of tort.

There are few problems in applying the law where the activities alleged to have been conducted negligently are of a type common to both public and private bodies. Liability for careless driving, dangerous premises or unsafe working practices is the same for public and private defendants. But difficulties may arise where the claim arises out of the exercise by a public authority of statutory powers of a type that private individuals do not have. Complaints about the exercise of such powers are principally dealt with by judicial review. This may provide adequate redress where the authority's action can be halted or reversed, by remedies such as injunction or quashing orders. But to claim compensation it is necessary to establish liability in tort. In *Dunlop v Woollahra Municipal Council* **[1982] AC 158**, the plaintiff established that the Council's decision was ultra vires and had it quashed, but he was unable to obtain any compensation, because he could not establish any form of tort liability.

What then is the relationship between judicial review and tort liability? Is it necessary to prove breaches of both laws or is tort liability alone sufficient? These questions have been addressed by the House of Lords in several cases, but their judgments have not always been consistent. In *Anns v Merton LBC* [1978] AC 728, the court drew a distinction between claims based on the negligent operation of statutory powers, for which tort liability alone needed to be proved, and claims based on policy decisions made by the public authority. In this situation, it would be necessary to prove that the policy decision was unlawful in public law terms before there could be any question of going on to establish liability in tort. This decision provided a rough test but was rendered problematic by the difficulty of deciding where the line between policy and operation could be drawn in practice.

The House of Lords returned to the problem in *X v Bedfordshire CC* [1995] 2 AC 633, a group of cases in which public authorities were alleged to have been negligent in the exercise of their child care and education powers. Rather than applying the *Anns v Merton LBC* distinction between policy and operation, the court held that some policy decisions, such as how to allocate limited resources, are regarded as non-justiciable in the context of judicial review. Cases like *R v Secretary of State for the Environment ex parte Nottinghamshire CC* [1986] 2 AC 240 had established that the courts would not be willing to challenge the political judgments of public authorities in such areas. That being so, the House of Lords felt that such policy decisions could not give rise to a duty of care to any individual. This decision must be correct, as it is inevitable that decisions on the allocation of what are always limited resources must mean that some individuals do not receive benefits or services that they might otherwise have received. Legal action by one disappointed claimant could only be satisfied by creating another dissatisfied claimant who would have an equally valid claim.

For claims falling outside this non-justiciable area, whether regarded as policy or operational, the House of Lords felt that cases should be dealt with on the basis of the normal principles of tort liability laid down in *Caparo Industries v Dickman* [1990] 2 AC 605. These principles require the court to start by deciding whether it is just and reasonable to impose a duty of care. Public authorities were keen to argue that for policy reasons it would not be just and reasonable to impose any duty of care on them when exercising their statutory responsibilities, so that cases could be disposed of at an early stage and litigants deterred from pursuing actions against them. The courts were initially sympathetic to this view. In *Hill v Chief Constable of West Yorkshire* [1989] AC 53, the House of Lords held that the police owed no duty of care to members of the public in respect of the prevention and investigation of crime; any other decision would have lead to resources being taken away from policing and given to the victims of crime, probably creating more victims in consequence. The decision in *Hill v Chief Constable of West Yorkshire* [1989] AC 53 has been confirmed in two subsequent House of Lords cases, *Brooks v Commissioner of Police of the Metropolis* [2005] 2 All ER 489 and *Van Colle v Chief Constable of Hertfordshire Police* [2008] 3 All ER 977. The latter case extended the ruling in *Hill*, in that the police still owed no individual duty of care, even if an individual alerted them to threats from a third party against that individual. Similarly, in those of the *X v Bedfordshire* CC cases that concerned the immensely difficult question whether or not to take a child into care on suspicion of abuse, the court held that it would not be just and reasonable to impose a duty of care on social service departments, as such decisions are normally taken after discussion with all the agencies concerned. A duty of care was held not to exist in *Jain v Trent Health Authority* [2009] 1 All ER 957, where Trent wrongly used a statutory procedure to close a retirement home run by the Jains, ruining their business. Trent should not be inhibited from using their statutory power, which was designed to protect the residents of such homes.

As a result of these precedents, it became common for public authorities to apply to strike out claims in these areas before the facts were established. In *Osman v United Kingdom* (1998) 29 EHRR 245, the European Court of Human Rights ruled that striking out a claim in this way was a breach of *Article 6 of the European Convention on Human Rights*. This decision was widely criticised as revealing a misunderstanding of the legal process. But the European Court of Human Rights revisited the issue in *Z v United Kingdom* [2001] 2 FLR 612, a case brought by one of the unsuccessful claimants in *X v Bedfordshire* CC. This time the Court held that to strike out a claim after considering whether it is just and reasonable to impose a duty of care is not a breach of *Article 6*, as that very consideration is the fair trial to which the individual is entitled.

Although there may not be any liability in negligence, that does not prevent there from being liability for the breach of human rights themselves. The European Court of Human Rights held that there was a breach of *Article 2*, the right to life, in *Osman v UK* (1998) 29 EHRR 245 and a breach of *Article 3*, freedom from torture and inhuman and degrading treatment, in *Z v UK* (2002) 34 EHRR 3. The English courts have declined to develop and change the tort of negligence, to take into account the additional Convention rights, despite the spirited dissent of Lord Bingham in *Van Colle v Chief Constable of Hertfordshire Police* [2008] 3 All ER 977. According to that case it is possible to bring an action for breach of a human right, when it is not possible to bring a claim in negligence.

There have been many cases in which the courts have found it just and reasonable to impose a duty of care, especially where the claim is based on the failure of a public authority to put into effect the decisions it had made. In *X v Bedfordshire* CC itself, the court imposed a duty of care on education authorities that had taken responsibility for dealing with pupils' problems but had failed to do so. Similarly, in *Barrett v Enfield LBC* [1999] 3 All ER 193, the court imposed a duty of care on an authority that, having rightly decided that a child needed to be taken into care, failed to ensure that he was properly cared for. But the court emphasised how difficult it was for them to deal with these cases when only the preliminary issue of whether to impose a duty of care was before them, and none of the facts were established.

The House of Lords returned to this question in *Phelps v London Borough of Hillingdon* [2000] 4 All ER 504, a group of cases alleging that education authorities had failed to identify and deal with pupils' problems, such as dyslexia. The local authorities had argued that policy considerations, such as the complexity of any litigation and the danger of a flood of vexatious claims, should preclude the imposition of a duty of care. But the House of Lords held that a duty of care should be held to exist; genuine claims should not be rejected out of hand. Instead, the court felt that policy considerations would only be material at the later stage of deciding whether the duty of care had been breached, and this would only be done once the facts had been established by evidence.

This decision makes it far more likely that cases will go forward to trial. For example, in *Connor v Surrey County Council* [2010] EWCA Civ 286, a public authority owes a duty of care to its employees. So using its statutory powers to institute an unnecessary public inquiry, which caused stress and psychiatric damage to a head teacher, was negligent.

Although all the above cases were dealt with using just tort principles, it seems to be possible that, in limited circumstances, public law principles may remain relevant in establishing liability. An example is the case of *Stovin v Wise* [1996] AC 923, where the local authority had a statutory power to remove obstructions adjoining the highway, but had not removed the obstruction in question. The House of Lords held that the claimant had to show that the local authority had acted irrationally and that the statute required compensation to be paid to those injured, when the power to remove was not used. It could not be shown that the local authority had acted irrationally.

In conclusion, the courts face difficult problems in dealing with actions in negligence against public authorities. There is constant pressure from litigants who choose to sue public authorities even in situations where someone else (with less money) is primarily liable. One thinks of the borstal boys in *Home Office v Dorset Yacht Co* [1970] AC 1004, the negligent builder in *Anns v Merton LBC* [1978] AC 728 or the careless driver in *Stovin v Wise* [1996] AC 923. Recent cases show the courts trying to steer a careful course between offering the victims of negligence appropriate compensation, and keeping vexatious claims out of court. The law in this area is likely to show further development.

Question 4

Consider the following situations in the light of the doctrine of public interest immunity.

(a) Smith was employed by Proton plc in their factory making nuclear warheads for Britain's missile defence system. He was killed in an explosion in the factory. His widow wishes to establish that the defective design of the warheads, or of the system for making them, caused the explosion, and so recover damages from Proton plc.

(b) A charity wishes to seek judicial review of the Home Office's plan to lock up young offenders in secure training centres. It believes that civil servants in the Home Office research department advised the Home Secretary that the scheme would make the offenders more delinquent, not less. The Home Office says all advice to ministers is confidential.

(c) Farmer Giles was shocked to receive a visit from animal welfare inspectors from the RSPCA, who said they had been informed that he was keeping veal calves in illegal crates. This accusation was wholly untrue. When Giles tried to discover the source of the accusation, the RSPCA said that it was their policy never to reveal the identity of their informants, in order to encourage people to inform them of cases of cruelty to animals.

Commentary

As the question makes clear, its principal concern is the doctrine of public interest immunity (PII). It is therefore appropriate to begin with a brief introductory paragraph explaining what public interest immunity is and how it developed, though it would be wrong in such a problem question to write a detailed history. In each part of the question, the student needs to identify briefly the subject matter of the litigation and the parties to it, but the bulk of the answer should be devoted to PII. Because it is a matter for the discretion of the court whether the claim to PII is upheld in any case, the student will be assessed not on the correctness or otherwise of the final conclusion, but on the quality of the arguments deployed, and the depth of knowledge of decided cases.

Answer plan

- Court to decide claims to PII
- Public interest in secrecy
- Public interest in fair litigation
- Claims to PII from any source.

Suggested answer

The doctrine of public interest immunity (PII) is intended to ensure that documents are not revealed in the course of litigation if it is not in the public interest that they should be revealed. Originally such a claim could only be made by the Crown and was therefore known as Crown Privilege. In *Duncan v Cammell Laird* [1942] AC 624, the House of Lords laid down the unfortunate rule that any claim made by the Crown had to be accepted by the courts, but in *Conway v Rimmer* [1968] AC 910, this rule was reversed, and the courts themselves took the responsibility of assessing whether or not it would be in the public interest for the documents to be disclosed.

(a) In this problem, Mrs Smith will be suing her late husband's employers, Proton plc, for negligence in failing to provide him with a safe system of work. She will therefore need the plans of the warheads and of the manufacturing system in order to identify the defects that gave rise to the explosion. But the Ministry of Defence is certainly going to claim that it would be against the public interest for these plans to be disclosed. That claim may be made in spite of the fact that the ministry is not a party to the case. Because of the adversarial nature of English legal proceedings, disclosing the documents means revealing them to the parties, their solicitors and barristers as well as to the judge. The possibility of hearing the case in camera does not eliminate the danger of the documents getting into the wrong hands.

In *Conway v Rimmer*, the House of Lords laid down that, in deciding whether documents should be disclosed or not, two aspects of the public interest had to be balanced. Firstly, there was a public interest in ensuring that no harm was done to the national interest by disclosing documents that should be kept secret. But secondly, there was a public interest in ensuring that the conduct of litigation was not frustrated. The court distinguished between claims based on the contents of the particular documents and those based merely on the class to which the documents belonged. Contents claims would generally be much stronger than class claims. As a consequence of the Scott Inquiry into the Matrix Churchill affair, the government announced that it would no longer make class claims, but only claims based on the contents of particular documents. At the same time, in *R v Chief Constable of the West Midlands Police ex parte Wiley* [1995] 1 AC 274 the House of Lords showed little enthusiasm for the idea that whole classes of documents should be kept secret or that the holder of a class of documents was legally obliged to claim public interest immunity. If necessary, the court could inspect the documents to identify the strengths of the arguments for and against disclosure.

Applying these principles to the case of Mrs Smith, it seems very probable that her chances of establishing liability will be almost completely dependent on access to the documents, which, if they do reveal design flaws, will virtually prove her case by themselves. The litigation will be frustrated if she cannot gain access to them. But the arguments against disclosure are particularly powerful. The PII claim will be based on the contents of the documents themselves, and it is hardly possible to dispute an assertion that it would pose a grave threat to national security if the plans of the nuclear deterrent fell into the wrong hands, or if designs indicating how to build a nuclear warhead came into the possession of terrorists. Inspection of the documents is not likely to be necessary to convince the court that these are genuine state secrets. Comparison may be made with *Duncan v Cammell Laird* (above) where the Admiralty was clearly justified in wishing to keep secret the plans of its latest submarine.

There is no doubt that the courts do have the power to order the disclosure even of documents as sensitive as these in the interest of justice, but it is doubtful whether they would do so in this case.

(b) The charity's appliction for judicial review may be based on the unreasonableness of the Home Office's decision or on the failure to take relevant considerations into account. Under the principle laid down in *Conway v Rimmer* (1968) it will be for the court to decide whether the public interest in confidentiality or the public interest in the fair conduct of litigation should prevail.

It appears that the Home Office's objection to the disclosure of documents in this case is based not on the contents of the particular documents, but on the claim that documents containing advice to ministers are a class that need to be kept confidential. The justification for this claim has been explained as the danger that officials might be deterred from being completely candid in their advice to ministers if they knew that such information might one day be revealed to the world through its use in litigation. But the courts have generally been unsympathetic to such assertions. In *Conway v Rimmer* (1968) such an argument was advanced in respect of the reports prepared by police officers on the conduct of a probationer, but the court rejected it. They pointed out that any such report would be protected by qualified privilege, so the official would have nothing to fear provided the report was honest. This point was also raised in *Williams v Home Office* [1981] 1 All ER 1151, where the court ordered the Home Office to disclose various documents including advice to ministers on the development of penal policy, rejecting the argument that the candour of public servants might be hindered by the remote chance of later disclosure in litigation. It would therefore appear that, unless some other, stronger argument for non-disclosure is presented to the court, the court may feel that the case for secrecy has not been made out.

Turning to the other side of the balance, the court will need to be satisfied that the disclosure of the documents is necessary for the fair conduct of the litigation. In *Air Canada v Secretary of State for Trade* [1983] 2 AC 394, this was interpreted as meaning that the applicants must show that it is very likely that the documents sought do contain material supportive of their case; applicants cannot embark on 'fishing' expeditions by demanding any document whether or not they have any grounds for thinking it material evidence. But once the applicants have passed this threshold, it may well be appropriate for the court to inspect the documents, because if they do not in fact assist the applicants' case, there is no need to order disclosure.

In this problem, the applicants seem to have good grounds for suggesting that the documents from the research department will assist their case, by demonstrating that relevant considerations were ignored. The court may feel that this is sufficient to justify an order for disclosure, given the weakness of the opposing case, or may feel it better to inspect the documents before coming to a conclusion. Only if the documents fail to support the applicants' case at all is it likely that disclosure will be refused.

(c) Before *Conway v Rimmer*, the term Crown privilege demonstrated clearly that claims for non-disclosure could be made only by the Crown. But in *Rogers v Home Secretary* [1973] AC 388, the claim was made by the Gaming Board which, though a public body, was not a government department. The House of Lords stated that claims based on the public interest could be made by any interested party, not just the Crown. This was applied in *D v NSPCC* [1978] AC 171, where the defendant, a charitable voluntary organisation, with a recognised status in the protection of children, was held able to claim PII in respect of certain confidential information. It would therefore be open to the RSPCA to raise an issue of PII in this case.

The basis of their claim is the need to offer complete confidentiality to informants who might otherwise be reluctant to contact them. Such claims have been accepted by the courts as being in the public interest. The case of *Rogers v Home Secretary* [1973] AC 388 concerned confidential information supplied to the Gaming Board about an applicant for a gaming licence. The court accepted that, in the sometimes murky world of gaming, informants needed to be given an absolute guarantee of confidentiality. In *D v NSPCC* [1978] AC 171 the charity was held to be justified in claiming that confidentiality served the vital function of encouraging people to report suspected child abuse. *R v Chief Constable of the West Midlands Police ex parte Wiley* [1995] 1 AC 274 also accepted that the identity of a police informer should be kept secret. The European Court of Human Rights has asserted, and the UK courts have accepted, that the trial judge should have the final say on whether, for example, the name of a police informant should be given to the defence: *Rowe v UK* (2000) 30 EHRR 1.

Whether the court would feel that the same justification applied in the case of cruelty to animals is not clear. But such activity can be criminal and the RSPCA is active in prosecution, so it seems that they could assert a public interest in the enforcement of the law. To set against this is the public interest in the fair conduct of litigation. Clearly Giles will be unable to bring proceedings for defamation against the informant if he cannot discover who the informant was, and this may seem unfair, particularly as the defamation may even have been malicious. But the court may feel, as they did in *D v NSPCC* [1978] AC 171 that this is a price worth paying for the better protection of the vulnerable.

Further reading

Bradley, A. and Ewing, K. *Constitutional and Administrative Law*, 15th edn (Longman, 2010), ch. 32.

Craig, P. *Administrative Law*, 6th edn (Sweet and Maxwell, 2008), ch. 28 and ch. 29.

Leyland, P. and Anthony, G. *Textbook on Administrative Law*, 6th edn (Oxford University Press, 2009), chs. 20, 21 and 17.6 (pp. 420–37).

Index

A

Accountability
see also **Judicial review**
conventions
  importance 10
  reasons for 14
individual ministerial responsibility
  government accountability to
    Commons 31–34
  overview 30–31
  questions to civil servants 33
  questions to ministers 33
  questions to Next Steps agencies 33–34
ministerial responsibility
  collective responsibility 36–37
  confidence votes 35–36
  overview 34–35
  personal misconduct 38
  responsibility for self and
    department 37–38
Prime Minister 23
role of House of Lords 80–81
role of select committees
  all-party cooperation 73
  enhanced powers 73
  membership 70–71
  overview 69–70
  power to call evidence 71
  role of civil servants 72
Acts of Parliament *see* **Statutes**
Additional Member System 60
Aggravated trespass 142
Aliens 50
Arrest powers 150–151, 150–151
Assemblies *see* **Freedom of assembly**

B

Bias 187–188
Bill of Rights
importance 9
main objectives 9–10
overview 5
parliamentary privilege 77
rejection by Dicey 103
UK proposals to replace human rights
  anti-terrorism considerations 124
  Coalition reform proposals 125–126
  development of privacy law 124–125
  effect on foreign policy 124
  fight against crime 124
  overview 120–122
  political advantages 122
  public opinion 123–124
  relationship between ECHR and
    HRA 1998 122–123
Breach of confidentiality
freedom of information 166–167
meaning and scope 171–175
official secrets 164
Breaches of the peace 137–138

C

Cabinet
adoption of policy 27–28
ministerial responsibility
  collective responsibility 36–37
  confidence votes 35–36
  overview 34–35
  personal misconduct 38
  responsibility for self and
    department 37–38
movement towards Prime Ministerial
  Government
  choice of government 23–24
  control of Cabinet and committees
    24–25
  conventional powers 22–23
  delegation of governance 25
  growth of powers 25–26
  overview 21–22
role of convention 12
Caravans 141
Certiori 178
Channel Islands 18
Civil liberties
see also **Human rights; Individual rights**
right to protest
  freedom of assembly 144–148
  overview 133–135

Civil liberties (*continued*)
    public order offences 135
    scope and limitations 140–144
  security in own home
    arrest powers 150–151
    entry and search 151–153
    overview 148–150
    seizure of evidence 153

Civil service
  see also **Public authorities**
  appearance before select committees 72
  importance of Downing Street staff 25
  questions in committee 33

Coalition policies
  electoral reform 60–61
  fixed term parliaments 87–88
  proposals to replace human rights 125–126
  sovereignty 93

Committees
  adoption of policy 27–28
  Prime Ministerial control 24–25
  questions to civil servants 33
  select committees
    pressure from MPs on government 68–69
    questions to civil servants 33
    scrutinizing role 69–70

Common law *see* **Judiciary**
Compatibility 131
Confidence votes 35–36
Confidentiality
  freedom of information 166–167
  meaning and scope 171–175
  official secrets 164

Constitutions
  benefits of written constitution
    adopted as break from past 8
    federal structures 8–9
    individual rights 9
    organisation of government 9
    procedures for change 8
    purpose and objectives 7–8
    US model 8
  conventions
    difficulties of identification 13
    enforcement 14–15
    examples 12
    importance 12
    individual ministerial responsibility 30–34
    overview 11
    process of change 15
    strengths and weaknesses of UK system 15
  doctrine if separation 105–108
  federal structures
    composition of UK 17

    devolved government in UK 17–20
    overview 15–16
    unitary structures compared 16–17
  importance of prerogative powers
    high policy 54–55
    judicial review 53–54
    limited Parliamentary control 55
    overview 52
    powers ill-defined 53
    use by and importance to government 52
  overview 5–6
  Parliamentary sovereignty 86
  sources
    Acts of Parliament 9
    common law 9
    conventions 10

Consultancies held by MPs 76–77
Contempt of court 159
Contractual liability 211–212
Conventions
  difficulties of identification 13
  enforcement 14–15
  examples 12
  importance 12
  individual ministerial responsibility
    government accountability to Commons 31–34
    overview 30–31
    questions to civil servants 33
    questions to ministers 33
    questions to Next Steps agencies 33–34
  ministerial responsibility
    collective responsibility 36–37
    confidence votes 35–36
    overview 34–35
    personal misconduct 38
    responsibility for self and department 37–38
  movement towards Prime Ministerial Government 22–23
  overview 11
  process of change 14
  Queen only acting on advice
    dismissal of Prime Minister 48
    'hung' Parliaments 46–48
    overview 44–45
    right to make personal choices 45–46
  Salisbury convention 29
  source of constitution 10
  strengths and weaknesses of UK system 15

Courts *see* **Judicial review; Judiciary**
Crown proceedings
  contractual liability 211–212
  immunities 208

public interest immunity 216–220
special rules of negligence 212–216
tortious liability 208–210

D

Declarations of incompatibility 131
Defence Advisory Notices 163
Delegated legislation
  collateral challenges 200–201
  failure to publish 200
  human rights 200
  illegality 199
  irrationality 199–200
  overview 196–197
  procedural impropriety 198–199
  statutory instruments 198
Democracy
  electoral voting systems 57
  freedom of information 164
  overview 5
  reason for conventions 14
Derogations
  anti-terrorist measures 115
  human rights 129
Devolution
  limited independence 20
  Northern Ireland 19
  Scotland 18
  Wales 18–19
Dicey, A.V.
  conventional view of constitution 6
  conventions
    comparison with moral rules 14–15
    difficulties of identification 13
    importance 12
  judicial review 179
  rule of law 99–100
  sovereignty 85, 89, 95
  statements of constitutional values 8
  unitarianism 16
Direct effect doctrine
  challenges to doctrine of implied repeal 95–96
  conditions for applicability 96–97
  enforcement 97–98
  overview 93–94
Discretionary powers
  judicial review
    fettering of discretionary powers 190–191
    misuse of discretion 191–192
    procedural *ultra vires* 183
  public order offences 135

E

Elections
  'hung' Parliaments 46–48
  voting systems
    Additional Member System 60
    First Past the Post 57–59
    overview 56–57
    Party List system 59–60
Enforcement
  conventions 14–15
  freedom of information 168–169
  individual ministerial responsibility 31
  parliamentary privilege 77
Entry and search powers 151–153
Equality before the law 101
EU law
  see also **International law**
  impact of UK membership on sovereignty
    effect of EU law within Member States 90–91
    express and implied repeal 92
    meaning and implications 83
    overview 88–89
    reconciliation between national and EU law 91–92
  parliamentary privilege 76
  supremacy of Parliament 9
Examination technique 1–4
Executive powers
  see also **Prerogative powers**
  doctrine if separation
    meaning and scope 104–105
    reform proposals 107–108
    relevance to UK 106–107
  extent of Prime Minister's powers
    adoption of policy by Cabinet 27–28
    control by Whips 28–29
    disputes between Lords and Commons 29
    media briefings 29–30
    overview 26–27
  movement towards Prime Ministerial Government
    choice of government 23–24
    control of Cabinet and committees 24–25
    conventional powers 22–23
    delegation of governance 25
    growth of powers 25–26
    overview 21–22
  pressure from first-time MPs
    lobbying 69
    overview 66
    Private Members Bills 67–68

Executive powers (*continued*)
    questions in the house 68
    scrutiny of legislation 67
    select committees 68–69
  role of House of Lords 80–81
  scrutiny by select committees
    all-party cooperation 73
    enhanced powers 73
    membership 70–71
    overview 69–70
    power to call evidence 71
    role of civil servants 72
  separation 5
  subject to rule of law 100–101
Expulsion of enemy aliens 50

F

Fair trial
  anti-terrorist measures 113–115
  derogation in emergency 129
  entitlement to fair hearing 186–187
Federal structures
  benefits of written constitution 8–9
  composition of UK 17
  devolved government in UK 17–20
  overview 15–16
  unitary structures compared 16–17
First Past the Post voting 57–59
Fixed-term parliaments 87–88
Foreign policy
  conclusion of treaties 51
  expulsion of enemy aliens 50
  judicial review 44
  overview 48–49
  passports 50
  requisitioning of property 51
  treaty-making powers 51
  UK proposals to replace human rights 124
  wartime prerogative 49–50
Freedom of assembly
  Convention guarantee 140
  Convention right 128
  meaning and scope
    Convention right 145
    highway obstruction 147
    overview 144–145
    peaceful assemblies 145–146
    positive State duties 148
    restrictions prescribed by law 146–147
    threats of violence 146
  public order offences 137
Freedom of expression
  conflict with privacy 173

  obscenity
    contempt of court 159
    depravity and corruption 158
    electronic data 158–159
    expert evidence 158
    'obscene' defined 158
    overview 156–157
    protection of morals 159
    qualified privilege 159–160
  official secrets
    breach of confidentiality 164
    communications to enemy 162
    damaging disclosures 162–163
    government property 163
    knowing receipt 163
    overview 160–161
  overview 155–156
  parliamentary privilege 75–76
Freedom of information
  breach of confidentiality 166–167
  enforcement 168–169
  exemptions 167–168
  Information Commissioner 169
  official secrets 166
  overview 164
  public requests 169
  release of government documents 165

G

Government *see* **Executive powers**
'Guillotine' 65

H

Harassment 136–137
Hereditary peers 29
High policy
  constitutional importance 54–55
  judicial review 44, 50
Highway obstruction 135–136, 141, 147
House of Commons
  confidence votes 35–36
  disputes with House of Lords 29
  modernisation
    enhanced public engagement 65–66
    Opposition obstruction 65
    overview 61–62
    Public Bills 65
    publication of draft legislation 64–65
    working conditions 62–64
  pressure from first-time MPs on government lobbying 69

overview 66
Private Members Bills 67–68
questions in the house 68
scrutiny of legislation 67
select committees 68–69

House of Lords
disputes over government policy 29
need for reform
    check on House of Commons 80–81
    overview 78
    relationship with House of Commons 82
    representation 79
    scrutiny of executive 81–82
    selection or election 79–80
role of convention 13

Human rights
see also **Civil liberties; Individual rights**
anti-terrorist measures
    detention without trial 113
    fair trial 113–115
    overview 110–111
    prohibition of torture 112–113
    right to life 112
    terrorism defined 111–112
    war and public emergencies 115
applicability to UK legislation
    detention without trial 128–129
    fair trial 129–130
    freedom of assembly 128
    liberty and security 128
    overview 126–127
contents of written constitution 9
Convention rights
    prohibition of torture 130
    public authorities 130
    right to life 130
declarations of incompatibility 131
delegated legislation 200
effect on English law
    compatibility 117–118
    individual rights 119–120
    judicial deference 118–119
    public authorities 119
    traditional civil liberties 116–117
fair trial
    anti-terrorist measures 113–115
    Crown proceedings 215
    derogation in emergency 129
    entitlement to fair hearing 186–187
    natural justice 163
freedom of assembly
    Convention guarantee 140
    Convention right 134, 145
    highway obstruction 147

overview 144–145
peaceful assemblies 145–146
positive State duties 148
public order offences 137
restrictions prescribed by law 146–147
threats of violence 146
freedom of expression
    obscenity 156–160
    official secrets 160–164
    overview 155–156
increased interest in rule of law 103
overview 109–110
privacy
    overview 170–171
    protection of English civil liberties 124
    public authority liability 205–206
    scope within UK law 170–175
public authority liability
    privacy 205–206
    right to life 207
replacement by UK Bill of Rights
    anti-terrorism considerations 124
    Coalition reform proposals 125–126
    development of privacy law 124–125
    effect on foreign policy 124
    fight against crime 124
    overview 120–122
    political advantages 122
    public opinion 123–124
    relationship between ECHR and HRA 1998 122–123
right to life
    anti-terrorist measures 112
    Convention right 130
    public authority liability 207
sources 9
'Hung' Parliaments 46-8

I

Illegality
see also **Rule of law**
delegated legislation 199
Immunities see **Privilege**
Imprisonment
detention without trial 124
Individual rights
see also **Civil liberties; Human rights**
benefits of written constitution 9
judicial review 184
protection by rule of law 101
Information Commissioner 169
see also **Freedom of information**

International law
see also **EU law**
  Parliamentary sovereignty 85
  treaties
    Parliamentary sovereignty 90
    prerogative powers 51
Irrationality
  delegated legislation 199–200
  scope of judicial review 192
Isle of Man 20

J

Judicial review
  delegated legislation
    collateral challenges 200–201
    failure to publish 200
    human rights 200
    illegality 199
    irrationality 199–200
    overview 196–197
    procedural impropriety 198–199
    statutory instruments 198
  foreign policy
    conclusion of treaties 51
    expulsion of enemy aliens 50
    overview 48–49
    passports 50
    requisitioning of property 51
    treaty-making powers 51
    wartime prerogative 49–50
  history and development 176–181
  natural justice
    bias 187–188
    entitlement to fair hearing 186–187
    legal representation 187
    notice of charges 186
    overview 185
  overview 176
  Parliamentary sovereignty 103
  prerogative powers
    common law power of Queen 42
    constitutional importance 53–54
    exercise 42–43
    existence and extent 42
    high policy 43
    individual rights 44
  procedural difficulties
    overview 193
    permission 194–195
    public private divide 193–194
    standing 195–196
    time limits 195

  procedural *ultra vires*
    balancing considerations 182–183
    consultation 183–184
    mandatory and discretionary conditions distinguished 183
    standing 184
  scope
    breaches of natural justice 189–190
    fettering of discretionary powers 190–191
    legitimate expectations 191
    misuse of discretion 191–192
    overview 188–189
    proportionality 190–191
    public authorities 189–190
    unreasonableness 192
Judiciary
  bias 187–188
  criticisms of rule of law 102
  deference on human rights 118–119
  doctrine if separation
    meaning and scope 104–105
    reform proposals 107–108
    relevance to UK 106–107
  revival of judicial review 180
  role of convention 13
  separation of powers 5

L

Legal representation 187
Legality principle *see* **Rule of law**
Legislative powers
  control of government policy by Whips 28–29
  delegated legislation
    collateral challenges 200–201
    failure to publish 200
    human rights 200
    illegality 199
    irrationality 199–200
    overview 196–197
    procedural impropriety 198–199
    statutory instruments 198
  devolved government
    Northern Ireland Assembly 19
    Scottish Parliament 18
    Welsh Assembly 18–19
  direct effect of EU law
    challenges to doctrine of implied repeal 95–96
    conditions for applicability 96–97
    enforcement 97–98
    overview 93–94

doctrine if separation
   meaning and scope 104–105
   reform proposals 107–108
   relevance to UK 106–107
impact of UK membership of EU
   effect of EU law within Member States 90–91
   express and implied repeal 92
   overview 88–89
   reconciliation between national and EU law 91–92
modernisation of House of Commons
   enhanced public engagement 65–66
   Opposition obstruction 65
   Public Bills 65
   publication of draft legislation 64–65
Parliamentary sovereignty
   'constitutional statutes' 86
   implied repeal 86
   law-making powers 84–85
   obedience by courts 85
   power to repeal or amend laws 85–86
pressure from first-time MPs on government
   Private Members Bills 67–68
   scrutiny of legislation 67
separation 5
Legitimate expectations 191
Liberty and security 128
Lobbying 69
Local authorities
   judicial review 189–190

M

Mandamus 178
Media
   attention on Prime Minister 25–26
   knowing receipt of official secrets 163
   parliamentary privilege 77
   qualified privilege 159–160
   use by Prime Minister 29–30
Members of Parliament
   electoral voting systems
      Additional Member System 60
      First Past the Post 57–59
      overview 56–57
      Party List system 59–60
   membership of select committees 70–71
   parliamentary privilege
      controls over consultancy 76–77
      enforcement 77
      freedom of speech 75–76
      overview 74–75

      reports of proceedings 77
   pressure on government
      lobbying 69
      overview 66
      Private Members Bills 67–68
      questions in the house 68
      scrutiny of legislation 67
      select committees 68–69
   questions in Parliament
      individual ministerial responsibility 33
Ministers
   enforcement of conventions 14
   individual ministerial responsibility
      government accountability to Commons 31–34
      overview 30–31
      questions to civil servants 33
      questions to ministers 33
      questions to Next Steps agencies 33–34
   ministerial responsibility
      collective responsibility 36–37
      confidence votes 35–36
      overview 34–35
      personal misconduct 38
      responsibility for self and department 37–38
   Prime Minister's choice of government 23–24
Misfeasance in public office 204–205
Monarchy
   see also **Prerogative powers**
   conventions
      changes over time 14
      enforcement 14
      importance 12
   Crown proceedings
      contractual liability 211–212
      public interest immunity 216–220
      special rules of negligence 212–216
      tortious liability 208–210
   Queen only acting on advice
      dismissal of Prime Minister 48
      'hung' Parliaments 46–48
      overview 44–45
      right to make personal choices 45–46

N

Natural justice
   bias 187–188
   entitlement to fair hearing 186–187
   legal representation 187
   meaning and scope 189–190
   notice of charges 187
   overview 184–185

Negligence
    general principles 206–207
    special rules for public authorities 212–216
Next Steps agencies 33–34
Northern Ireland
    devolved government 19
    limited independence 20
    union with England 17
Nuisance
    public authority liability 203–204
    right to protest 141

O

Obscenity
    contempt of court 159
    depravity and corruption 158
    electronic data 158–159
    expert evidence 158
    'obscene' defined 158
    overview 157
    protection of morals 159
    qualified privilege 159
Official secrets
    breach of confidentiality 164
    communications to enemy 162
    damaging disclosures 162–163
    freedom of information 166
    government property 163
    knowing receipt 163
    overview 160–161
Ombudsmen *see* Parliamentary Commissioner for Administration

P

Parliament
    see also House of Commons; House of Lords; Legislative powers; Members of Parliament
    electoral voting systems
        Additional Member System 60
        First Past the Post 57–59
        overview 56–57
        Party List system 59–60
    modernisation of House of Commons
        enhanced public engagement 65–66
        Opposition obstruction 65
        overview 61–62
        Public Bills 65
        publication of draft legislation 64–65
        working conditions 62–64
    pressure from first-time MPs on government
        lobbying 69
        overview 66
        Private Members Bills 67–68
        questions in the house 68
        scrutiny of legislation 67
        select committees 68–69
    reform of House of Lords
        check on House of Commons 80–81
        overview 78
        relationship with House of Commons 82
        representation 79
        scrutiny of executive 81–82
        selection or election 79–80
    sovereignty
        conflict with rule of law 102
        direct effect of EU law 95–98
        impact of UK membership of EU 89–93
        meaning and implications 83–88
        overview 83
Parliamentary Commissioner for Administration 32–33
Parliamentary privilege
    controls over consultancy 76–77
    enforcement 77
    freedom of speech 75–76
    overview 74–75
    reports of proceedings 77
Party List system 59–60
Passports 50
Permission for judicial review 194–195
Police powers
    arrest 150–151
    detention without trial
        anti-terrorist measures 113
        Convention right 128–129
    entry and search 151–153
    overview 148–150
    public order offences 135
    seizure of evidence 153
Prerogative powers
    constitutional importance
        high policy 54–55
        judicial review 53–54
        limited Parliamentary control 55
        overview 52
        powers ill-defined 53
        use by and importance to government 52
    convention that Queen only acts on advice
        dismissal of Prime Minister 48
        'hung' Parliaments 46–48
        overview 44–45
        right to make personal choices 45–46
    foreign policy
        conclusion of treaties 51
        expulsion of enemy aliens 50

overview 48–49
passports 50
requisitioning of property 51
treaty-making powers 51
wartime prerogative 49–50
judicial review
  common law power of Queen 42
  exercise 42–43
  existence and extent 42
  high policy 43
  individual rights 44
overview 40–41
Prime Minister's source of power 23

Prime Minister
conventions
  dismissal of Canadian Prime Minister 14
  enforcement by 14
  importance 12
dismissal by monarch 48
extent of powers
  adoption of policy by Cabinet 27–28
  control by Whips 28–29
  disputes between Lords and Commons 29
  media briefings 29–30
  overview 26–27
full constitutional position 10
movement towards Prime Ministerial Government
  choice of government 23–24
  control of Cabinet and committees 24–25
  conventional powers 22–23
  delegation of governance 25
  growth of powers 25–26
  overview 21–22

Privacy
development of UK law 124–125
overview 170–171
public authority liability 205–206
scope within UK law
  breach of confidentiality 171–175
  conflict with freedom of expression 173
  effect of HRA 1998 173
  public interest 174
  traditional view 171

Private Members Bills 67–68

Privilege
Crown immunities 208, 212
good faith discussions 159–160
parliamentary privilege
  controls over consultancy 76–77
  enforcement 77
  freedom of speech 75–76
  overview 74–75
  reports of proceedings 77

public interest immunity
  claims against interested parties 220
  judicial review 219–220
  negligence claims 218–219
  overview 216–217
  public authority liability 206
  rationale 217–218

Procedure
constitutional change 8
Crown immunities 212
delegated legislation 198–199
judicial review
  overview 193
  permission 194–195
  public private divide 193–194
  standing 195–196
  time limits 195
ultra vires
  balancing considerations 182–183
  consultation 183–184
  mandatory and discretionary conditions distinguished 183
  standing 184

Prohibition of torture
anti-terrorist measures 112–113
Convention right 130

Prohibitions 178

Proportional representation 59–60

Proportionality 190–191

Public authorities
applicability of human rights 130
Crown proceedings
  contractual liability 211–212
  immunities 208
  overview 208
  procedural immunities 212
  tortious liability 208–210
freedom of information 169
grounds for liability
  misfeasance in public office 204–205
  negligence 206–207
  nuisance 203–204
  overview 202–203
  privacy 205–206
  right to life 207
human rights obligations 119
meaning and scope 189–190
overview 202
procedural *ultra vires*
  balancing considerations 182–183
  consultation 183–184
  mandatory and discretionary conditions distinguished 183
  standing 184

Public authorities (*continued*)
   public interest immunity
      claims against interested parties 220
      judicial review 219–220
      negligence claims 218–219
      overview 216–217
      rationale 217–218
   tortious liability
      special rules of negligence 212–216

Public interest
   conflict between privacy and freedom of expression 174
   immunity
      claims against interested parties 220
      judicial review 219–220
      negligence claims 218–219
      overview 216–217
      public authority liability 206
      rationale 217–218

Public nuisance 141

Public opinion
   media attention on Prime Minister 25–26
   media briefings 29–30

Public order *see* **Freedom to protest**

Q

Qualified privilege
   good faith discussions 159–160
   Parliamentary proceedings 77

Questions in Parliament
   individual ministerial responsibility 33
   pressure from first-time MPs on government 68

R

Raves 141
Representation
   reform of House of Lords 79
   voting systems
      Additional Member System 60
      First Past the Post 57–59
      overview 56–57
      Party List system 59–60

Right to life
   anti-terrorist measures 112
   Convention right 130
   public authority liability 207

Right to protest
   freedom of assembly
      Convention right 145

      highway obstruction 147
      overview 144–145
      peaceful assemblies 145–146
      positive State duties 148
      restrictions prescribed by law 146–147
      threats of violence 146
   overview 133–135
   public order offences
      assemblies 137
      breaches of the peace 137–138
      harassment 136–137
      highway obstruction 135–136
      police discretion 135
      processions 138
      riot 137
      threatening behaviour 136
      violent disorder 137
   scope and limitations
      aggravated trespass 142
      Convention guarantee 140
      disorder or crime 140–141
      overview 140
      public nuisance 141
      unlawful assemblies 141–142

Riot 137
Royal Assent 12
Royal prerogative *see* **Prerogative powers**
Rule of law
   authority for government action 100–101
   constitutional principle 100
   constitutional role 5
   equality before the law 101
   failure to deal with supremacy 102
   protection of individual liberties 101

S

Salisbury convention 29
Scotland
   devolved government 18
   electoral voting systems 60
   limited independence 20
   Parliamentary sovereignty 86
   union with England 17
Search powers 151–153
Select committees
   pressure from first-time MPs on government 68–69
   Prime Ministerial attendance 13–14
   questions to civil servants 33
   scrutinising role
      all-party cooperation 73

enhanced powers 73
membership 70–71
overview 69–70
power to call evidence 71
role of civil servants 72
Separation of powers
meaning and scope 104–105
overview 5
reform proposals 107–108
relevance to UK 106–107
Sovereignty
Channel Islands 18
Coalition proposals 93
conflict with rule of law 102
direct effect of EU law
  challenges to doctrine of implied repeal 95–96
  conditions for applicability 96–97
  enforcement 97–98
  overview 93–94
impact of UK membership of EU
  effect of EU law within Member States 89
  express and implied repeal 92
  overview 88–89
  reconciliation between national and EU law 91–92
meaning and implications
  'constitutional statutes' 86
  implied repeal 86
  law-making powers 84–85
  obedience by courts 85
  power to repeal or amend laws 85–86
overview 83
re-affirmed by common law 9
Standing 184, 195–196
Statutes
see also **Legislative powers**
'constitutional statutes' 86
source of constitution 9
Statutory instruments *see* **Delegated legislation**
Supremacy *see* **Sovereignty**

T

Terrorism
defined 111–112
detention without trial 113
fair trial 113–115
overview 110–111
prohibition of torture 112–113

right to life 112
UK proposals to replace human rights 124
war and public emergencies 115
Threatening behaviour 136
Time limits for judicial review 195
Tortious liability
Crown proceedings 208–210
special rules of negligence 212–216
Treaties
Parliamentary sovereignty 90
prerogative powers 51
Trespass
protection of privacy, 170–171
right to protest 142
Tribunals
bias 187–188
entitlement to fair hearing 186–187
legal representation 187
notice of charges 186
overview 185–186

U

Ultra vires
balancing considerations 182–183
consultation 183–184
mandatory and discretionary conditions distinguished 183
standing 184
Unitarianism 16, 19
Unreasonableness
delegated legislation 199–200
scope of judicial review 192

V

Violent disorder 137
Voting systems
Additional Member System 60
Coalition proposals for reform 60–61
First Past the Post 57–59
overview 56–57
Party List system 59–60

W

Wales
devolved government 18–19
electoral voting systems 60
limited independence 20
union with England 17

Wartime
  expulsion of enemy aliens 50
  judicial review
    history and development 179
    prerogative powers 51
  prerogative powers 49–50
  requisitioning of property 51
Whips 28–29

Written constitutions
  adopted as break from past 8
  federal structures 8–9
  human rights 9
  organisation of government 9
  procedures for change 8
  purpose and objectives 7–8
  unwritten constitutions compared 11
  US model 8

Candidate No.

EXAM PAPER

If you're serious about exam success, it's time to *Concentrate!*

Each guide in the **Concentrate** series shows you what to expect in your law exam, what examiners are looking for, and how to achieve extra marks.

* Written by experts
* Developed with students
* Designed for success

For a full list of titles available and forthcoming please visit the website

If you're struggling with your course or worried about exams, don't panic, just *concentrate!*

Buy yours from your campus bookshop, online, or direct from OUP www.oxfordtextbooks.co.uk/law/revision

Visit **www.oxfordtextbooks.co.uk/orc/concentrate/** for a wealth of online resources including a podcast of exam and revision guidance, diagnostic tests, understanding your marks, interactive flashcard glossaries and cases, and multiple choice questions with instant feedback.